GALILEO, DARWIN, AND HAWKING

Galileo, Darwin, and Hawking

The Interplay of Science, Reason, and Religion

PHIL DOWE

WILLIAM B. EERDMANS PUBLISHING COMPANY
GRAND RAPIDS, MICHIGAN / CAMBRIDGE, U.K.

© 2005 Wm. B. Eerdmans Publishing Co.
All rights reserved

Wm. B. Eerdmans Publishing Co.
255 Jefferson Ave. S.E., Grand Rapids, Michigan 49503 /
P.O. Box 163, Cambridge CB3 9PU U.K.

Printed in the United States of America

09 08 07 06 05   7 6 5 4 3 2

ISBN-10: 0-8028-2696-2
ISBN-13: 978-0-8028-2696-1

www.eerdmans.com

Contents

Acknowledgments — viii

Introduction: Harmony or Conflict? — 1

1. **Cosmology and Scripture** — 9
   Cosmology — 10
   Genesis and Hermeneutics — 16
   Augustine's Hermeneutics — 22
   Calvin's Hermeneutics — 26
   Galileo and the Church — 29
   Bellarmino's Dilemma — 33
   Galileo's Reconciliatory Hermeneutics — 35
   Conclusion — 38

2. **The Hermeneutics of Science and Religion:
   Realism and Antirealism** — 40
   Osiander's Preface — 41
   Antirealist Accounts of Science — 42
   Scientific Realism and Inference to the Best Explanation — 46
   Antirealism in Philosophy of Religion — 49

v

CONTENTS

3. Knowledge and Power   57
   The Heritage of Greek Logic and Geometry   57
   The Image of God   59
   Descartes, Rationality, and the Perspicuity of Nature   62
   Francis Bacon's Vision of Science and Technology   66
   Bacon and the Cultural Mandate   70
   Twentieth-Century Critiques of the Baconian Vision   72
   From God to Science and Back:
   The Mutual Relevance of Science and Religion   79

4. Miracles   82
   Hume's Theory of Rational Belief   83
   Testimonial Evidence   86
   The Concept of a Miracle   87
   Hume's First Argument against Miracles   91
   A Problem for Testimony   93
   Hume's 'Limitation'   94
   Hume's Second Argument against Miracles   97
   Schlesinger's Defence of Miracles   99

5. Creation and Evolution   104
   Teleological and Mechanical Explanation   104
   Paley's Design Argument   109
   Darwin's *The Origin of Species*   113
   Natural Selection or Special Creation?   118
   Darwin and God   125
   Darwin and Asa Gray   127
   From the Monkey Jibe to the Monkey Trial   131
   Creation Science   137

6. Big Bang Cosmology and God   142
   Kalām Cosmological Argument and the Infinite Universe   143
   Big Bang Cosmology   146
   The Anthropic Principle   148

Contents

God as an Explanation — 154
Chance and Many Worlds Explanations — 158
The Inverse Gambler's Fallacy — 160
The Observer Selection Effect — 164
Denial of the Need for Explanation — 167

7. **God and Chance** — 170
The Chance Worldview — 170
Providence — 173
Three Models of Providence — 175
Quantum Chance — 178
Chance and Providence — 183
Physical Chance, Divine Cause — 184
Physical Chance, No Divine Cause — 186
Meaningless Coincidences — 187
Conclusion — 189

8. **The Interaction of Science and Religion** — 191
Mutual Interaction — 191
Defeasibility and the God of the Gaps Objection — 193
Conclusion — 195

Bibliography — 196

Index — 203

Acknowledgments

I would like to thank Marguerite La Caze, John Colman, Roger White, Damian Cox, Stephen Coleman, Bruce Langtry, and especially Paul Helm for commenting on various sections. I would also like to thank Angela Rosier, Gwen Nettlefold, and David Luttrell for their considerable help with this manuscript. I dedicate this to the memory of Gwen.

INTRODUCTION

Harmony or Conflict?

The pairing of science and religion evokes strong images in the popular imagination. One such image is that of the dejected Galileo Galilei (1564-1642), convinced by scientific experiment that the earth is in motion around the sun, but being forced to recant by a powerful and obscurantist church hierarchy.

Another powerful image is that of Samuel Wilberforce (1805-1873) denouncing Darwin's theory of natural selection in a debate at Oxford University in 1860 without properly understanding the theory or how the evidence was supposed to support it. Although there is no written record of Wilberforce's speech, popular mythology has it that he asked his opponent, Thomas Huxley (1825-1895), whether it was his grandmother or grandfather who had descended from an ape, when in fact Darwinian theory claims that humans and apes are descended from a common ancestor. So Huxley replied that he would prefer to claim descent from an ape than from any human who could ridicule science in such an ill-informed way.[1] This incident branded Wilberforce as a symbol of an ignorant church ridiculing the discoveries of science without fully understanding them.

In his book *A Brief History of Time* leading twentieth-century theoretical physicist Stephen Hawking attempts to paint himself as Galileo's heir. Hawking relates a story in which, on the anniversary of Galileo's trial, he attended a cosmology conference at the Vatican at which the Pope suggested that scientists would be wise to avoid investigation of the early mo-

---

1. White 1960, vol. 1, p. 71.

ments of the big bang, as these were part of the mystery of God. Hawking writes that it was fortunate that the Pope had not read his recent paper on that very subject, in which he had shown that the big bang provides no grounds for believing in God![2]

Each of these images portrays the relationship between science and religion as one of sharp conflict, involving a political struggle over what people will and should believe. This perception paints religion as the enemy of scientific progress, inciting free spirits to rise in rebellion against it.

This book deals with the relationship between science and religion. But this is, in fact, a controversial issue. The popular perception of conflict is but one view of the matter. There are other views, some of which hold that the relationship between science and religion is not necessarily one of conflict, but rather that they can and generally do coexist in some sort of harmony. We should start by outlining some of these opposing views.[3]

First, let's consider some versions of the view that the relationship between science and religion is one of conflict. On the conflict view, science and religion are seen as competing attempts to come to grips with one domain of human discovery and thought. One version of this conflict view is what I will call *naturalism*. Naturalism as understood here is the view that only this spacetime world exists, and everything in it is in principle open to scientific explanation.[4] So the advocate of naturalism claims that there is only one domain of truth, and it is science alone which can supply us with the correct view about that one domain. Religion, on the other hand, provides rival, or contrasting views in that domain, and must therefore be incorrect.

Naturalism also involves the view that as science progresses it will continue to reveal the mistakes of religion. This view was prominent in the nineteenth century, where religion came to be seen as a primitive attempt to explain natural phenomena, which would in due course be replaced by science. A popular example of this naturalist view can be found in Sir James Frazer's *The Golden Bough*,[5] (written 1911-1913) which, from an anthropological perspective, relates the stories of various religions — including Hebrew, Egyptian, Greek, and Babylonian — and attempts to explain

2. Hawking 1988, ch. 7.
3. This follows, roughly, the tradition of the so-called 'Barbour typology' (Barbour 1966). For some critical comments of the same, see below.
4. Armstrong 1980.
5. Frazer 1911-1913.

them as primitive attempts to understand natural processes and phenomena. For example, the stories of the Greek tradition used 'the gods' as devices to explain earthquakes, thunder, and so on, but we now have new explanations for these things, based on science. That is not to say, however, that the religious stories were of no value. They were instrumental in the journey to scientific discovery. But scientific advancement now warrants the discarding of the religious stories. So now, according to the naturalist view, science is the replacement for religion.

Naturalism has been promoted by philosophers such as David Hume (1711-1776), Thomas Huxley (1825-1895), and in our century Bertrand Russell (1872-1970) and John Mackie (1917-1981). Stephen Hawking also fits into this camp. According to Hawking science is on the path to a complete understanding of the universe,[6] when we will "know the mind of God."[7] "What place, then, for a creator?"[8] he asks.

So according to naturalism, science and religion are competing for the role of provider of the total explanation of reality. They are in conflict, but science will succeed, and religion will be shown to have been a pretender.

A particularly radical version of naturalism called logical positivism flourished in the first half of the twentieth century. The logical positivists were interested in how religious and scientific assertions can be meaningful. They proposed a criterion of meaning, based on verifiability,[9] and if an assertion fell into the category 'non-verifiable' or 'non-testable,' it was deemed meaningless (with the exception of analytical statements, which are true in virtue of the meanings of their terms). Using this criterion, the positivists concluded that since religious assertions are non-verifiable, they are meaningless. So, under this strong version of naturalism, not only are science and religion in conflict, but religious assertions are meaningless and make no legitimate contribution to human knowledge, thought, or life.

A second type of conflict account is what I will call *religious science.* According to this view, naturalism is right that there is one domain, which both science and religion attempt to address. It is also true that the claims

---

6. At least, this is how Hawking is popularly understood, but see Hilgevoord 1994, especially the articles by Barrow and Hooft.

7. Hawking 1988, p. 185.

8. Hawking 1988, p. 149.

9. Ayer 1936.

of science are often found to be in conflict with claims of theology. However, when the religion is well based, we are forced to reject the claims of science in favor of those of religion, which have the status of infallible truth.

According to popular tradition, one example of religious science is Cardinal Bellarmino, a representative of the Catholic Church and a key figure at Galileo's trial. In 1615 Bellarmino claimed[10] that because Scripture and the Church Fathers endorsed the view that the earth is stationary, at the center of the universe, and because the Scriptures cannot be in error, the claims of science (particularly those of Galileo) must be wrong. Consequently the church banned Galileo's books and instructed him not to teach Copernicus' theory as if it were true.

A prominent twentieth century example is 'creation science.' According to one proponent, Henry Morris,[11] creation science insists that the story of the creation of the world found in the Bible in Genesis chapters 1 and 2 is literally true. God created the world in a period of literally six days about 6000 years ago, and in the order described in Genesis chapter 1. Morris is critical, for example, of theistic evolution (the position that God created the world through the process of evolution),[12] claiming that anyone who takes the teachings of the bible seriously must reject the theory of evolution. Many critics therefore take this to be an instance of religious science. Thus, like naturalism, religious science sees the relationship between science and religion as one of conflict but, unlike naturalism, settles on the side of religion.

The alternative to conflict I will call *harmony*. According to this view, science and religion stand in a relationship of compatibility rather than conflict, in which both the claims of science and the claims of religion can be true, if understood properly. One version of the harmony view I will call the *independence* version. This view advocates the existence of two autonomous, independent domains. Religion is the field of discourse that speaks to one domain, and science is the field of discourse that speaks to the other. Each field is subject to its own standards and methods, and so science and religion do not impact on one another.

The influential philosopher Ludwig Wittgenstein (1889-1951) held an

10. Bellarmino 1955.
11. Morris 1974.
12. Morris 1974, pp. 215-220.

independence version of the harmony view. Early in his career Wittgenstein subscribed to logical positivism and agreed that verifiability was the correct criterion for meaning. However, after reflecting on the nature of language, Wittgenstein changed his mind, concluding that there are different 'forms of life' or aspects of human existence.[13] One of these forms of life is factual, and, within this form, verifiability is the appropriate criterion of meaning. But there are also other dimensions to human life that have different criteria of meaning. Religion is an example of a different form of life, having its own standards and criteria. If religion and science are two independent domains of reality, then any conflict between them is merely apparent. According to Wittgenstein the illusion of conflict is the result of our confusion as to which form of life we are dealing with.

Another version of the harmony view I will call the *interaction* account. According to this view science and religion are neither in conflict nor completely compartmentalized. Rather, there is genuine interaction between the two. But what kind of interaction? One answer to this question is that the interaction between science and religion takes the form of a kind of mutual promotion. One idea here is that if we are serious about religion we will naturally become more serious about science. An example of this mutual promotion between science and religion can be seen in the writings of Francis Bacon (1561-1626),[14] who held that taking certain Judeo-Christian beliefs seriously should lead people to carry out science and develop technology.

According to the mutual promotion view, science can also have positive implications for religious belief. An example of this is the plethora of scientifically based arguments for the existence of God, such as the design argument. Examples include Sir Isaac Newton's (1642-1727) view that cosmology implies the existence of a mathematical designer. In another famous example, William Paley (1743-1805)[15] gave the classic formulation of this argument based on biological adaptation. In the twentieth century, Albert Einstein (1879-1955) thought cosmology, including the theory of relativity, had various implications about the nature and existence of God. These are cases of religious belief being prompted or spurred on by science.

A stronger version of the interaction view I will call *dependence*. This

13. Wittgenstein 1958.
14. Bacon 1905.
15. Paley 1890a.

view maintains that science and religion are not only compatible, but are dependent on one another in some way; for example, that science is needed to provide a rational basis for religion, and that religion is needed in science, for example, to provide the answers to important ethical questions.

Another important question in the independence-versus-interaction debate concerns methodology. A key claim of the independence position is that the two are different domains with different methodologies, different standards for assessing evidence, and so on. The question therefore arises as to what continuity of methodology exists between the two domains, and whether there are similarities, and what significance may be attached to any similarities.

Figure 1: Four views of the relationship between science and religion

So the relation between science and religion is a controversial issue, with a number of competing views. How are we to decide which (if any) of these is correct? Each of these views of the relationship between science and religion — naturalism and religious science on the conflict side, and independence and interaction on the harmony side — is well represented in contemporary thought. So how do we go about resolving the issue? What method can we use to determine a resolution to such controversies?

We can — as we will — turn to case studies found in the history of the development of science and religion such as those of Galileo, Darwin, and modern cosmology. But what will this prove? How does the consideration of such historical case studies help establish the relation between science and religion? These are questions for philosophical analysis. There are two extreme positions on how to approach case studies and what they can tell us.

First, the answer might be that scrutinizing various case studies serves no purpose whatsoever. If each of us has her own set of fixed presuppositions about the relation between science and religion which she will inevitably bring to bear on the case studies, then these presuppositions will lead different people to different assessments of the cases. This may not mean that the case studies are a complete waste of time; rather, what we have — and this is typical of philosophy — is different people engaged in philosophical debate, each with her own different views about the world. We can investigate the implied commitments, consequences and points of convergence and divergence of our various positions. This in itself is a productive activity. However, the case studies will not resolve the dispute over the relation between science and religion.

A second way to approach case studies is to put aside precommitments and to remain open to historical evidence. If we want to find out whether science and religion stand in a relation of conflict or harmony, we simply look to the case studies for empirical evidence of either conflict or harmony. As a result of this we may actually find that we need to revise our presuppositions and original views. Those who do not endorse an empirical approach may instead look to independent philosophical reasoning and arguments to illuminate the problem. Such a method would combine scrutiny of the case studies with independent analysis.

There may even be a correlation between the kind of view a person has of the relation between science and religion, and his methodological preference. For example, naturalists sometimes suggest that those who favor naturalism tend towards an empirical approach, while religious scientists and advocates of the independence version of the harmony view often favor the view that we have fixed presuppositions.

In this book we will visit in some detail each of the three case studies — Galileo, Darwin, and Hawking. In particular, we will examine the various responses that religious figures have made. However, in each case we eventually come back to the central philosophical questions about the relation between science and religion. So how can philosophical analysis contribute? I take it that philosophical analysis is needed to clarify the issues — for example, in setting out possible alternative philosophical perspectives, and the considerations in favor of each.

For example, it will help to distinguish 'philosophical conflict' from 'social conflict.'[16] By 'philosophical conflict' I mean a clash of beliefs or

---

16. Perhaps a weakness of Barbour's analysis is that it fails to make this distinction clearly enough.

ideologies, such that there is a logical inconsistency in the strongest case or some kind of cognitive dissonance in weaker cases. By 'social conflict' I mean an explicit and heated clash of interests within society. So, for example, suppose that special relativity and quantum mechanics are in conflict because of difficulties in resolving, let's suppose, the issue of non-locality; but suppose also that there is no social problem at all, as scientists in these fields labor together in seeking to resolve the problem. This is philosophical conflict, but not social conflict. On the other hand suppose nuclear physics and molecular biology, two areas with remarkably little conceptual conflict, are involved in acrimonious competition for research funding over some major large-scale international research initiatives, to the point where each criticizes the other publicly; and suppose popular journals are divided, *Nature* taking up the cause of biology and *Scientific American* defending physics; and suppose otherwise sane adults refuse to speak to each other in university meetings, and so on. This is social conflict, not philosophical conflict. Of course, there could be cases where both kinds of conflict are present. It should be clear how philosophical conflict could easily spark social conflict. Our concern in dealing with case studies will be to look for genuine philosophical incompatibility behind the obvious social tensions.

Throughout this book we will meet proponents of all the various positions on the relationship between science and religion. The intention is to allow each to get a fair hearing, although my own view is that an open minded look at the case studies will show that the best account of the relation between science and religion is that they are in harmony, with a considerable amount of fruitful interaction. I will defend the view that religious belief as given in Western traditions — not only the theism of classical theism but even many of the orthodox tenets of Christianity — is neither incompatible with nor a hindrance to science: there is no philosophical conflict. At least, that is so in the famous cases of Galileo, Darwin, and Hawking.

CHAPTER 1

Cosmology and Scripture

As we have seen, one of the most potent images of conflict between science and religion in Western history is that of the trial of Galileo. We are tempted from our perspective to think of this as a fight between a lone scientist's attempt to replace outdated religious explanation and a desperate church's effort to retain its place of dominance within intellectual life. But this would be 'Whiggish' history[1] — reading back into Galileo a modern naturalism that isn't in fact there. We need instead to understand the conflict in its context. Galileo was, of course, a scientist, but on all the evidence he was also a serious Catholic. There just was no one in the debate who was trying to replace religion with science.

One common Whiggish response to this fact is to say that figures such as Galileo 'had to' say that they believed in God because there would be political consequences if they didn't. But again, there just is no evidence that Galileo was insincere in his belief in God or in his membership in the church.

As we will see, the debate surrounding the Galilean controversy concerned the interpretation of Scripture on the one hand and science on the other. There was no question that either should be given up. The controversy concerned *how* to show their consonance; that is, how to give a unified understanding of science and religion. It centered on the issue of how

1. A reference to an alleged tendency by the Whigs, an English political party, to rewrite history purely in the light of present circumstances and interests. See Butterfield 1931 and Hall 1983.

we are to read Scripture, and what our understanding of the relation between Scripture and the discoveries of cosmology should be.

To understand the context of the conflict in which Galileo was involved we need to understand a little about the development of cosmology (in which Galileo played a significant part), a little about Genesis and the debate over how it is to be interpreted, and a little about the ways Galileo's predecessors, especially Augustine, construed the relation between science and religion. We start with an account of some of the various developments in cosmology leading up to Galileo.

Cosmology

Cosmology starts for our purposes with Eudoxus (408-353 B.C.) and Aristotle (384-322 B.C.). Aristotle was both a philosopher and a scientist, and his system included a remarkable synthesis of many fields of knowledge. In his cosmology Aristotle divided the subluminal area, or the earthly area, from the heavens, and according to his physics these two regions are fundamentally different. The heavens are perfect and are not subject to decay, but down on earth we have both imperfection and decay. Earthly things are made up of four basic elements: earth, air, water, and fire.

According to Aristotle's physics, things move in natural motions according to certain principles that are connected to those things' natures. In other words, the motions of an object depend on the kind of thing that object is. If that object's nature is earthy, its natural motion will tend towards the earth. This also applies to objects that possess a water nature, since water's nature is to move to the center of the universe, which is in fact the earth. On the other hand, objects whose natures are connected with air or fire have a different natural motion, namely to move away from the earth, that is, straight up. Violent motion is any motion that is not a natural motion. For example, pushing a physical object upwards, away from the earth, is a violent motion, since that goes against that object's natural motion. In Aristotle's physics, a violent motion requires a force to make it happen and continue to happen. To make a physical object keep moving in violent motion, one must continue applying a force to that object.

On the other hand, the so-called heavenly motions involve a different kind of motion, because the heavenly things are made of a different element, the fifth type of element, the ether. According to Aristotle, things that are made of the ether possess a perfectly circular, constant, continuous, and unforced motion. This idea is important in Aristotle's overall physics and cosmology.

Eudoxus, a friend of Aristotle's teacher Plato, had offered a schema for the movements of the heavenly bodies centered on the earth. Eudoxus' model depicts the universe as something like a beach ball, with the fixed stars painted on the inside and the earth in the exact centre. In the area between the earth and the fixed stars move what we would call the planets and the sun and the moon.

All these heavenly bodies move in spheres, which, being in the heavens, have the nature of ether and move in circles. The total system involves a series of concentric spheres. Saturn, Jupiter, Mars, Venus, Mercury, the sun, and the moon are all embedded in their own (sometimes interpenetrating) spheres, each sphere rotating slowly around the earth at its own speed. The fixed stars, on the other hand, rotate together once a day.

Now this system of Eudoxus' encountered several problems in accounting for all the data of astronomy. The biggest problem concerned what were known as the 'wandering stars' (that is, the planets). When astronomers observed Mars move, say, for six months, they noticed that it appears to travel forward and then loop back on itself, and then go forward again. Such phenomena needed to be explained within the concentric circles schema.

Aristotle attempted to solve this problem by introducing more spheres of movement, moving in different directions. The looping motions are explained if the planet transfers to a different sphere of motion (moving at the same distance from the center), and back again, just as if two trains are passing each other in opposite directions you can have a looping trajectory by jumping from one train to the other, and then back again. Aristotle's hope was that these additional spheres might help to explain the actual observations of the wandering stars. In all, Aristotle had to posit the existence of fifty-five spheres of motion, a system far more complicated than the original scheme proposed by Eudoxus.

There was, however, another problem with the Eudoxus/Aristotle model. According to this system, all the planets or wandering stars should appear to be the same brightness at all times because they are traveling in perfect circles. But according to observation the planets vary in brightness as though they are actually closer and further away at different times of the year. Aristotle's system had no obvious way of explaining this anomaly.

The Greek astronomer Ptolemy (A.D. 100-170) didn't question Aristotle's physics, but he did offer a new, more sophisticated mathematical system to explain the looping motion and the variation in brightness of the planets. He introduced several new devices. One was the epicycle. Ptolemy, like Aristotle, worked under the assumption that cosmology could be explained in terms of circular motions, and took this to be the basic motion of the heavenly bodies. However, Ptolemy added another smaller circular motion, or epicycle on that basic circle, on which the planet's motion is the sum of these two circles. This device allowed Ptolemy to explain the motions of the wandering stars and the variations in apparent brightness, by arranging various epicycles in the right way.

However, Ptolemy found that to account for observations he had to allow the planetary motions to be eccentric, meaning that the earth is not exactly in the center of the motion of the planetary spheres. He recognized that if the earth is not quite in the center of the circular motions of the planets, then Aristotle's fundamental principle of constant motion about the earth is violated. So Ptolemy introduced the notion of the equant to preserve this principle of constant motion, and to make his system more consistent with observation of the planets. The equant is a point near the earth, and also not quite at the center of the planetary revolution, but from which point the major epicycle of that planetary motion has constant angular velocity.

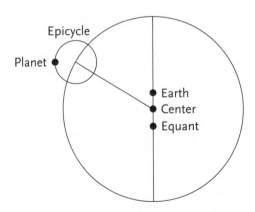

Figure 2: Ptolemaic Model of an Outer Planet

Followers of Ptolemy, and even Ptolemy himself, were equivocal about whether this system was intended to be a mathematical device for explaining observation, or a physical hypothesis about the way things really are. Aristotle, on the other hand was clear on this point. He maintained that his system was intended to be a physical hypothesis and explanation of the way that the cosmos really works.

By the time of Nicholas Copernicus (1473-1543), the Ptolemaic system had been the dominant view for more than a thousand years, although in the Renaissance it again became an ongoing, developing project. Copernicus was a priest in the Roman Catholic Church and a sincere, dedicated member of the church. His main work, *On the Revolutions of the Celestial Spheres,* is dedicated to the Pope. In that dedication, Copernicus also feels a need to offer ancient support for his theories, and so goes to great lengths to name Greek philosophers (among them Pythagoras and others of Heraclitus' followers) who had held heliocentric views similar to his own.

Copernicus' interest in cosmology arose within an ecclesiastical (church) setting. A church council had been convened to reform the calendar, which was based on predictions of the motions of the planets. The council determined that it was incapable of facilitating this reform, as not enough was known at that point about cosmology. This, then, became Copernicus' vision: to provide a cosmology adequate for the ecclesiastical reform of the calendar. Thus he saw his work in astronomy as being part of his service to the church.

But Copernicus found the Ptolemaic system most unpalatable, a "monster," a mish-mash of bits and pieces with no clear unifying concept. In particular, since it deals with the motions as they appear from the equant point, it gives no insight into the way the world really is. Further, the different cycles have their own principles of operation and epicycles, leaving the system with no unifying principle that explains how all the motions work as a whole. To Copernicus, Ptolemy's theory appears

> as if someone were to collect hands, feet, a head, and other members from various places, all very fine in themselves, but not proportionate to one body, and no single one corresponding to others, so that a monster rather than a man would be formed from them.[2]

2. Copernicus 1939a.

Aristotle's physics, on the other hand, had that unity, for in it all of the planets move by constant, circular motion.

On the Revolutions of the Celestial Spheres was published in 1543, although the ideas put forward in this work had been formulated by Copernicus as early as 1512.[3] The essence of the Copernican system is that the center of the cosmos is not the earth but (more nearly) the sun, and that the earth, and the heavenly bodies (except the moon) circle the sun. This enabled Copernicus to rescue the idea that the motion in the heavens is constant and circular, and, he claimed, to bring all of cosmology back to simpler motions.

But the Copernican system immediately causes problems for Aristotelian physics. If the earth is moving around the cosmos, loose objects will fly off (that is, be left behind), clouds will necessarily float toward the west, and a body in free fall next to a tower will land to the west of the tower. None of this in fact occurs. Worse still, the Copernican system makes the earth a heavenly body, when its nature is not to be in motion, and it places a heavenly body, the sun, at the centre of the cosmos and not strictly in the heavens.

It should also be noted that Copernicus' system did not make things particularly simpler. To make the system fit in with astronomical observation, Copernicus also introduced the epicycle. In fact, he introduced epicycles on epicycles on epicycles, resulting in a system even more complex than that of Ptolemy. (Real simplification did not come until the work of Kepler in 1609, who recognized that the planetary motions are better described by the ellipse.)

We now turn to Galileo's contribution. Galileo (1564-1642), who grew up in Pisa and taught in Padua and Florence, was a vocal defender of the Copernican system and equally vocal critic of Aristotelianism. (He was more impressed by philosophers such as Archimedes than by Aristotle.)

One of Galileo's chief contributions was to appreciate how the Copernican theory required a new physics, and he argued vigorously for a version of the 'impetus theory.' By the time of Isaac Newton this impetus theory had solved many of the physical problems or 'absurdities' facing the Copernican system — such as the fact that bodies in free fall fall in a straight line toward the earth — by utilizing the radical dynamic principle of impetus. In opposition to the Aristotelian notion that violent motion needs a sus-

3. Hooykaas 1974.

taining force, the impetus theory (in the version of interest here) says that without interference a 'violent' motion remains constant and rectilinear. The reason, therefore, why a ball dropped from a tower lands at the base of the tower and is not left behind as the earth moves on is that it already has the 'violent' motion and that motion continues in virtue of the impetus of the object. In other words, physical bodies show no effect of the earth's motion in virtue of their participation in the earth's motion.

On first glance the impetus theory appears to be contrary to the evidence. If I knock a ball, causing it to roll along the ground, then the ball eventually stops unless I continue to apply the force. Galileo himself solves this by distinguishing actual empirical motion and natural motion in an ideal sense. By ideal motion Galileo meant motion in which all external influences, such as friction and air resistance, are discounted. The natural ideal motion of the ball is to continue in motion, but empirically the ball stops because it is acted on by frictional forces.

In 1610 Galileo published his major work, *The Starry Messenger*,[4] in which he reports his observations of the heavens made with a telescope. The telescope had been in use for some time before Galileo, but only in either a commercial or military capacity. Galileo was the first to direct his telescope towards the heavens, and his discoveries made him a celebrity overnight. One of these was the fact that the moon is not a perfect sphere, immune to decay or change, but rather has a landscape that includes mountains and valleys. Other discoveries included the moons of Jupiter and a vast number of new stars that had never before been seen, which challenged the Aristotelian picture of a fixed, small universe with stars embedded in the outer shell like a beach ball.

While Galileo's discoveries made him a celebrity, they also put him in conflict with the Aristotelians, who were mainly centered in the universities, and sections of the church, as we will see in subsequent sections.

In the end, Isaac Newton (1642-1727) was able to systematize Galileo's ideas into what we today think of as Newtonian physics. Newton employed the basic assumption that bodies follow the same laws of motion everywhere, in opposition to Aristotle's idea of different natures having different motions, and in particular the heavens having different natural motion to that of the earth. Newton was able to use the Galilean assumption that bodies move in straight lines unless acted upon by a force to de-

---

4. Reprinted in Galileo 1937a.

rive universal laws of motion that applied equally well to planets and billiard balls.

However, Newton's system was not trouble-free. One problem is that it seems to be true empirically, not just ideally, that the planets do not decay in their motion, just as Aristotle had claimed. Newton's explanation was that the nature of planets is to run down, but God continually throws comets into the solar system, injecting the energy needed to keep the planets in continuous motion. (This problem was not really solved until the development of thermodynamics in the nineteenth century.)

In the one hundred and fifty years between Copernicus and Newton there was a complete overturning of a worldview, from the idea of a small, contained universe with humanity at its center, to a possibly infinite universe in which the earth is just one insignificant lump of rock that happens to circle around one insignificant star. The new cosmology raises further questions about the interface of science and religion. What is our place in this universe? Is it all made for us as the book of Genesis claims? Newton himself concluded that his discoveries pointed to the existence of God, as master mathematician and architect, as we will see in a later chapter. But first we turn to the immediate theological problem with Greek cosmology, and the issues of hermeneutics, Genesis, and the answers on science and religion given by Augustine and Calvin.

Genesis and Hermeneutics

The book of Genesis, especially chapters 1 and 2, is significant to several of the world's major religions, including Judaism, Christianity, and Islam. Chapters 1 and 2 of Genesis relate the story of the creation of the world. Although it was not the only account of creation available in its day, we will mainly focus on Genesis and the Judeo-Christian religious tradition because that is the context in which our case study is situated.

In fact, Galileo's defense of Copernican cosmology is not the only occasion Genesis 1–2 becomes a focal point for debate. We will find throughout this book that Genesis features in a number of the flashpoints between science and history in the Western tradition. Francis Bacon uses the idea of the 'image of God' in arriving at his influential views about the relation between humanity and nature, and about the significance of that for our attitude towards science and technology. In the Darwinian debate the 'seven days' of Genesis 1 are used to defend a young earth theory, and the idea that creatures were made 'according to their kind' is used to challenge Darwin's theory of the evolution of species.

Genesis is a Jewish piece of literature, written in Hebrew (by Moses, according to tradition). Genesis 1 describes God creating, in six days, heaven and earth from formlessness and void, speaking into existence light and the sky (called the 'firmament' or 'heaven'); dividing light from darkness and the earth from the sea; and adding vegetation, the sun, moon, and stars, the fish and birds, and the 'beasts of the earth.' Its climax is God creating the man and the woman and telling them to rule the earth, and its denouement is God resting on the seventh day.

The question of hermeneutics immediately arises. Should this all be read literally, or to some extent metaphorically? This question cannot be avoided if we are to address the relationship between science and religion. On the one hand, if you hold that Genesis is true, you will still need to ask what is the appropriate way to interpret it. On the other hand if you hold that religion is in effect a primitive scientific account that is in due course replaced by a better scientific one, then you are assuming that Genesis was intended to be read literally, as a scientific account, and it is on that basis that it is mistaken. Either way, the issue of hermeneutics cannot be avoided.

Hermeneutics is the theory of interpretation, the study of the interpretation of a text. As a discipline it has its roots in theological discussions about how to interpret texts such as Genesis, but hermeneutics has today become a major issue in contemporary philosophy, with its scope reaching far beyond questions regarding the interpretation of Scripture. Every book we read, every newspaper article, every assertion we hear someone make requires interpretation in the sense that we have to know whether it is to be taken literally or metaphorically. To take a sentence literally means reading each word in that sentence according to an accepted, 'dictionary' meaning (context indicating which meaning if there is more than one), and applying the rules of grammar to yield a unique meaning for that sentence. To take something metaphorically is to take the sentence to be making a different point than the literal. Saying, for example, "That's a dog of a car," makes a point other than about a literal animal nature of your car.

An allegory is a kind of extended metaphor, in which an entire story has a higher, additional meaning other than the literal one. Many familiar texts contain allegory; for instance, George Orwell's *Animal Farm* contains political allegory, and C. S. Lewis' *Chronicles of Narnia* expresses a Christian allegory. It is possible to read such works without recognizing the intended allegory, but lurking behind the story lies a higher meaning fully intended by the author.

Given that to understand a text we always need to decide whether it is to be interpreted literally or metaphorically, is it arbitrary how a text is read? According to one philosophical movement, so-called 'postmodernism,' it is, because the intended meaning of the author is either inaccessible to us or a meaningless notion. French intellectual Roland Barthes therefore announces the 'death of the author.'[5]

But this sort of skepticism runs up against the brute fact that we do successfully communicate. This is so regardless of whether we can explain how we do it. Somehow or other we know in many cases what the author intends, and to know that we must know whether the text is intended literally or metaphorically. When I say, "That's a dog of a car," it is clear that I want this to be taken metaphorically.

In fact we can identify several ways to tell whether something is to be read literally or metaphorically; some are internal and others are external. By *internal* I mean internal to the text: we discover the intentions of an author by staying within the confines of the text. So, if I send you a letter in which I have written "That's a dog of a car," you may be able to tell by what else is contained in the letter, if not by the sentence itself, that this is not intended to be taken literally. There can also be *external* reasons, from the context outside of the text. For instance, in reading my letter, that you know me and know that I own a certain car and so on helps fix the meaning. In this way, you can discover my intentions and what I mean.

There is also a third way of fixing a meaning: by *policy*. For example, the person who for some *a priori* reason says that a text is to be taken literally has a fixed policy on the interpretation, and is not influenced by the details of the text or context in coming to that judgment. Alternatively, someone might have a Marxist or feminist policy for interpretation that in effect fixes the kind of interpretation independently of the text or context.

It will be helpful to consider two kinds of interpretations of Genesis 1–2, namely the cosmological and the theological approaches. According to the *cosmological* approach we are to take Genesis 1–2 at face value, as a literal account of what actually happened, and of what is. This leads us to a particular cosmology, that is, to a particular account of the creation and

---

5. Gellner 1992; Wolterstorff 1995.

structure of the universe. For instance, when we read "And God said, let there be a firmament in the midst of the waters, and let it divide the waters from the waters" we are in fact reading a scientific account which specifies the shape of the universe. There is (or was), as a matter of fact, water above the sky. Similarly, since the moon is the lesser of the great lights, it is literally a luminous body with greater absolute brightness than any of the stars. This approach gives us the cosmology we see in figure 3.

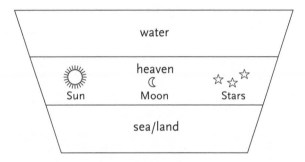

Figure 3: The Literal Cosmology of Genesis 1

Taken literally, Genesis also provides us with a specific time frame in which creation took place, namely six days and nights, and a strict order in which the various bits of the cosmology were added.

A *theological* reading of Genesis 1–2 takes the text to be revealed by God, but recommends that we do not take the text at face value, but instead, for internal and external reasons, read the cosmology metaphorically. These reasons include, firstly, the nature of the literature that we are concerned with, and secondly, the historical context of the text.

One of the first things that we notice about the literary nature of Genesis 1–2 is that it contains two very different creation accounts. The first account occurs through chapter one up to chapter two, verse two, whilst the second forms the subject matter of chapter two, from verse three onwards. There is a striking difference in the order of creation given in the two accounts. In Chapter 1 the plants are created before the animals, which are created before the man and woman. In Chapter 2 the man is created first and then the plants and animals, and then the woman. This indicates that the order is not intended to be taken literally.

The Two Accounts of Creation

Genesis 1–2:3	*Genesis 2:4-25*
trees, plants — day 3 (11-12)	man (7)
fish, birds — day 5 (20-21)	trees (9)
animals — day 6 (24-5)	animals, birds (19)
man and woman — day 6 (26-7)	woman (22)

Another difference is in literary style. The first account is a highly structured piece of literature, while the second is more straightforward discursive prose. Chapter 1 contains an introduction, middle, and conclusion, with the middle section being divided into six sub-sections corresponding to the six days, and marked off with the formula 'And the evening and the morning were the xth day.' Each day begins with a divine command, which is followed by the fulfillment or execution of that command, an evaluation of that fulfillment, the naming by God of what was created, and finally the counting of the day on which this has all occurred. Phrases such as "God saw that it was good" are repeated regularly. In other words, there is a distinctive formalism or regular patterning within the text.

There are also patterns of content. For example, if we arrange the objects of creation in two columns, according to days, like so:

1. light	4. sun, moon, stars
2. sky	5. birds
3. land	6. animals and humans

a certain symmetry appears. The column on the left is the 'forms', and the column on the right the 'content' of those forms; the two correspond perfectly.[6] So, the sun, moon and stars are instances of light; the birds fill the sky, and the animals the land.

There is also a great deal of symbolism in the first account. If we count the number of times that certain words and phrases such as "and it was so," "God," "earth," and "heaven" appear in the original Hebrew text, we will see that they are always present in multiples of seven. Also, in the Hebrew text, the first sentence of chapter one contains seven words, and verses one to three of chapter two (the last sentence of the first account) contain thirty-five words — a multiple of seven. The number seven was an

6. Wenham 1987, p. 7.

important symbolic number in Hebrew thought, symbolizing God, perfection, and eternity much in the same way that the number thirteen might symbolize bad luck to us. This indicates that the number of days of creation — seven — serves to highlight the divine origin of the activity described rather than having any literal significance.

According to the theological interpretation, the structure of Genesis 1 emphasizes the orderliness of creation — its regularity and order. Nature as we know it is not chaotic but obeys laws, and this order tells us that its creator is an orderly, rational God. In other words, creation reveals the rationality and wisdom of God.

The historical context of Genesis provides external clues about its interpretation. Israel was surrounded by powerful political forces: Egypt to the south, Babylon to the east, the local Canaanites, and later on Assyria and then Greece to the north. These nations had their own religious traditions, mostly polytheistic. In Egypt under the Pharaohs many gods were worshiped, including the sun god Ra, the god of the underworld Osiris, and many others in both human and animal forms; the king was associated with the falcon god Horus. The Mesopotamian pantheon included deities associated with heaven, the moon, the sun, the morning and evening star, the winds, fresh water, various regions on earth, and the netherworld.

These religions had their own creation stories, such as the Babylonian Atrahasis epic and the Enuma Elish,[7] which share various similarities with Genesis 1–2.[8] The Atrahasis epic, like Genesis, gives the story of creation as a prelude to a universal flood. The later Enuma Elish shares with Genesis stories of the creation of light, firmament, lights, and dry land.

However, the distinctive features of Genesis are even more significant. In Genesis God is in complete control, without rival, creating at will in an orderly and purposeful fashion. In the Babylonian stories the gods fight for supremacy, and the outcome depends on various contingencies. In the Atrahasis epic the gods originally had to work for their food; angry about this, they rebelled against their leader. The eventual solution was to create human beings to do the work, so a god was killed and his blood mixed with clay to form a man.[9]

---

7. This 'folk' title derives from the first words of the Babylonian creation myth, meaning 'when on high.'

8. Heidel (trans) 1954.

9. Jacobsen 1987.

Against this context, the Jewish story asserts a monotheism involving the supremacy of the God of Israel over all creation. The sun, moon, and stars are expressly created for the purpose of marking time, in deliberate contrast to the deification of these in Mesopotamian and Egyptian religions. Thus Genesis is best seen as a polemic against alternative religious ideas of the day. This helps us see that details may not be literally significant, since they are just the vehicle for expressing the distinctively Hebrew monotheistic doctrine of God's unrivalled sovereignty. That is, the details of the story are not the point, but rather the details are the vehicle for the point.

So, to summarize, the cosmological interpretation takes literally the details of the description of the world and how and when it came into being. The theological interpretation takes the details to be a product of a literary and polemical expression of central theological truths about God's rationality, wisdom, power, and sovereignty.

Augustine's Hermeneutics

Augustine's (A.D. 354-430) mature thought was influenced by two main factors, Christianity and Greek philosophy. Early in life he was influenced by the Manicheans, who taught a version of the Zoroastrian doctrine that there are good and evil forces of similar power whose cosmic struggle produces the world as we know it, including the good human soul and the evil physical body. But on being converted to Christianity, Augustine set about to effect a synthesis of neo-Platonic philosophy and Christian theology.

One aspect of this synthesis is Augustine's integration of the Christian notion of God with the Platonic theory of forms. By a 'form' Plato means the universal quality associated with any group of particulars that share that quality. A particular, say a dog, is just one of the class (of dogs). The true definition of a dog — that it has four legs and so on — captures the form or nature of the dog. The form, definition, or true nature of a circle is that each of its points are equidistant from its center. For Plato the form is the true reality, while the particular is real only in so far as it shares in that true reality. A particular dog is a dog in virtue of the fact that it participates in the form of dogness, which exists in the realm of the forms. No actual circle that we could draw on earth, no matter how carefully, could ever be a true, perfect circle. The true circle that we cannot draw is the Platonic form of the circle. For Plato, everything has a perfect form that exists in 'heaven.'

For Plato, the Form of the Good, mathematized as the One, is greater than all the other forms and 'subsumes' them all in important respects. For example, in order to know any form we must first know the Good. Augustine identified Plato's Form of the Good with the personal Judeo-Christian God. All other forms have their ultimate existence in the mind of God, their Creator.

Augustine's best known works are the *Confessions*,[10] which was completed in about A.D. 400, and *City of God*,[11] which was completed near the end of his life. Here, however, we will focus on another of Augustine's works, *De Litteram* or, in translation, "On the Literal Interpretation of Genesis"[12] (A.D. 415), a massive volume that took Augustine fifteen years to complete.

In *De Litteram* Augustine says his major aim is to demonstrate a one to one correlation between Scripture and true science. In Augustine's day the Aristotelian-Ptolemaic model of the cosmos was dominant, and Augustine does not question that.[13] On the other hand, Augustine sees Scripture as coming uncorrupted from God. Although it has human writers and therefore bears human characteristics, it is infallible. This still leaves open how Scripture is to be interpreted. According to Augustine, we should in the first instance read all of Scripture literally, because Scripture is a 'faithful record' of what has actually happened. However, Augustine's readings are often allegorical. A case in point is his interpretation of Genesis 1.

According to Augustine's reconstruction of Genesis, God created everything at the beginning in one instantaneous, all-encompassing act of creation. The six day structure of the Genesis narrative is thus not intended to be the literal historical sequence of creation, but rather a topically ordered set of revelations to angels. It is not sequentially the way that events occurred in time, but is doctrinally ordered in the way in which those events were revealed. (Augustine's focus on the part played by angels comes from the tradition that the book of Genesis was received by Moses from angels.) Augustine also claims that the six days of creation have

---

10. Augustine 1961.

11. Augustine 1972.

12. Augustine 1982.

13. Virtually all Christian writers from the first century down to Copernicus held to the Aristotelian-Ptolemaic cosmology. One notable exception was Lactantius (d. ~A.D. 330), who taught a flat earth on the basis of Scripture, and in opposition to Greek cosmology.

mathematical significance, six being a perfect number because it is equal to the sum of all of its factors. (Earlier, we noted that the Hebrew tradition saw seven as the perfect number; indeed it seems here that Augustine was more in tune with Pythagorean philosophy than with Hebrew thought.)

According to Plato in the *Timaeus*,[14] the 'Demiurge,' a poorly-esteemed craftsman god, created the visible world by copying the forms, imposing them on matter which already existed. Augustine's God is very much more exalted. All the creaturely forms exist firstly in the mind of God. In creation God created all of the matter that makes up the material world, and all the substantial forms of every kind of thing that would ever come into existence. These substantial forms are physical instantiations of the forms that already existed as ideas in God's mind. This does not mean that all created things were present at that instant of creation; rather they were all there in embryo in order that they would develop at a later time. Thus there is a kind of blueprint for everything that will later come to be. There may be no actual dog in the original creation, but the substantial form of 'dogness' is there, and so the dog exists potentially at that moment. Augustine expressed this in terms of the idea of a 'seed' or causal reason, a premature instantiation of the creaturely form.

Augustine's account is an evolutionary theory of creation. It is historical but teleological evolution, operating not by chance but by an inbuilt driving rational principle that will certainly lead to its goal. It is not Darwinian evolution in that it carries no possibility for modification of kinds; dogs cannot turn into cats. It involves rather the coexistence of all of the potential kinds together at the original point in time.

According to Augustine's stated hermeneutics of Scripture, we should always take the literal reading of Scripture to be the true one unless we have conclusive reasons to do otherwise. There may be cases where science provides a proof of something contrary to the teaching of Scripture interpreted literally. In such cases this shows that Scripture is intended to be taken metaphorically. This approach is warranted by the underlying premise there is one God who is the author of both creation and Scripture, so that it is impossible that we should find science contradicting Scripture, or Scripture contradicting science.

For example, Scripture says that God stretches out the heavens like an animal skin, whereas astronomy tells us that the heavens are spherical.

14. Plato 1971.

Augustine notes that these rival claims are in opposition but adds: "Let it be opposed if [the astronomers'] statement is false."[15] In other words, accept Scripture over against science, if that science has not been proved conclusively. But if the science has been proved, we must show that Scripture is not opposed to it by reading that Scripture metaphorically rather than literally. In any case, in another part of Scripture heaven is described as being suspended like a dome or a vault. Since these two Scriptures are contradictory and incompatible, we also have an internal reason for reading these parts of Scripture metaphorically.

Augustine also urges that Christians not be what he calls "doggedly literal minded" and insist on a literal interpretation of Scripture in the face of proven science, or in ignorance of science. This only brings Scripture into disrepute among those who need it. A related theme in *De Litteram* is that the main purpose of Scripture is spiritual and not cosmological. For instance, on the question of the shape of the heavens, Augustine concludes that

> in the matter of the shape of heaven the sacred writers knew the truth, but that the Spirit of God, who spoke through them, did not wish to teach men these facts that would be of no avail for their salvation.[16]

Ernan McMullin[17] finds in Augustine two contradictory hermeneutical themes. The 'relevance principle' says to take Scripture literally, including its apparently cosmological claims, unless it is contradicted by conclusively proven scientific findings, in which case we should read that Scripture metaphorically. But the 'neutrality principle' urges that Scripture is concerned with spirituality and salvation rather than cosmology, which presumably entails that all apparently cosmological passages are to be interpreted metaphorically.

These two principles are consistent in cases of apparent conflict, on a matter where science is proved. Both say to read Scripture metaphorically, not as literal cosmological claims. The conflict arises in cases of apparent conflict on matters where science is not conclusively proved. Then relevance recommends a literal, cosmological reading of Scripture while neutrality recommends a metaphorical, spiritual reading.

15. Augustine 1982, bk. 2, ch. 9, v. 21.
16. Augustine 1982, bk. 2, ch. 9, v. 20.
17. McMullin 1981.

However, this may be a little unfair on Augustine, as there are ways to read these principles consistently. One way is simply to take the neutrality principle to apply in those problematic cases where science has proved the literal reading wrong. Another more sophisticated conciliation is to take Augustine as recognizing two aims in Scripture. The first, primary aim is spiritual, to lead people to God. This is for the benefit of everyone and the Church has the responsibility to teach Scripture to that end. The second, however, allows the learned legitimately to glean from Scripture cosmological and metaphysical truths (such as Augustine's neo-Platonic account of creation). This gives Scripture considerable importance — outweighing merely probable scientific results. However, one should realize that by 'Scripture' Augustine on this view seems to mean allegorical constructions more than literal cosmological assertions; and further, that 'proven science' means things like Aristotelian-Ptolemaic cosmology, and that 'merely probable science' means speculative cosmological/metaphysical philosophy such as that of the Manicheans. According to this reconciliation of Augustine's views, then, neutrality is a safe, general approach for the non-learned, and cosmological speculation should only be undertaken by the qualified few.

Calvin's Hermeneutics

The Protestant Reformation began in 1517 when Martin Luther (1483-1546) posted his Ninety-Five Theses on the door of Wittenberg Cathedral. Over the following hundred years the Reformation developed in different places throughout Europe. The result was a Europe that was split both geographically and religiously into Protestant and Roman Catholic spheres of influence.

John Calvin (1509-1564) was a reformer, a theologian, and a leader in the Protestant movement in Geneva, Switzerland. Calvin published his main work, *Institutes of Christian Religion*,[18] in 1536 but he also wrote an extensive commentary on the Bible which runs to many volumes.[19]

Calvin held that there is an innate and universal religious instinct present in all human beings, which is such that everyone can discern in the

---

18. Calvin 1949.
19. Calvin 1846; Calvin 1847.

natural world evidence which points to the existence and nature of God. Therefore, any person anywhere has an innate capacity to be able to know that God exists. This is part of his doctrine of common grace, according to which God gives every person, Christian or otherwise, abilities to do and know certain sorts of things, for example, scientific ones. Calvin held the view that science is a noble and admirable enterprise that should be pursued, as it "unfolds the admirable wisdom of God."[20] Those privileged few who have the ability to do science have an obligation to pursue it. (We will return to this idea when we look at Francis Bacon.) The doctrine of common grace also allowed Calvin, in keeping with Renaissance humanism, to recognize and acknowledge the value of the literary and scholarly Greek heritage.

Nevertheless Calvin was skeptical about the capacity of the human intellect to grasp any kind of 'ultimate truth.' On the theological side, like Augustine, Calvin was skeptical about the capacity of the human intellect to grasp ultimate truths by the power of reason, because all humans are morally corrupt, and this moral corruption affects the understanding (the noetic[21] effect of sin). For true knowledge of God Calvin places a great emphasis on Scripture as an infallible, unique and necessary source of knowledge about God and salvation.

On the philosophical side, Calvin was a nominalist, denying Platonic forms on the grounds that the way language divides groups of particulars into classes, such as dog, circle, and so on is a matter of convention. This led to skepticism with regard to the human intellect's capacity to do philosophy and metaphysics, a skepticism that later influenced the British empiricists and their forerunner Francis Bacon.

Copernicus' findings were published in 1543, but Calvin makes little mention of the Copernican system, and what he does say is unfavorable. At the time, the theory was of course merely one among many, and Calvin himself was pre-Copernican, firmly in the grip of Aristotelian-Ptolemaic cosmology. But Calvin's focus was not generally directed toward the details of cosmology.

Calvin recognized that a literal reading of Scripture might sometimes be in conflict with science. For instance, Genesis apparently de-

20. Calvin 1847, pp. 85-86.
21. 'Noetic' refers to the intellect, hence the 'noetic effect of sin' refers to the alleged distorting impact, due to sin, on the human capacity for rational thinking.

scribes one expanse of the heavens, but science teaches us that the heavens contain a number of spheres. In Genesis the sun and the moon are called the great lights, whereas astronomy teaches us that Saturn is in fact greater than the moon. And Genesis describes the 'water above the heavens,' whereas astronomy and common sense tell us that there is no such water above the heavens.[22]

But Calvin insisted that we should not search for a detailed cosmology in Scripture because cosmology is not the topic of Scripture, and he completely resisted the common approach of reading Greek cosmology into Scripture. Calvin's general principle is that nothing is discussed in Genesis except the visible form of the world. Calvin's idea of 'the visible form of the world' involves a distinction between how things appear to us, and the way things really are, which we can discover through science. Scripture deals only in the language of appearance. The actual point of the Genesis account of the 'firmament' is to affirm the fact that God created the heavens, but not to say anything about exactly what the nature of the heavens is. Aristotelian science might be capable of showing us what the nature of the heavens is, but it is not the purpose of Scripture to teach such things. The same applies to 'the greater and lesser lights,' (the sun and the moon and planets, respectively). From the point of view of the way things appear to us, the moon does actually look brighter than, say, Saturn, although we know that this is not really the case. So Calvin concludes: "He who would learn astronomy and other recondite arts, let him go elsewhere."[23]

The theological underpinning to this neutrality account of the relation between cosmology and Scripture is the Reformation doctrine that Scripture is written by God for everybody and not just for the learned. Every person has the right and ability to read and understand Scripture for themselves without needing the authoritative interpretation of the Church. In order to be relevant to everybody, Scripture must deal with appearance and not the way things really are from a scientific point of view. To teach about science is to exclude all but the learned few. Thus Scriptures speak in a language *accommodated* to the uneducated common person, so that everyone can understand them.

This applies not only to Genesis, but also, for example, to the Psalms,

22. Calvin 1847, ch. I, v. 6.
23. Calvin 1847, ch. I, v. 6.

where David speaks of a "deaf"[24] adder as though there really is such a thing as enchantment.[25] David writes in accommodation to the common people, making allowance for their mistakes.

There are similarities and differences between Calvin and Augustine. Both agree that Scripture is true and comes to us uncorrupted from God, and that its primary purpose concerns salvation and other spiritual issues. Both agree that Aristotelian cosmology is true and that Scripture should not be taken literally as denying what is proven by Aristotelian cosmology. But Augustine maintains that the Bible can teach the learned about cosmology and metaphysics, whereas Calvin claims that the Bible does not teach us about cosmology. Calvin holds that the whole message of Scripture is accessible to all people, a view that is not shared by Augustine.

Galileo and the Church

Copernicus published *On the Revolutions of the Celestial Spheres* in 1543. During that same year, the Catholic Church convened the Council of Trent in response to the Protestant Reformation, in which it articulated a hardened position against heresy. One of its directives recommended that Scriptures not be interpreted in a manner contrary to the common interpretation of the Church Fathers (which included Augustine).

Galileo's *Starry Messenger* was published in 1610;[26] in it he claimed to show that the heavens are imperfect. This served to stimulate much debate within the Church during the period between 1610 and 1616, over the Copernican system and over hermeneutics, that is, over how Scripture was to be read if the Copernican system was taken to be true.

In 1615 matters started to come to a head. A letter appeared, written by the priest Paolo Antonio Foscarini and circulated quite widely in Italy. Foscarini, a friend of Galileo, discusses the opinions of the Pythagoreans and of Copernicus concerning the motion of the Earth, and attempts to demonstrate the compatibility of these views with Scripture. Foscarini is not so much concerned with proving whether or not Copernicus' system is true; rather, assuming it is true he sets out a hermeneutics that will allow

24. This is a reference to a "deaf" death adder.
25. Psalm 53.
26. See Hooykaas 1974.

an interpretation of Scripture that is compatible with the Copernican system. Foscarini was of the view that if we properly understand the true meaning of Scripture, we will discover there something like the Copernican system. However, on a surface level, Scripture is saying something that has been adapted, or accommodated, to everyday people: "the words of Scripture are adapted to the way of speech of daily life."[27]

In April of that same year, Cardinal Bellarmino, a more senior figure in the Church than Foscarini, replied to the letter, advising Foscarini directly (and therefore Galileo indirectly) that he should speak hypothetically, not absolutely, about the Copernican system. Bellarmino's tone is not one of friendly advice, but more of serious warning.

To speak 'hypothetically rather than absolutely' was a common way of viewing astronomy and mathematics during this period. Aristotelian philosophy and metaphysics dictates that the Earth is in the center of the universe and that the heavenly bodies move in spheres and so on, but the mathematics of the epicycles was often taken as a mere tool for making predictions. It was quite common to say that one could speak hypothetically and propose a system that would enable predictions to be made. The idea can be found in the preface that was (anonymously) added to Copernicus' *On the Revolutions of the Celestial Spheres*[28] in 1543 by Osiander, the man responsible for its printing. Osiander wrote that the entire Copernican system should be taken as a hypothesis, and as not speaking absolutely about what really is the case.

Also in 1615, Galileo wrote his *Letter to the Grand Duchess Christina*,[29] in which he spells out his views on the relation between cosmology and Scripture. Like Foscarini, his aim is to allow for both the Copernican theory and Scripture. Galileo appeals directly to Augustine to furnish a hermeneutic that will achieve this aim.

It is important to again emphasize that this period — from the publication of *The Starry Messenger* in 1610 through to 1615 — was a time of torrid debate within the ranks of the Church regarding these sorts of issues. However, Bellarmino's letter was a signal that it was not to be a matter of debate for much longer.

In 1616 the Catholic Church officially banned the Copernican sys-

27. Hooykaas 1974, p. 75.
28. Copernicus 1939b.
29. Galileo 1937b.

tem, by way of the "Congregation of the Index,"[30] a censorship council that determined which books were contrary to the faith and to be banned, and which books were allowable. The council ruled the Copernican system was

> foolish and absurd philosophically and formally heretical inasmuch as it expressly contradicts the doctrine of holy Scripture in many places, both according to the literal meaning and according to the common meaning of the Holy Fathers and doctors.[31]

In so doing, the council took up the hermeneutic dictated by the Council of Trent and applied it to the Copernican issue. It directed that the Copernican system was not to be taught in any Catholic country. Part of the decree was that Copernicus' book *On the Revolutions of the Celestial Bodies* was to be corrected so that it could be read as a mere hypothesis for making predictions rather than as truth. It also decreed that Foscarini's letter was to be completely banned, and that Galileo was not to teach the Copernican system as though it were true. Fortunately, it does not appear that the censorship council had access to Galileo's *Letter to the Grand Duchess Christina* at this stage. If it had, the council certainly would have banned it in the way that it had banned Foscarini's letter.

Meanwhile Galileo went on with his scientific work. He thought that he had found further evidence for the Copernican system in his studies of the tides, and so in 1632, he published his most famous work, *Dialogue on the Two Chief World Systems*.[32] The 'two chief world systems' are the Ptolemaic-Aristotelian system and the Copernican-Galilean system, and the *Dialogue* is written as a dialogue between different characters who represent these different views. Galileo was granted permission to publish this book on the condition that he presented the Copernican system as a hypothesis only.

Galileo obeyed the letter of this command. The Copernican system was presented as a hypothesis in that the work was a dialogue in which different views were being presented, and that at the close of the *Dialogue* Galileo explicitly said that everything that he had said was merely hypothetical.

---

30. See Hooykaas 1974, pp. 109-10.
31. Hooykaas 1974, p. 109.
32. Galileo 1967.

However, in spirit Galileo did not comply. The *Dialogue*'s support for Copernicanism was very thinly veiled. For instance, the Ptolemaic system was represented by a character called Simplicio — which means 'stupid' — introduced on the first page as "the stout defender of Aristotle." Even worse, Simplicio seemed to bear an unfortunate resemblance to Cardinal Bellarmino! And the content of the *Dialogue* is in effect a solid refutation of the Ptolemaic system.

It did not fool the Inquisition. In 1633 there was a Papal Inquisition directed solely at Galileo. By this time it was well established that the Catholic Church took the position that the Copernican system was to be seen merely as a hypothesis, and Galileo had flouted this. He was required by the Inquisition to recant his views and to agree that the Copernican system was nothing but hypothesis. From that time onward — from 1633 until his death in 1642 — Galileo was confined to his house in Arceti, where he nevertheless continued his scientific work. At the Inquisition, Galileo was declared

> suspected of heresy, namely of having believed and held the doctrine — which is false and contrary to sacred and divine Scriptures — that the sun is the center of the world and does not move from east to west, and that the earth moves and is not the centre of the world.[33]

Galileo did recant at the Inquisition, with lines that had been written for him. He was forced to say: "with sincere heart and unfeigned faith I abjure, curse, and detest the aforesaid errors and heresies."[34] But we know from Galileo's subsequent correspondences that it was not with a sincere heart. Although confined to his house, he was permitted to continue his work, and was even able to smuggle out his books and have them printed in other countries, such as Holland, where censorship was less strict.

In 1893, some 250 years later, Pope Leo XIII proclaimed that the correct way to read science and Scripture is to adhere to something close to the neutrality principle, that Scripture does not give us information about scientific cosmology.[35]

33. Hooykaas 1974, p. 75.
34. Hooykaas 1974, p. 75.
35. McMullin 1981.

Bellarmino's Dilemma

Foscarini had put forward the view that if the Copernican system is true, it must be that Scripture was written in a non-literal way to accommodate common sense. Bellarmino's response to this is to advise Foscarini to see the Copernican theory as merely hypothetical, rather than absolutely true. Bellarmino elaborates:

> Such a manner of speaking is enough for a mathematician. But to want to affirm that the Sun, in very truth, is at the centre of the universe and only rotates its axis without going from east to west, is a very dangerous attitude and one calculated not only to arouse all Scholastic philosophers and theologians, but also to injure our holy faith by contradicting the Scriptures.[36]

At the close of his letter Bellarmino goes on to say: "As you are aware, the council of Trent forbids the interpretation of the Scriptures in a way contrary to the common opinion of the holy Fathers."[37] In Bellarmino's view, because the Fathers all agreed on the matter, Scripture should be interpreted literally as teaching that the sun is in the heavens and revolves around the earth. It is hardly surprising then, that Bellarmino was committed to saying,

> Consider, then, in your prudence, whether the Church can tolerate, that the Scriptures should be interpreted in a manner contrary to that of the holy Fathers and of all modern commentators, both Latin and Greek.[38]

However, in the third section of his Letter to Foscarini, Bellarmino goes on to say that

> If there were a real proof that the Sun is in the centre of the universe, that the Earth is in the third heaven, . . . then we should have to proceed with great circumspection in explaining passages of Scripture which appear to teach the contrary, and rather admit that we did not understand them.[39]

36. Bellarmino 1955, p. 99.
37. Bellarmino 1955, p. 99.
38. Bellarmino 1955, p. 99.
39. Bellarmino 1955, p. 99.

This appears to contradict Bellarmino's earlier comments, and is really a re-expression of the views of Augustine, that if science is absolutely proven, and it is in conflict with Scripture, then we must take Scripture metaphorically. However, Bellarmino goes on to say: "But, as for myself, I shall not believe that there are such proofs until they are shown to me."[40] Bellarmino is actually following Augustine quite closely when he says that it is only in cases where there is a definite proof that we need to read Scripture in any way other than literally. This was the main line that Augustine took.

So Bellarmino has a dilemma. On the one hand, he wants to retain Augustine's hermeneutic principle and maintain that if we really do find proof for that science we need to look again at Scripture. If, as Galileo claimed, the Copernican theory had been proved, then the hermeneutics of the Fathers forced Bellarmino to accept Copernicanism as cosmological truth. However, on the other hand, Bellarmino must hold onto the decree laid down at the Council of Trent which demands that Scripture be interpreted according to the Holy Fathers. It is clear that the Holy Fathers thought that the sun was in motion whilst the earth remained stationary. Therefore, by the Trent decree Bellarmino was forced to adhere to the Aristotelian system.

Augustine was a product of his time, and his times were Aristotelian and Ptolemaic. The science of Augustine's day showed that the sun moves around the earth, and Augustine found some Scriptural texts that seemed to support this. Thus Augustine could hold that Scripture is in harmony with (Aristotelian) science. Bellarmino's dilemma is that if Copernican hypothesis is proved, he cannot follow Augustine both in his hermeneutics and in his interpretation of Scripture.

To be fair to Bellarmino, he does have a point about proof. The Copernican system had not, as yet, been conclusively proven by science, from the perspective of Aristotelian physics. There were various difficulties, such as the problem of bodies in free-fall discussed above. So, as Augustine's relevance principle recommends, Bellarmino may reasonably claim that until he has seen proof of the Copernican system he is going to take it as just a hypothesis. Read in this way, Bellarmino's account appears to be not a conflict theory of the relation between science and religion, but rather an Augustinian harmony account.

40. Bellarmino 1955, p. 100.

Galileo's Reconciliatory Hermeneutics

In the *Letter to the Grand Duchess Christina,* Galileo quotes Augustine fourteen times as his authority for his account of how to read Scripture in matters concerning cosmology. In that letter he also accuses his opponents of moving away from Augustine's hermeneutics:

> Contrary to the sense of the Bible and the intention of the holy Fathers, . . . they [that is, Bellarmino] would extend such authorities until even in purely physical matters — where faith is not involved — they would have us altogether abandon reason and the evidence of our senses in favor of some biblical passage, though under the surface meaning of its words this passage may contain a different sense.[41]

Here Galileo attributes to his opponents the view that science cannot inform us about the appropriate interpretation of Scripture, a view that contradicts Augustine's relevance principle. Recall that this principle says that where science proves something that contradicts a literal interpretation of a biblical passage, we should take a metaphorical interpretation of that passage. (Now this is not quite fair to Bellarmino, who never advocated that we abandon reason and evidence altogether, as we have seen.)

According to McMullin,[42] there are three streams to be discerned in Galileo's thought. The first is that one is to follow cosmology where and only where it has been proven (Augustine's relevance principle). McMullin claims that this theme can be found in various sections of Galileo's writings. The second is that we are to follow cosmology or science where it can be proved in principle. As McMullin says, this is a very much broader or weaker relevance thesis than Augustine's relevance principle. The third is the neutrality principle, the idea that the Bible, properly read or interpreted, does not teach cosmology (a secondary theme in Augustine).

However, it is not quite right to say that there are three principles at work here. The second and third principles are actually very similar in content, since the kind of facts covered by 'cosmology' — such as what the shape of the heavens are and how they move — are the sorts of facts for which we could, in principle, provide scientific proofs. If this is right then we find the same two themes in Galileo's writings as we saw in Augustine.

41. Galileo 1937a, p. 179.
42. McMullin 1981.

But the dominant theme in Augustine's thought is the relevance principle, whereas the dominant one in Galileo is the neutrality principle. In the *Letter to the Grand Duchess Christina,* each of the fourteen times Galileo quotes Augustine an interpretation is given along the lines of the neutrality principle. Galileo thus chooses not to quote those sections of Augustine's work that express the relevance thesis, and when he does, they are given a neutrality interpretation.

McMullin is not clear on this. The quotes that he provides from Galileo that are supposed to show that Galileo really held the relevance thesis do not really show any such thing.[43] What Galileo says is that where merely speculative philosophical writings conflict with Scripture we should always follow Scripture. McMullin claims that in this Galileo is following Augustine's relevance principle. But this overlooks a significant difference between Galileo and Augustine, and a distinction in Galileo's thought which became an important issue in the sixteenth and seventeenth centuries between the scholastic writings of philosophers and the empirical findings of science. This is not a distinction that we find in the writings of Augustine (in Aristotle, we find that physics, science, and philosophy are all bound up together), but in the sixteenth and seventeenth centuries the emerging view is anti-Aristotelian and anti-scholastic. Galileo claims that if scholastic philosophy conflicts with Scripture, then we should follow Scripture. However, that is not to say that Galileo is claiming that the kinds of things that experimental science deals with should ever be held in question on the grounds that they conflict with Scripture. Where he does in fact discuss experimental science, Galileo never equivocates. He always maintains that religion is not in a position to make any assertions regarding these issues.

In the light of this, the best way to see Galileo's position is as offering a fairly strong case for a neutrality view of the relation between science and religion.

Ironically, Galileo devised a way to save Bellarmino from his dilemma.[44] In his *Letter to the Grand Duchess Christina,* Galileo wrote,

> I question the truth of the statement that the church commands us to hold as matters of faith all physical conclusions bearing the stamp of

43. McMullin 1981, pp. 22-24.
44. Contrary to the assessment of Duhem (1969, p. 106).

harmonious interpretation by all the Fathers. I think this may be an arbitrary simplification of various council decrees [such as the Council of Trent]. . . . So far as I can find, all that is really prohibited is the perverting into senses contrary to that of the holy Church or that of the concurrent agreement of the Fathers those passages, and those alone, which pertain to faith or ethics, or which concern the edification of Christian doctrine.[45]

Galileo is claiming that the findings of the Council of Trent do not assert that we must always hold with the common interpretation of the Fathers, but only that we must hold with the common interpretation of the Fathers in matters relating to faith or ethics. In fact, a careful reading of the *Canons and Decrees of the Council of Trent* confirms that Galileo's interpretation of Trent was more accurate than Bellarmino's. Bellarmino was correct only inasmuch as the Council of Trent *proposed* that interpretation of the Scriptures must have approval from the Fathers. The proposal recommended

> that it should be forbidden to interpret the Scriptures contrary to the declared sentiment of the Church, and to the unanimous consent of the Fathers; and that the license of certain ecclesiastical censors should be required, previous to the publication of any commentary on holy writ.[46]

Without clarification to the contrary, it is easily assumed that consent of the Fathers is required on any matter whatsoever when it comes to interpretation of the Scriptures. However, when it comes to reading the actual *decrees* of the Council it is evident that Galileo's escape clause is present, and that such interpretation is only forbidden in "matters of faith." The Council actually decrees that

> no-one, relying on his own skill, shall, — in matters of faith, and of morals pertaining to the edification of Christian doctrine, — . . . presume to interpret the said Scripture contrary to that sense [of the] church.[47]

---

45. Galileo 1937a, p. 203.
46. Waterworth 1848, p. xc.
47. Waterworth 1848, p. 19.

Thus Galileo rescues Bellarmino from his dilemma. Bellarmino was free to follow Augustine's relevance principle, rejecting Copernicus until there was adequate proof, but accepting it when there was. This does not conflict with Trent after all, since it is not a matter of faith or morals.

The other side to this is that it is not at all clear that there ever needed be any condemnation of Galileo, even when Bellarmino's commitments to the Church are taken into account.

Conclusion

So how are we to take this episode in history? As was noted earlier, there are broadly speaking two ways of looking at the relationship between science and religion — the conflict model and the harmony model. There are also two ways to approach historical episodes. One way is to start, from the outset, with either a harmony or a conflict model in place, being convinced, for example, that there is a harmony between science and religion; and then to turn to the case in question and attempt to read everything in terms of that position. The alternative is to begin with an open mind in regard to which model is correct, being thereby free to approach the episode as a way to determine which model is correct. (There are also shades of grey between these two alternatives.)

In Galileo there is a bold commitment to the idea of unity — that there is one God behind both Scripture and nature. For Galileo the same God who created the things that we discover through science also wrote all of the Scriptures. So Galileo says of Copernicus,

> He did not ignore the Bible, but he knew very well that if his doctrine were proved, then it could not contradict the Scriptures when they were rightly understood.[48]

The assumption of unity leads Galileo to a harmony view of the relation between science and religion: since there is one God behind the book of nature and the book of Scripture, then there is a harmony between true science and true religion, once science is properly proved, and Scripture properly interpreted. If we begin from the presupposition of unity, then it

48. Galileo 1937a, pp. 179-180.

is inevitable that we will be led to a metaphoric interpretation of anything that apparently contradicts what we are learning in the new science. This type of argument is valid: but since it begins from the presupposition of unity, it does nothing to answer the question about which is the appropriate way to approach these episodes.

The neutrality principle of Galileo and Calvin guarantees harmony by insulating religion from scientific advances, via the blanket understanding that Scripture teaches us how to go to heaven, not how the heavens go. Neutrality is an independence view of the relation between science and religion, offering a global recipe for reading Scripture. However, this is not simply an *ad hoc* response to new developments in science, invented to avoid the Church's censure. It is rather the natural outworking of a fundamentally religious, and universally unquestioned view of the world: that one and the same mind created the world and wrote Scripture.

This holds also for Augustine, whose relevance principle leads him to an interactionist view in which science tells us in piecemeal fashion what the intent of Scripture is. On either approach — the interactionist, piecemeal relevance principle, or the independence/global neutrality principle — harmony is ultimately guaranteed by the premise of unity. This premise was never questioned in the sixteenth century.

CHAPTER 2

The Hermeneutics of Science and Religion:
Realism and Antirealism

In the previous chapter we looked at the question of hermeneutics in terms of the interpretation of particular sentences of Scripture. However, we can also think about hermeneutics in terms of the whole enterprise of science or religion. Such questions regarding the appropriate way in which to interpret science or religion as a whole bring us to the topic of realism and antirealism.

Realism about a certain discourse is the view that a discourse in question is to be understood as asserting the reality of the key concepts of the discourse, taken literally,[1] and in particular, as asserting the existence of the central objects of that discourse, again understood literally. Antirealism about that discourse therefore denies *either* the existence of such objects taken in a strict literal sense, or, more radically, that the discourse needs to be taken as asserting the existence of those objects taken in any sense, that is, that the existence of those objects is not at issue (assuming that is a meaningful question at all).

In this section we consider how antirealist accounts of science, such as those of Osiander, Duhem, and van Fraassen, allow for a harmony account of the relation between science and religion. We also consider antirealist accounts of religion, such as those of Feuerbach, Tillich, and

---

1. For discussion of the realist requirement that references to the central objects be taken literally see Leplin 1984, p. 2. Alternative formulations of the realism/antirealism distinction — for example, as commitment to/denial of the mind-independence of such objects — may lead to different classification of the positions discussed below.

Wittgenstein, to see whether they can serve the same function of allowing a harmony account of science and religion. However, for various reasons we will find that antirealist accounts are untenable.

Osiander's Preface

Andreas Osiander apparently wrote the preface for Copernicus' *On the Revolutions of the Celestial Spheres*[2] without Copernicus' authorization.[3] Copernicus himself was sick and had appointed an assistant named Rheticus, in 1543, to see to its publication, but when Rheticus became embroiled in a scandal involving a homosexual affair with one of his students and was forced to quickly find alternative employment, the job of ensuring publication was left to Osiander by default. Osiander was a Lutheran theologian who had been involved in discussions with Copernicus and Rheticus about how they were going to publish the book in the light of certain difficulties that were being posed by the Aristotelians.

According to legend, reading the preface hastened Copernicus' death in 1543, the year that his book was published. The legend has it that Copernicus died on seeing the printed version of his book, in particular the contents of Osiander's preface,[4] when it was handed to him on his sickbed.

In the preface Osiander writes that the hypotheses of Copernicus' book are not to be read as telling us what is literally true about the world, but rather as mere hypotheses or mathematical devices for accommodating all of the astronomical calculations and perhaps telling us what predictions we can make. They are not intended to tell us the truth about whether or not it is the earth or the sun that is in motion, nor about the cause of these apparent motions. So, Copernicus' hypothesis is not true, strictly speaking, but is simply a useful fiction that is scientifically productive.

In addition, Osiander's preface contains scientific arguments that the Copernican theory, if taken literally, is not true. The orbit ascribed to Venus by Copernican theory would make that planet appear sixteen times as large when Venus is close to the Earth, as it would appear when it is furthest away from the Earth. Osiander claims that this is contradicted by ex-

2. Copernicus 1939b.
3. See Koestler 1959, pp. 165-172.
4. Koestler 1959.

perience; Venus does not appear to be that much brighter. So Copernicus' theory cannot be taken as being true, but it can be taken as being a very valuable scientific hypothesis because it produces a far better theory than others for fitting the observational data. Osiander says

> these hypotheses need not be true nor even probable; if they provide a calculus consistent with the observations, that alone is sufficient.[5]

On this view, astronomy may be valuable and capable of progress, but it does not tell us the way reality really is. Astronomical theories are ways of 'saving the phenomena,' but we must turn to physics and philosophy to tell us about reality. This is a radical antirealist interpretation of a scientific theory because the question of the reality of a central concept in the theory, namely the various motions, is taken to be beside the point.

Antirealism neatly resolves the apparent conflict between astronomy and religion discussed in the previous chapter. Suppose, for argument's sake, that Scripture tells us that the earth is in the center of the universe and that the sun moves around it, but that astronomy tells us that the earth revolves around the sun. Instead of changing our readings of the biblical text we can change the way we interpret the scientific theory, taking *it* 'antirealistically.' On this view, the findings of astronomy (that the earth is in motion) are not literally true, but are only true in the sense that they operate effectively as tools. If the antirealism applies to all astronomy, then it is a broader kind of hermeneutical issue than one that only deals with the interpretation of a particular text.

So, for Osiander, the project of science is interpreted in such a way that both science and religion can be maintained. In this case it is science, rather than religion, that gives way in order that the two can be held together.

Antirealist Accounts of Science

Osiander's antirealism is part of a larger history. Antirealism — or 'instrumentalism' or 'fictionalism' — as a philosophy of science has been a significant option since the Greeks, at least, if Pierre Duhem (1861-1916) is

---

5. Osiander 1939, p. 24.

to be believed. In *To Save the Phenomena* Duhem argues that the view that the aim of astronomy is just to 'save the phenomena' — that is to adequately represent all the observational data — can be traced from Plato, through Ptolemy, Maimonides, to Osiander and Bellarmino. Duhem credits Ptolemy with the following comment on wooden models of the heavens:

> So long as we attend to these models, which we have put together, we find the composition and succession of the various motions awkward. To set them up in such a way that each motion can freely be accomplished hardly seems feasible. But when we study what happens in the sky, we are not at all disturbed by such a mixture of motions.

Duhem comments,

> Certainly Ptolemy means to indicate in this passage that the many motions he compounds in the *Syntaxis* to determine the trajectory of a planet have no physical reality.[6]

Duhem contrasts this antirealist trend with a realist, 'metaphysical' approach found in Aristotle, Copernicus, and Galileo. For Galileo, Duhem says,

> the hypotheses of the new system were not to be mere contrivances for the calculation of astronomical tables but propositions that conform to the nature of things. He wanted them established on the ground of physics.[7]

At fault in the whole Galileo episode was Galileo's inadequate philosophy of science. Duhem then concludes:

> The condemnation carried through by the Holy Office resulted from the clash between two realist positions. This head-on collision might have been avoided, the debate between the Ptolemaists and the Copernicans might have been kept to the terrain of astronomy, if certain sagacious precepts concerning the nature of scientific theories and the hypotheses on which they rest had been heeded. These pre-

6. Duhem 1969, p. 17.
7. Duhem 1969, p. 105.

cepts, first formulated by Posidonius, Ptolemy, Proclus, and Simplicius, had, through an uninterrupted tradition, come down directly to Osiander, Reinhold, and Melanchthon. But now they seemed quite forgotten.[8]

Duhem himself articulated a fictionalist account of scientific theories as formalisms — logical constructs — deduced from a small number of principles, and having the aim not of explaining anything, but of representing the phenomena in the simplest and most elegant manner possible. The theoretical aspect of the theory does not represent anything, it is neither true nor false, but is a more or less effective instrument facilitating the representation of data.

Duhem rejected the idea that science could grasp ultimate truth about the universe, and therefore rejected any attempt at metaphysics based on science. He gave the role of providing access to ultimate truth to theology.[9] His own theological views were strongly Catholic, Thomist, and conservative. Nevertheless, Duhem's anti-metaphysical instrumentalism was very influential in the early half of the twentieth century.

In the second half of the twentieth century the leading antirealist was probably Bas van Fraassen (b. 1941). Van Fraassen offers an antirealist philosophy of science that he calls 'constructive empiricism,' characterized as follows:

> Science aims to give us theories which are empirically adequate; and acceptance of a theory involves as belief only that it is empirically adequate.[10]

Firstly, 'empirically adequate' here refers to the theory's fit with current observational data — a theory is empirically adequate insofar as it fits all of the observational data. If Kepler's theory fits considerably more data than did Ptolemy's theory, then Kepler's theory is more empirically adequate than Ptolemy's.

Secondly, van Fraassen introduces the notion of 'acceptance of' as opposed to 'belief in' a theory. Here, van Fraassen is distinguishing between two psychological states — literal belief and what he calls 'acceptance.' Such

8. Duhem 1969, p. 106.
9. Duhem 1954.
10. van Fraassen 1980, p. 12.

a distinction is crucial to this kind of antirealism. Van Fraassen's point is that one can be a dedicated Copernican, and fully accept that theory, and yet not necessarily believe that theory literally. One can remain agnostic about whether the hypothesis corresponds to the way things are. To accept a theory is simply to believe that the theory is empirically adequate.

Thirdly, van Fraassen's constructive empiricism relies heavily on a distinction between observables and unobservables. Van Fraassen claims that we should literally believe in the world as it appears to us, in the realm of observables — for example, that there is a sun. His antirealism applies specifically to the unobservable world, things such as atoms, electrons, genes, quarks, and the like, which we can't observe with the naked eye. For van Fraassen, when we accept a theory about those entities, we can be satisfied with acceptance without having to literally believe that those entities exist.

Van Fraassen is not claiming that we can choose not to believe a theory if we want to. Nor is he claiming that we would be irrational to believe in a theory literally. Van Fraassen's view is not that we are necessarily irrational if we believe that atoms exist, but rather that we are not compelled to believe in them by virtue of the fact that we accept modern theories of atomic structure and so on.

One main argument in favor of antirealism urged by both Duhem and van Fraassen concerns the underdetermination of theory by evidence. According to this thesis, there is always a range of possible scientific theories available, although we may for pragmatic reasons focus on just one particular theory. In fact, for any scientific phenomenon there are always going to be an infinite number of possible theories. For any set of data, or evidence (E), there may be any number of theories ($H_1 \ldots H_n$) that all fit E equally well. We may have reasons for preferring one theory rather than another, but this will be nothing but a matter of taste, because all of the theories equally save the appearances. So, the data cannot logically determine which of these theories is correct simply because they are all empirically adequate. (Of course, there are also many other theories, which are not empirically adequate and must be rejected.)

For example, one of the leading astronomers in Galileo's day was Tycho Brahe (1546-1601). (Kepler was Brahe's young assistant and successor). Tycho Brahe had a large observatory in Denmark, the best of his day (which he built himself), and consequently the best collection of observational data. He could not bring himself to accept the Copernican hypothe-

GALILEO, DARWIN, AND HAWKING

sis, for various reasons. He saw problems with both the Ptolemaic and Copernican systems, and suggested an alternative model, according to which
the Earth is at the center of the universe, the moon and sun revolve around
the Earth, but all of the other planets revolve around the sun. Each of the
theories — those of Ptolemy, Brahe, and Copernicus — uses the concept
of circular motion to account for the observations available to Brahe. The
Ptolemaic and Copernican systems can be adjusted to fit the data by adding additional epicycles to the circular motions of the planets.

All three theories appear to fit the set of observational data equally
well. The antirealist claims that since this is often the case in science, we are
never compelled to believe literally in any of these theories.

Scientific Realism and Inference to the Best Explanation

According to the formulation of van Fraassen,[11] scientific realism is the
view that the best current scientific theories are at least approximately
true, and the entities they describe really exist. By 'best scientific theories,'
the realist is referring to scientific theories that are well accepted and for
which there is a strong body of confirmatory evidence. The realist claims
that if a theory falls into this category, it is at least approximately true.
When the realist says 'true,' she means that the theory as it describes the
world, taken literally, corresponds to the way that the world really is.

The truth of a scientific theory is 'approximate' because the contemporary realist does not want to say that the best current scientific theories
are conclusive; the expectation is that in time there may be a new theory
that will provide a closer approximation to the truth. This idea of progress
is sometimes called 'convergent realism.' Copernicus and Galileo claimed
that the sun is at rest and that the Earth moves around it in circles with
epicycles added onto these circles. The realist claims that this description
of the motion is approximately true, although an improved theory would
later replace it, when Kepler added the hypothesis that the planets move in
ellipses, a closer approximation to the way things really are.

One argument in favor of scientific realism utilizes reasoning called
'inference to the best explanation.'[12] This reasoning is one that is used

11. van Fraassen 1980, pp. 8.
12. van Fraassen 1980, pp. 19-23.

widely in science, where we are often interested in trying to explain why things are the way they are. When Galileo proposed that the light and dark regions visible on a full moon are best explained by the hypothesis that the moon has mountains and valleys on its surface, he was utilizing inference to the best explanation.[13]

Take the question, "Why is the sky blue?" The evidence (E) here is the way that the sky appears to us on a clear day. There is a range of different theories that explain why. The ancients believed, for example, that there was water above the heavens, and since water is blue the sky is blue. Another explanation, sometimes attributed to the Australian Aborigines, is that we live in a massive emu egg shell, the inside of which is blue. According to modern science, light from the sun is scattered by molecules throughout the atmosphere, and blue light is scattered towards us whereas light of other colors continues on unscattered. So, we have three theories, each of which (if true) explain why the sky appears blue to us. We need to ask which is the best explanation.

There are two important criteria for assessing rival explanations. The first is how probable or likely is the theory (H) in and of itself, quite apart from the issue of the relevant evidence. In other words, what is P(H), the 'prior' probability or initial plausibility? How probable is it that we live inside an emu egg, that there is water above us, and that there are molecules in the sky that selectively scatter light? This criterion asks how plausible each of these explanations is, independent of any particular evidence that we are trying to explain. To us the hypothesis that there are molecules in the sky which selectively scatter light is very much more plausible than the hypotheses that we live inside an emu egg or that there is water above us. So, on this first criterion the modern theory is easily the best one.

The second criterion concerns how probable the evidence (E) is given that the theory (H) is true. That is, we need to determine the conditional probability P(E|H), for each of the rival explanations. If it is true that we live inside an emu egg (H_1) how likely is it that the sky will be blue (E)? The answer: very likely; so, on this score, H_1 does very well. If there really is water in the sky, and water is blue (H_2), how likely is it that the sky is blue? Again, very likely; so, on this score H_2 also does well. Or, given H_3, the theories concerning light scattering are true and there are molecules of the right sort in the sky, how likely is it be that the sky is blue? The answer is,

13. McMullin 1978.

very likely. So, all three explanations do well on this second criterion. To put this point another way, all three qualify as possible explanations on this second criterion; but on the first criterion the modern theory seems well ahead.

These two criteria form the basis of Inference to the Best Explanation.[14] Put more formally, if

1. $P(H) > P(H')$ and
2. $P(E|H) > P(E|H')$

for two rival hypotheses, H and H', then we should infer the truth of H, on the grounds that it is the best explanation.

Suppose that a professor is handed two exactly identical assignments by two of her students (E). The professor forms a theory (H) to explain this phenomenon, namely that one of the students has copied the other's work or they have both copied from a common source. She summons the students, and is surprised to find that they maintain a different theory (H'), that the similarity in the two essays is due merely to the fact that the two students had often discussed the issues in the course in great detail. Which theory is the best explanation? On the first criterion the students' explanation fares better than the professor's. It is actually very rare that students copy each others' work, while presumably it is very common for students to discuss issues in the course in detail. But in terms of the second criterion the professor's does much better, since if copying has occurred it is very likely that the professor is going to receive identical essays; but even if it was true that the two students discussed the course at length it would still be highly unlikely that the professor should receive two identical essays. So H' is a better theory on the first criterion, but H is better on the second.

The argument for scientific realism is that it provides the best explanation for the success of science, in comparison to antirealism or constructive empiricism.

This argument focuses on the idea of success. A scientific theory is successful insofar as it fits the relevant data, and in particular in making successful predictions. For example, the Newton-Kepler theory predicted the 1759 return of Halley's comet to within one month. It also predicted the

14. van Fraassen 1980.

48

existence of a new planet, which was also later found to be true. These predictions are very impressive examples of the success of science.

The fact that the Newton-Kepler theory is able to produce such successful predictions, the realist claims, is explained by the fact that these theories are approximately true. If the earth really does move around the sun then that explains why the heliocentric theory, in conjunction with Newton's theory of gravity, is so successful in explaining the known data and successfully making novel predictions. On the other hand, the rival theory, antirealism, does not explain at all why the theory is successful. If the earth isn't really moving around the sun, then why would the Newton-Kepler theory make successful predictions? In terms of inference to the best explanation, realism makes the evidence (science's success) likely, where antirealism does not.[15]

This approach also answers the underdetermination objection to scientific realism. There may indeed be many rival hypotheses, but we simply need a reason to prefer one of those we know about, and we should believe that one until such time as we come across a preferable hypothesis.[16]

Antirealism in Philosophy of Religion

We have seen that antirealism about science provided a blanket escape from conflict between astronomy and Scripture for Osiander. If astronomy is a tool for representation and prediction, but not a picture of reality, then it cannot conflict with the picture of reality found in Scripture. This is an independence picture of the relation between science and religion: the two are in harmony because they have such different aims that conflict is impossible. But we have also seen that this account of science is inadequate because it fails to explain why science has been so successful. In this section we examine the possibility that there is a correlative escape available that involves being antirealist about religion rather than about science. Can antirealism about religion secure harmony between science and religion?

Firstly, is this in effect what Augustine does, when he takes as metaphorical points in Scripture which conflict with science? No, simply because to take a locally antirealist attitude to a particular element of Scrip-

15. See Leplin 1984.
16. For further debate see van Fraassen 1989.

49

ture is not a global antirealism (that is, one that takes the entire discourse antirealistically) of the sort that provides a blanket escape from conflict of the sort Osiander's antirealism provides. Such elements are not necessarily key concepts of the discourse. For example, holding that the 'days' of the Genesis 1 story do not literally correspond to anything but are just the vehicle for claims about God's wisdom and power is compatible with a realist view of the discourse — that there really is a God out there and a world which that God literally created, and so on. Augustine's relevance principle may lead to antirealist interpretations of elements of the Genesis account, but his position on science and religion is still very much one of realism and interaction, where science informs us piecemeal about how to interpret Scripture. Similarly, scientific realists sometimes take non-central elements of a theory in an antirealist fashion — such as the imaginary numbers used in calculating electric fields — without being antirealists about the theory per se.

The neutrality position of Calvin and Galileo, on the other hand, unlike Augustine's relevance principle, is global. They do have a blanket escape from conflict: it is not the purpose of Scripture to teach about cosmology so it will never conflict with astronomy. This is a genuine independence position. Is this a kind of antirealism correlative with Osiander's scientific antirealism? No, not strictly speaking; again because the *key* terms of the account are taken literally and realistically. Terms such as God, the world, creation — the most central concepts in Genesis on anyone's view — are all taken by Calvin and Galileo as corresponding to what is really out there. So it would be a little strange to call their accounts 'antirealist' just as it would be strange to label physicists antirealist about the classical theory of electrodynamics just because they discard solutions involving imaginary numbers as 'unphysical.'

But there have been more radical accounts of religion that more closely mirror Osiander's global scientific antirealism (although none of these approaches to religion would have been taken seriously in the sixteenth century).

Ludwig Feuerbach (1804-1872) offers a prescription for the rational construal of religion that allows it to function in a valuable way in modern society. According to Feuerbach, religion has developed historically, but in most religious belief consciousness of the object is indistinguishable from consciousness of the self. Unlike empirical knowledge, which is indifferent and impersonal, knowledge of God has the object as subject — personal, moral, and free. God loves, is wise, is kindly, is just. Indeed, religious belief is a projection, a taking of our qualities and extrapolating them beyond limitation, to the point of perfection. We create God in our image, Feuerbach thinks, making God what we want ourselves to be — a person like us but perfect, infinite, almighty. Of course the believer is not directly aware of this. It is important to faith that it is ignorant of the true explanation; so true understanding is not normally available to the believer. But the religious need is genuine, and the function important.

However, Feuerbach argues that we don't have to "fixate on the concrete." The intellectual history of humanity can in fact be traced as a movement from the literal to the metaphorical. We don't have to remain in our infantile stage of religion, taking it in a literal way. We can instead in maturity recognize the metaphorical nature of the true understanding of religious discourse — as a way to recognize our nature within ourselves, within material nature. What was regarded as objective is now regarded as subjective: "What today is atheism, tomorrow is religion."

Feuerbach's idea of religion is to see in humanity the freedom from the restriction and limitations of its individual members via the fiction postulated in literal religions. We can project onto ourselves ourselves. In our human race we can find all the aspirations and needs of the human soul. And now it can be a fully conscious, self-aware activity — and as such more effectively aimed at the common good of humanity.

This vision of religion can be seen as a kind of materialist reductionism, where religion is 'reduced to' the fulfillment of human aspirations. In one sense Feuerbach's account is an extrapolation of Augustine's, in that it removes from religion what Feuerbach took to be disproved by modern science, and tries to make sense of what is left. Moreover, it is a type of antirealism because while it retains belief in the existence of the core religious concepts, such as 'God,' it does so only by refusing to take the concept literally as referring to a transcendent being. It takes 'God' to refer metaphorically to the personification of human aspirations.

Because Feuerbach rejects Augustine's fundamental premise, that there is one mind who is the author of both Scripture and nature, Feuerbach is open to the charge of atheism. Indeed, his ideas belong to a tradition which can be traced from the writings of David Hume through Feuerbach himself to Marx and Freud — a tradition of explaining religion away on the assumption that it is literally false, and offering an explanation of belief in terms of individuals' psychological motivations for believing. Hume in his *Natural*

History of Religion[17] offers explanations of various polytheisms in terms of the fears and hopes of the human mind, and the resultant need to explain various phenomena — earthquakes, thunder, and so forth. Marx explains religion as the "opiate of the people" — something which serves to alleviate the pain that comes to the exploited social classes, and so as something which plays a significant role in the development of history since it serves to help maintain exploitative labor relations. Freud explained religion in terms of the unconscious repressed drives and wishes. These are all natural or material explanations — that the explanation does not appeal to anything apart from what is given in the natural, material world. It can be hard to tell the difference between the atheist materialist who explains why religion is needed and the reductionist who redefines religion in purely material terms.

In fact, since Feuerbach rejects what believers once believed, his view is really a conflict thesis rather than the interactionist harmony of, say, Augustine: science proves that earlier forms of religion were false. Indeed, Feuerbach, along with Hume, Marx, and Freud, was an influence behind the conflict thesis that flourished at the end of the nineteenth century in the thought of writers such as A. D. White and was popularized in books such as Frazer's *The Golden Bough*.[18]

A harmony version of this sort of reductionism that flourished in the early twentieth century is the 'liberal' or 'modernist' theology of Paul Tillich and others, which was popularized in England by Bishop John Robinson in his 1960s bestseller *Honest to God*.[19] According to Tillich and Robinson the old 'levels' way of thinking about God cannot be taken seriously in the age of modern science. People no longer picture God as 'up there,' but rather as 'out there,' which was once a helpful way of thinking, but which is too misleading if taken literally. In reality, God is not a supernatural person at all, but 'that which a person takes uncompromisingly as ultimate reality.' God is, in the words of Tillich, the "ground of our being." But as such God is beyond all positive predication, literally speaking, so we speak of God in symbolic terms — that is, in our common religious language. But, for example, when we say 'God loves me,' we aren't literally referring to a bearded old man in the sky, but rather to the ultimate fact that love is of central importance in the universe.

17. Hume 1976.
18. Frazer 1911-1913.
19. Robinson 1963.

Harmony can be maintained if one insists that this was what was intended all along. Robinson claimed to be giving the account that apostles such as St. Paul really held. This puts liberal theology in one sense into the tradition of Calvin and Galileo, in that it takes a metaphorical reading of traditional Christianity, which guarantees independence, although it does so on a grander, more ambitious scale.

However, neither reductionist approaches — neither Feuerbach's conflict account nor Tillich's harmony account — are as radically anti-realist about religion as is the approach of Osiander, Duhem, and van Fraassen to science, since they take the key concepts to refer (non-literally) to *something*, albeit something immanent rather than transcendent. The later philosophy of Ludwig Wittgenstein, on the other hand, offers a genuinely antirealist approach to religious concepts, which thereby guarantees harmony between science and religion.

Wittgenstein's two major works, the *Tractatus*,[20] written in 1921, and *Philosophical Investigations*,[21] a collection of writing not published until 1953, two years after his death, record a self-conscious change in philosophical direction. The *Tractatus* is often associated with logical positivism (see Chapter 1), for our purposes the view that meaningful statements are those which can be verified in principle and that this provides a criteria for distinguishing between science and non-science. For example, in *Language, Truth, and Logic*[22] logical positivist A. J. Ayer places religion firmly in the camp of non-science, as non-meaningful and therefore the sort of thing that we should just get rid of as a whole big mistake.[23] Logical positivism, we saw, is an example of the conflict view about science and religion. In it, science is enshrined as the paradigm of meaningful discourse, and religion banished as pointless. According to the *Tractatus:* "whereof we cannot speak thereof we must be silent."[24]

In *Investigations,* however, we find a different picture. The catch cry is that 'philosophy leaves everything as it is,' so the philosopher's role does not include telling people what they should or should not believe. Philoso-

20. Wittgenstein 1961.
21. Wittgenstein 1958.
22. Ayer 1936.
23. Not all positivists took this view — one who didn't was Braithwaite.
24. Others have read this as being as much an invitation to mysticism as an expression of an Ayer-style rejection of religion, which puts the early Wittgenstein much closer to the later Wittgenstein.

phy studies life, human life, but does not make verdicts about what is good and what is not, nor about what is true and what is not. It is descriptive, not prescriptive, merely offering clarification and codification of belief and meaning, focusing on what people mean and explicating that meaning without making any verdicts about the truth or value of the belief.

Wittgenstein offers a broader theory of meaning than that of logical positivism. He claims we need to see how terms or concepts are used in order to understand what their meaning is. Here he draws on the notion of an ostensive definition. If we want to know the meaning of a word like 'chair' and we look it up in the dictionary, we find a definition in terms of some other word, say, 'seat.' If we then look up the word 'seat' we may find additional terms, but in the end we are going to come to a circle: for example, we look up 'seat' and it says 'a chair'. But we can break that circle by an ostensive definition, the non-verbal pointing to a chair. In the case of theories, or entire 'ways of life', Wittgenstein says that it is insufficient to ask for a definition in terms of some metaphysical theory; we need to understand how it is practiced in its context. This means that different areas of life, having different purposes and practices, may have different 'language games,' or ways that meaning operates.

According to Wittgenstein, understanding how meaning operates in actual practice — for example how concepts such as 'God exists' serve a certain function in a particular context — requires a distinction between surface and depth grammar. At times it is inappropriate to simply read something quite literally according to its surface grammar. The surface grammar of "you give me the creeps" is exactly the same as "you give me the coins." In such a case, however, the meaning is quite different so we need to appeal to depth grammar, moving beyond the literal meaning and logic of sentence itself to the context in which the practice occurred.

D. Z. Phillips relates a story of the philosopher Norman Malcolm in which Malcolm was walking with Wittgenstein one day and as they passed a tree Wittgenstein said to Malcolm, "This is your tree, I now give it to you — but you cannot chop it down, you cannot mark it in any sort of way, you are not allowed to trim it or do anything to it. And since the tree is in somebody else's garden, you are not allowed to sit under it." His idea was that the concept of ownership has been so removed from any of its usual contexts, that it becomes quite meaningless.

Wittgenstein says that the task of philosophy is like holding up a mirror. He says:

I ought to be no more than a mirror in which my reader can see his thinking with all its deformities and so be helped in this way he can put it right.[25]

According to Wittgenstein, the mistake of philosophy has often been to push everything of human life into one area, the scientific. Indeed, this is the case with the conflict thesis of science and religion. The criterion of meaning in science may well be verifiability, but this clearly is not the criterion of meaning in religion. To apply the scientific criterion to religion, as logical positivism does, simply confuses two disparate areas of life.

According to Wittgenstein 'there is a God' cannot simply be read in terms of the surface grammar, as in, for example, 'there is a chair,' because this would make no sense of how belief in God actually operates for believers. As D. Z. Phillips, the foremost twentieth-century articulator of the Wittgensteinian view of religion, writes,

> Instead of stipulating what *must* constitute intelligible uses of language, one should look to see how language is in fact used. If one does, one comes across the use of language found in magic and religious rites and rituals. Such language is not based on opinions or hypotheses, but is expressive. . . . Faced by it, the philosopher's task is not to attempt to verify or falsify what he sees, for that makes no sense in this context. His task is a descriptive one; he gives an account of the use of language involved. He can only say that these language games are played.[26]

According to Phillips the nature of belief is expressive, not fact stating. The surface grammar looks indicative — cognitive, fact stating — but the depth grammar, the true nature, is revealed by the function of the language in the context of the language game — and that is expressive. For example, religious belief is immune from revision, whereas fact-stating language is open to refutation.

On prayer Phillips writes,

> When deep religious believers pray *for* something, they are not so much asking God to bring this about, but in a way telling him of the strength of their desires. They realize things may not go as they wish,

25. Phillips 1991, p. 135.
26. Phillips 1976, p. 41.

but they are asking to be able to go on living whatever happens. In prayers of confession, and in prayers of petition, the believer is trying to find a meaning and a hope that will deliver him from the elements in his life which threaten to destroy it: in the first case his guilt, in the second case, his desires.[27]

This is a radical version of the independence view of the relation between science and religion. Science and religion belong to different domains, ways of life, and so what happens in one is incommensurable with what happens in the other — it can have no bearing at all. Religion is not a fact-stating domain.

As such we have found the correlative of Osiander's antirealism. Wittgenstein offers a blanket antirealism about religion[28] which guarantees harmony with science. Religion is not a fact-stating enterprise; rather, beliefs and creedal statements are like tools, they serve a certain function. It is either meaningless, or at least unnecessary, to ask whether they are successfully fact-stating.

Is this a satisfactory account? It would seem, by Wittgenstein's own lights, that it cannot be. The reason is simply that Wittgenstein's mirror destroys what it reflects. It is not part of the self-understanding of a religious believer such as Augustine, Calvin, or Galileo that it doesn't matter whether or not God exists. When Augustine prays he thinks God hears, and the idea that that belief is literally false would count as atheism. So to analyze religion in terms of a global antirealism is hardly to 'leave everything as it is.'

Admittedly, in the quote given above, Wittgenstein is discussing how philosophy can help by showing up 'deformities' in human thinking. But whether or not God is really there is central to the whole enterprise for most religious believers, so that to correct that deformity is so violent a 'help' that there is no possibility of taking this contribution of philosophy as 'leaving everything as it is.'

This means that Wittgensteinian antirealism about religion cannot be a satisfactory harmony account of religion and science. It does not harmonize religion with science; it changes it to the point of being unrecognizable, at least to traditional theists such as Augustine, Calvin, and Galileo.

---

27. Phillips 1965, p. 121.
28. In our sense of 'realism.' Not all scholars follow this usage.

CHAPTER 3

Knowledge and Power

Galileo was only one of many important figures in the rise of modern science in the seventeenth century — René Descartes and Francis Bacon were others — who tended to hold to the independence of science and religion. God wrote two books, the book of Scripture and the book of nature, but their purposes were different; hence, they could be expected to cover different subject matter. But this did not mean that science and religion were independent in every respect. In fact, there were other, more subtle points of interaction. In this chapter we will investigate the way in which religious ideas influenced the way figures in the seventeenth century approached science.

The Heritage of Greek Logic and Geometry

The legacy of Greek logic, especially the Aristotelian deductive pattern of reasoning and the Euclidean vision of geometry, produced differing responses among the leaders of the new science and philosophy of the seventeenth century. On the one hand Descartes and Galileo adopted with enthusiasm the Euclidean vision as the pattern for all physical science; yet on the other hand the empirically-minded, such as Francis Bacon, painted their vision of science as a reaction to Aristotelian deductivism. Yet Euclid's achievement was no more than a remarkable instance of the Aristotelian vision.

Aristotle's views on scientific reasoning and logic are found in a number of works known collectively as *The Organon*.[1] These are based around the concept of the syllogism, a set of three propositions, the first two of which are premises and the third the conclusion. For example, one particular form of syllogism is:

> All planets are heavenly bodies.
> All heavenly bodies move in circles.
> Therefore all planets move in circles.

Followers of Aristotle called this form of argument 'AAA' because each of the premises and also the conclusion are 'universal affirmative' (A) statements. There are also universal negative (E), particular affirmative (I), and particular negative (O) statements, so altogether there are 64 possible argument forms, or 'moods.'

Some of the 64 moods are valid forms, some not. AAA is valid but IIA, for example, is not:

> Some planets are heavenly bodies. (I)
> Some heavenly bodies move in circles. (I)
> Therefore all planets move in circles. (A)

What makes valid forms deductively valid is that the truth of their premises guarantees the truth of their conclusion, or to put it another way, that it is impossible for the conclusion to be false if the premises are true.

According to Aristotle, scientific reasoning essentially involves deducing certain truths from the right kinds of premises via deductive reasoning. (He did recognize a kind of argument whose conclusion is not guaranteed by the premises, but is made plausible by them; but such arguments he thought inappropriate for scientific inquiry.) True science is the demonstration of necessary truths, or as Aristotle calls them, basic or primary truths. For Aristotle, these might be something like "rocks are heavy," from which it is possible to establish scientific knowledge such as "rocks fall towards the earth if not obstructed," by deductive reasoning.

But how do we arrive at this kind of basic primary premise? There

---

1. *The Organon* is an umbrella term for the logical works of Aristotle, including *Categories, On Interpretation, Prior Analytics, Posterior Analytics, Topics,* and *Sophistical Refutations.*

seems to be a fundamental flaw in a purely deductive system: the so-called 'problem of premise regress.' A valid argument tells me that if the premises are true, then the conclusion must also be true; but how do I know the premises are true? Well, I could have another deductively valid argument with the premise of the first as the conclusion. But again, that would just tell me that if the premises are true, then the conclusion is true, but how do I know those premises are true? This leads to a regress. How do we ever reach a starting point, premises which are certainly true, on which knowledge can be built via deductive inferences based on those certain truths?

According to Aristotle, primary truths are known by an 'intuition' which comes from our experience. This intuition is an insight into the essence, or essential nature, of objects. Because we have this insight into the essence of things, we can be certain of the truth of these basic, primary premises; and from there, using the deductive method of the syllogism, we can deduce all the truths of science.

Euclid's *Elements*[2] is possibly the most influential example of deductive reasoning ever produced. Influenced by Aristotle, Euclid (c. 300 B.C.) was able to show how to deduce numerous geometric theorems from a few fundamental axioms of geometry, including the distinctively Euclidean axiom that parallel lines never meet. In this way he built up a system of geometry whose rigor and systematic organization has inspired mathematicians ever since. Euclid is alleged to have replied, when the ruler Ptolemy (not the Ptolemy of cosmology) asked him whether the *Elements* was the shortest way to prove those theorems, that "there is no royal road to geometry."

The Greek heritage, especially Aristotelian logic, dominated European thought throughout the Middle Ages, and deductive logic was a focus of university learning. The art of disputation, in which one tries to prove various theses and defend them from objections, was an application of the *Organon*. The Greek heritage held sway until the seventeenth century, at which point it sparked two quite different responses.

The Image of God

The idea of the image of God in humanity derives from Genesis, where we read,

---

2. Euclid 1926.

And God said, Let us make man in our image, after our likeness: and let them have dominion over the fish of the sea, and over the fowl of the air, and over the cattle, and over all the earth, and over every creeping thing that creepeth upon the earth. So God created man in his own image, in the image of God created he him; male and female he created them.[3]

Here we have the makings of a theory of human nature. On the one hand, humans are like other creatures and unlike God: we are finite, created beings. This doctrine is reinforced in Genesis 1 by the literary structure: humans are created on the sixth day, along with the other animals. But on the other hand, humanity, male and female, are made in the image of God, and nothing else is. There is a qualitative difference between us and other animals, in virtue of which we are like God and unlike the rest of nature. Thus we arrive at a standard religious view of human nature: our essence derives from God in such a way as to elevate us above all creation.

Human nature in Genesis

This is to be contrasted with naturalistic accounts of human nature, according to which there is no God and humanity belongs with the rest of nature. In other words, there is no qualitative difference between Homo sapiens and any other species.

But if 'the image of God' does mark a qualitative difference between humanity and the rest of nature, what exactly does this entail? What does the phrase mean? There are many theories.[4] The Hebrew word 'likeness' refers to family resemblance — for example, the sort of facial similarity one might have to one's parents. Virtually no one takes this literally, thinking that God actually has a face or that all human beings somehow resem-

3. Genesis 1:26-27 (King James Version).
4. See Wenham 1987, pp. 28-32.

ble God in the literal sense of 'likeness.' All theories take it metaphorically in some way. We can briefly mention three, all of which have some support in Genesis.

Some take 'image of God' to refer to moral capacity. We, like God, have the capacity to understand what is right and wrong, and the freedom to act in a way that is right or wrong. Other animals, according to this theory, do not have this capacity. My cat, for example, doesn't do things that are right or wrong — even though I sometimes speak as if she does — since she doesn't have such a capacity. That this is the correct interpretation of Genesis 1 has some support from the fact that humans are the only ones that are given commands about what they can and cannot do.

Secondly, others take 'the image of God' to refer to rationality. Genesis 1 has a tight literary structure which is logical and organized according to very strict and rigorous form, which, as we have seen, conveys the concept of a God who is orderly, rational, and highly structured in his thinking and therefore in his creating. The phrase, "Let us make man in our image, after our likeness," then means that God chose to create human beings who also are rational, orderly, and reasonable — that is, who possess a mind similar to that of God and in contrast to those of animals. In Genesis 2 the man and woman are given the task of naming the animals. Unless this is to be taken just at face value, it seems to indicate that they are to be scientists, involved in classification and study of the rest of nature. Only they have this role, so it seems only they have this capacity. On this view the rest of nature lacks the ability to reason, to think logically, or to calculate.

Thirdly, some take 'in the image of God' to be a reference to the function of being a ruler. On this view the qualitative difference between us and the rest of nature is functional — we alone are designed to govern others. This has specific support from the verse in which the phrase 'image of God' is found, where the command to "have dominion over" the rest of nature is explicitly given to the man and woman. No other part of creation is given responsibility of that sort.

Although it seems strange to twenty-first-century ears, in the words of Edward Craig, the idea of the image of God was "axiomatic" in the seventeenth century.[5] Today the question is more easily recognized if it is put as "what makes us different from animals?" — but this, of course, is only

---

5. See Craig 1987, ch. 1.

half of the matter. According to Craig the idea of the image of God, or the 'Similarity Thesis,' as he sometimes calls it, is

> one very deep and pervasive feature of the thought of the seventeenth and early eighteenth centuries, something which can clearly be seen as a central concern of nearly all the major philosophers of that period, even though they concerned themselves with it for different purposes and reacted to it in widely varying ways. If anything can properly be called the 'dominant philosophy' of these hundred or so years, this is it.[6]

According to Craig, "commentators to whom this dominant philosophy has, for historical reasons, ceased to mean anything, frequently fail to recognize its role in the thought of those whose works they discuss, and that the failure can and does lead to serious superficiality and distortion."[7] In particular, we might add, commentators tend to read naturalism back into early modern philosophy, taking the religious elements in the latter as less-than-serious lip service to the dominant ideology of the day.[8] As we will see, for Descartes, Galileo, and Bacon[9] the notion of the image of God in humanity played a fundamental motivating role in an optimistic view of science.

Descartes, Rationality, and the Perspicuity of Nature

Descartes is generally thought of as one of the main proponents of 'rationalism' as opposed to 'empiricism.' Rationalists claim we can acquire knowledge through sheer reasoning alone. Empiricists, on the other hand, claim that we cannot know anything by pure reasoning alone — in order to gain knowledge we need to have some actual experience of the world. But this division can mask important similarities that all the early moderns share in comparison with later centuries, as we will see.

6. Craig 1987, p. 13.

7. Craig 1987, p. 13.

8. Cottingham, for example, attributes to Descartes a disrespect (although not overt) for religious belief, citing as evidence Descartes' comments that Genesis should be read metaphorically (Cottingham 1986, pp. 95-100). But this overlooks the tradition of hermeneutic integration that we have seen in earlier chapters.

9. Whom, interestingly, Craig does not discuss.

Descartes was impressed by Euclid's *Elements*,[10] and thought that all knowledge could be derived as part of a systematic deductive edifice based on certain truths which cannot be doubted. In particular, the foundation of the Cartesian system is my first person knowledge that I am thinking, from which I can deduce, Descartes says, my own existence *(cogito ergo sum)*. I can also deduce God's existence from my idea of God, since my idea of God contains perfection and to exist is more perfect than to not exist (the ontological argument). If a perfect God exists then that God wouldn't systematically deceive me about the proofs I derive in mathematics, so mathematically proven truths about the world are certain.

Descartes proves, he thinks, that human beings are made up of two sorts of substances — the rational mind or soul (the 'I' which thinks), and the physical body (comprised of the brain, reflexes, nervous system, and so on). The essence of soul is reason and thought, whereas the essence of body is extension — to be in some place and take up a certain amount of space.

The proof in the *Meditations on First Philosophy*[11] for the claim that the essence of material bodies is extension illustrates the sense in which Descartes thought we could have 'mathematical' truths about the world. According to the famous "wax argument," a piece of wax has certain properties, hardness, a certain shape, color, smell, and so on — but when it is melted it has none of those properties. Those things cannot be essential properties, since the wax doesn't always have them. The only property that it always has is extension — so that must be its essential nature. This is a 'mathematical truth' in the sense that the argument exhibits, in Descartes' view, Euclidean rigor and simplicity of assumptions. More generally, Descartes' ideal for physics is that it deals with measurable quantity, which is amenable to mathematics.

So Descartes believed in the perspicuity of nature. On the Cartesian view, the empirical world is orderly, rational, and indeed mathematical. The book of nature is written in the language of mathematics, and we rational souls have a truth-reaching capacity for reading that book. Nature's essences are at least in some cases an open book. Nature is perspicuous — transparent to the rational mind.

Descartes himself made some major contributions to the develop-

---

10. Euclid 1926.
11. Descartes 1986.

ment of mathematics, particularly coordinate geometry; and physics, notably his attempts to formulate laws of collision.

The natural world in Descartes' materialism consists purely of matter and motion, the only exception being human souls. Animals, according to Descartes, do not have minds; being purely material, or physical, they have no capacity for reason. This difference accounts for the superiority of human nature, that only humans are made in the image of God — that is, with a rational soul. We are like God in that we are rational. This idea of the image of God is implicit in Descartes' claim in *Meditations on First Philosophy*,[12] at the end of the Third Meditation, that

> the mere fact that God created me is a very strong basis for believing that I am somehow made in his image and likeness and that I perceive that likeness, which includes the idea of God, by the same faculty which enables me to perceive myself.

The existence of the image of God in humanity explains why nature is perspicuous to us. Because we have a rational mind, which is like the mind of God, we can expect to be able to understand the rationality of the world he created. Thus in Descartes' philosophy there is optimism about our ability to understand and have knowledge about the world. We expect that the world is transparent, perspicuous to the rational mind. Descartes' argument in the *Meditations*, of course, appeals more explicitly to God's moral qualities, such that God would not deceive us about what we clearly and distinctly perceive. But also underlying this seems to be the pervasive doctrine of the image of God in humanity.[13]

Galileo takes this line of reasoning even more seriously than Descartes. In the words of Galileo's spokesman Salvatio in *Dialogue Concerning Two World Systems*,

> I say that the human intellect does understand some [propositions] perfectly, and thus in these it has as much absolute certainty as nature itself has. Of such are the mathematical sciences alone; that is, geometry and arithmetic, in which the divine intellect indeed knows infinitely more propositions, since it knows all. But with regard to those few which the human intellect does understand, I believe its knowl-

12. Descartes 1986, p. 35.
13. See also Craig 1987, p. 15.

edge equals the divine in objective certainty, for here it succeeds in understanding necessity, beyond which there can be no greater sureness.[14]

So in mathematics our understanding reaches a standard of infallibility that mirrors God's understanding, although God perceives such things immediately whereas we have to follow through chains of reasoning. Galileo was also more serious than Descartes about using mathematical formulations in his scientific work.

There is an obvious problem here that Galileo doesn't address, namely that we do make mistakes in mathematical reasoning. Descartes, however, does wrestle with this. In the end his answer is to take the image of God to be more fully manifest in our will, rather than our rationality. Error arises, then, because our wills are able to go beyond our intellects, having the power to believe things that are not proven.[15]

This point notwithstanding, Descartes agrees with Galileo that human cognition is capable of Godlike knowledge in some cases:

And now that I know Him I have the means of acquiring a perfect knowledge of an infinitude of things, not only of those which relate to God Himself and other intellectual matters, but also of those which pertain to corporeal nature in so far as it is the object of pure mathematics.[16]

So Descartes in fact goes further than Galileo in one respect: this mathematical knowledge yields certainty about propositions concerning the world itself, not just pure mathematics.

With such a notion of the image of God in humanity, it is of no surprise that there is a confidence about in the seventeenth century that through the use of mathematical methods we can come to genuine knowledge of the world. What is perhaps surprising is that this same outline of thought can also be found in the radically empiricist vision of Bacon, even though the intermediate steps about how the mind knows nature are so different.

14. Galileo 1967, p. 103. See also Craig 1987, pp. 18-20.
15. Descartes 1986, Meditation IV.
16. Descartes 1986, p. 49.

Francis Bacon's Vision of Science and Technology

Francis Bacon has traditionally been credited as the "father of modern science and technology," one who "has permanent importance as the founder of modern inductive method and pioneer in the attempt at logical systematization of scientific procedure."[17] Although he lacked Galileo's and Descartes' appreciation of the importance for mathematics in science, his vision for actual experimentation and application has justly secured his reputation.

As the title of one of Bacon's works, *The New Organon*,[18] suggests, his account of scientific method and logic was developed with the explicit intention of its replacing Aristotle's. He begins the Preface to *The Great Instauration* with the claim, "That the state of knowledge is not prosperous nor greatly advancing, and that a different way must be opened for the human understanding entirely different from any hitherto known."[19] Bacon claimed that the whole scholastic scheme, with its Aristotelian base, was not producing any knowledge at all, as evidenced by the fact that it never produced anything of practical benefit for humanity. He thought of the scholastic university as an 'ivory tower,' dominated by obscurantist texts and deductive logic and possessed of a disregard for the hands-on knowledge of the things of the humble artisan, a disregard possibly derived from a Greek disdain for manual labor. In the mechanical arts (of, say, the silversmith), Bacon saw genuine practical ability and knowledge of the workings of nature.

On the other hand, Bacon also thought that this practical knowledge was not enough for genuine understanding of the world. What was needed was a synthesis of these two types of knowledge, the hands-on knowledge of nature and the academic pursuits of literacy and numbers, to produce a so-called "marriage of practice and discourse."

So how is one to go about attaining this new knowledge? There are three requirements. The first is a willingness to discard all personal biases and a desire to know nature as it is undistorted by theories and presuppositions. Bacon outlines four 'idols of the mind' — habits and ideas that corrupt our capacity for knowledge. The 'idols of the tribe' are tendencies

17. Russell 1946, p. 526.
18. Bacon 1905.
19. Bacon 1905.

toward self-deception that are an innate part of human nature. 'Idols of the den' are distortions that arise from our particular perspective — our environment, temperament, education, and so on. 'Idols of the market-place' are deceptions we share with one another through the abuse or inherent shortcomings of words. Finally, 'idols of the theater' are errors associated with grand theories such as Aristotelianism.

The second requirement is that a large sampling of all relevant data be gathered. Indeed, *The New Organon* was part of a scheme that was to have produced one huge encyclopedia of nature, incorporating all data of observation and experiment available in Bacon's day. Toward the end of the *New Organon,* Bacon sets out the general plan for what is to be included in this encyclopedia.

For example, suppose we are studying heat and want to know everything about heat in a way that is completely free from biases and presuppositions. The method involves formulating what Bacon calls the 'Tables of Investigation.' The first Table of Investigation is the 'Table of Affirmation,' in which we should list all the things that contain heat, following the 'Rule of Presence,' — the sun's rays, blood that circulates around the body, certain chemicals, iron after it has been in fire, chili peppers, and so on. In the second, the 'Table of Negation,' we should list according to the 'Rule of Absence' all the things that do not contain heat, such as the moon's rays, the blood in a dead body, or chemicals that are cold. At this point we can formulate a 'Table of Comparisons,' in which the different types of data are compared. The 'Prerogative Instances' are twenty-seven kinds of ways that something might stand out when we are studying a particular case. For example, the 'Solitary Instance' is one in which two things are very similar in many ways but differ in one; the 'Glaring Instance' is one in which there is just one feature of a particular thing that is conspicuous — say, the weight of quicksilver. In the preface to *The New Organon* we find a catalogue of 130 'Particular Instances' by title, including the history of the heavenly bodies, the history of comets, the history of air as a whole, the history of sleep and dreams, the history of smell and smells, the history of wine, the history of cements, the history of working with wood, and so on.

Bacon's third requirement concerns the method for deducing from this collection of facts certain sorts of generalizations about nature — in other words, scientific laws. For example, in studying heat, we may discover the generalization that metals expand when heated. The process will be something like this:

This piece of iron expands when heated
This second piece of iron expands when heated
This piece of copper expands when heated
This second piece of copper expands when heated
This piece of bronze expands when heated
Etc.

Therefore, all iron expands when heated

All copper expands when heated
All bronze expands when heated
Etc.

Therefore all metals expand when heated

From sufficient observations of iron expanding we draw the conclusion that all iron expands when heated. Then, from the generalizations of various kinds of metals expanding when heated we conclude that all metals expand when heated.

This method of simple enumeration is one kind of inductive as opposed to deductive inference. The premises, or particular observations, do not guarantee the truth of the conclusion in the logical sense, since it is logically possible for the premises to be true and the conclusion to be false. The premises instead just render the conclusion probable. But the problem of premise regress is overcome, since the entire process is grounded in simple particular observations, which, according to empiricism, are the ground of all knowledge. So by following the Baconian inductive method, we arrive at generalizations from observation.

Bacon believed that true knowledge always leads to practical application, since true knowledge of nature gives us power over nature. (Of course, he recognized that such practical application might not be immediate.) If I understand metal to the point that I know reliably that if I heat a certain piece of copper it will expand, then that gives me power to control it. If I want it expanded, I can heat it up. If I don't, I can prevent it from being heated. For example, suppose part of the deck of a ship is made from metal, and I want to prevent expansion because that tends to warp the wood, which could cause a leak. Knowing what I know about metal, I can prevent that expansion by preventing the heating — by shielding the metal from the sun if that is the source of heat. In this way, Bacon thought, understanding of nature would automatically lead to control of nature with practical benefit to humanity. In a real sense, knowledge is power. As Bacon claims in *Novum Organum* (in a rather self-satisfied tone),

> I may hand over to men their fortunes, now their understanding is emancipated and come as it were of age; whence there cannot but follow an improvement in man's estate and an enlargement of his power over nature.[20]

In *The New Atlantis,* Bacon describes a utopia in which scientists work very hard at applying their science to the improvement of the quality of human life. Bacon cites three inventions as evidence that such a utopian vision is actually going to come about if his vision of science is followed. The first is the printing press, which aids the dissemination of knowledge; the second is gunpowder, an obvious source of power; and the third is the compass, which improves navigation. For Bacon, these three inventions demonstrated conclusively the capacity of scientific knowledge to give power over nature. They give us good reason to think that if we pour our efforts into true science, it will reward us with these sorts of technological advances, which in turn improves the quality of life. Bacon's optimistic view about the possibility of human achievement marks the early stages of a trend that dominated Western thought until the early twentieth century.

Unlike Descartes and particularly Galileo, Bacon did not himself make very much progress in any actual scientific projects. He is seen rather as a philosopher of the scientific method and its technology who succeeded in specifying the methodology and research program required for successful science. But it was not long before the kind of scientific successes that Bacon had hoped for did in fact arise. Eighty years after Bacon's death, his vision of the way in which science should be done was adopted by the Royal Society in London, which set itself up deliberately and explicitly in order to carry out the work that Bacon had envisioned, adopting Bacon as a kind of patron saint. At their meetings, the Royal Society reported on experiments, discussed those experiments, collected data, and so on. Its members included figures such as Boyle, Hooke, Newton, and Harvey — in other words, many of the founders of modern science.

---

20. Bacon 1905, p. 387.

Bacon and the Cultural Mandate

The Baconian vision of science and technology may seem to the modern mind to be a long way from religion. After all, isn't Bacon in effect criticizing the dominant religious ideology and seeking to replace it with science? At a glance it may seem so, but this naturalistic perspective seriously misunderstands Bacon. In fact, as with Descartes, Bacon's vision is underpinned and motivated by a number of related religious themes.

In the passage from the Preface of *The Great Instauration,* cited earlier, Bacon spells out the purpose of his 'new way.' He claims

> [t]hat the state of knowledge is not prosperous nor greatly advancing; and that a way must be opened for the human understanding entirely different from any hitherto known . . . in order that the mind may exercise over the nature of things the authority which properly belongs to it.[21]

In other words, as we have seen, when bankrupt Aristotelian 'science' is replaced by genuine, inductive science we will find that we gain authority, that is, power over nature. But notice that Bacon speaks of the mind having an authority "which properly belongs to it." Here Bacon alludes to Genesis 1 where, having created man and woman, God immediately decrees that they

> Be fruitful, and multiply, and replenish the earth, and subdue it: and have dominion over the fish of the sea, and over the fowl of the air and over every living thing that moveth upon the earth.[22]

This command to rule over nature is known, quaintly, as the 'cultural mandate.' Bacon takes this to mean that God has told the human race that it has the job of ruling over the rest of nature, a job that requires the development of science and technology. We rule nature better when we understand it better. Bacon continues,

> For man by the fall fell at the same time from his state of innocence and from his dominion over creation. Both the loss of the state of in-

21. Bacon 1905, p. 243.
22. Genesis 1:28

70

nocence and loss of dominion over creation or nature can, however, even in this life be in some part repaired. The former is to be regained through religion and faith, whereas the latter is to be regained through the arts and sciences.[23]

Here Bacon refers not to Genesis 1 but to Genesis 3, to the 'fall,' in which Eve and Adam eat the fruit of the tree of knowledge of good and evil, which they had been told not to eat. This fall is not just a moral or spiritual matter; it also affect our ability to rule creation, Bacon asserts. But true scientific endeavor can help us regain that aspect of paradise. Bacon explains:

> For creation was not by the curse made altogether and forever a rebel, but in virtue of that charter "In the sweat of thy face shalt thou eat bread," it is now by various labours (not certainly by disputations or idle magical ceremonies, but by various labours) at length and in some measure subdued to the supplying of man with bread; that is, to the uses of human life.[24]

Behind Bacon's use of the cultural mandate lies a view of human nature with an accompanying theory of 'the image of God.' We have already met the theory that says that God, as a ruler, has dominion over all things, and because humanity is made in the image of God, we too have dominion and must rule over the rest of nature. This is Bacon's view. The image of God in humanity, and therefore human nature itself, is understood in terms of power, and the function of ruling.

So Bacon's use of the image of God differs from Descartes' in telling ways. Descartes conceived the image of God in terms of rationality alone, which makes human beings spectators — we seek knowledge for knowledge's sake.[25] But Bacon's vision of humanity is not of spectators, but of hands-on rulers who bring nature under control, making a practical difference to the world.

A related theme, which is perhaps even more alien to a naturalistic mindset, is the idea of 'adamic wisdom.' According to this notion, Adam engaged in scientific study of nature in the Garden of Eden, reaching a

23. Bacon 1905, p. 387.

24. Bacon 1905, p. 387.

25. But see Descartes (1984, pt. 6), where Descartes espouses a very Baconian view (see Lloyd 1994, pp. 151-54).

high point in human knowledge and understanding that was largely lost and which has never been reclaimed. Adamic wisdom was not only partially lost at the fall but also continued to be lost over the centuries. In fact, for Bacon, the progress of knowledge from Adam through Aristotle to Aristotelian scholasticism was one long downhill slide. So figures closer to Adam may have known more than their descendants. Indeed, since one of Aristotle's projects was to attempt to refute all of the earlier philosophers, it seemed to Bacon that Aristotle was cutting us off from adamic wisdom. Bacon proposes that this slide can be reversed, and although we will never attain the pristine, uncorrupted wisdom of Adam, we may get back closer to that garden state.[26]

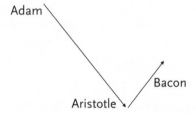

Figure 4: Scientific Progress

This will, no doubt, surprise casual readers of Bacon. When we first read of his disdain for Aristotelianism we may envisage a far more wide-reaching disrespect for the past and for religion. But it turns out that the cultural mandate and related religious ideas are the motivating ideological notions behind Bacon's vision of a scientifically-driven society.

Twentieth-Century Critiques of the Baconian Vision

The Baconian vision for science and technology has, arguably right up until today, continued to be the dominant ideology in the West. But in the second half of the twentieth century there was a sustained reaction against it, from sections of the environmental and feminist movements.

26. See the related Baconian use of 'Solomon' (e.g., Briggs 1996, p. 179).

Lyn White, in his 1967 article "The Historical Roots of Our Ecological Crisis,"[27] claims that within pre-Judeo-Christian Europe the dominant worldview was not the Baconian one of dominion but rather a pagan view that sees humanity as part of nature, in which nature is something to be revered — for example, the belief that in a certain group of trees there are resident spirits that must be placated before the trees can be cut down, or in a field an earth goddess that must be placated before heavy plowing can be undertaken. White writes,

> In Antiquity every tree, every spring, every stream, every hill had its own *genius loci,* its guardian spirit. These spirits were accessible to men, but were very unlike men; centaurs, fauns, and mermaids show their ambivalence. Before one cut a tree, mined a mountain, or dammed a brook, it was important to placate the spirit in charge of that particular situation, and to keep it placated. By destroying pagan animism, Christianity made it possible to exploit nature in a mood of indifference to the feelings of natural objects.[28]

White argued that even though it had become in many ways 'post-Christian,' the West in the twentieth century was still operating largely under a Baconian ideology. The implicit belief continued that we must (and can) seek to understand the world, in order that our knowledge will give us power over nature. If you own a book, for example, then you are free to do with it as you please; you can write in it, highlight it, or tear out pages. However, if the book is from the library, or belongs to a friend that you respect, then you will not. Ownership seems to sanction any action. According to White, the same applies to the way that we think of nature. If we think that we own it, and it was created for us, we feel that we can do with it as we please. The word commonly thought to be appropriate here is 'exploitation.'

So religion can take some credit for the development of science and technology, according to White, but it also must take the blame for the problems that technological development has brought — the various environmental disasters:

> The emergence in widespread practice of the Baconian creed that scientific knowledge means technological power over nature can scarcely

27. White 1967.
28. White 1967, p. 1205.

be dated before about 1850, save in the chemical industries, where it is anticipated in the 18th century. Its acceptance as a normal pattern of action may mark the greatest event in human history since the invention of agriculture, and perhaps in nonhuman terrestrial history as well. Almost at once the new situation forced the crystallization of the novel concept of ecology; indeed, the word *ecology* first appeared in the English language in 1873. Today, less than a century later, the impact of our race upon the environment has so increased in force that it has changed in essence. When the first cannons were fired, in the early 14th century, they affected ecology by sending workers scrambling to the forests and mountains for more potash, sulfur, iron ore, and charcoal, with some resulting erosion and deforestation. Hydrogen bombs are of a different order: a war fought with them might alter the genetics of all life on this planet. By 1285 London had a smog problem arising from the burning of soft coal, but our present combustion of fossil fuels threatens to change the chemistry of the globe's atmosphere as a whole, with consequences which we are only beginning to guess. With the population explosion, the carcinoma of planless urbanism, the now geological deposits of sewage and garbage, surely no creature other than man has ever managed to foul its nest in such short order.[29]

White therefore challenges the entire Baconian vision, suggesting that certain Judeo-Christian concepts, in particular dominion over nature, are to blame for the damage done to the earth by technology. The solution is by no means obvious. According to White, technology is something of a runaway train, out of control. It does not have within itself the capacity to remedy the problems that it has caused because any application of technology will lead to still bigger problems. For example, we spray to control a certain kind of insect but then that insect mutates, after which we need even more potent chemicals, and the problem simply escalates. Radical changes are needed.

White's solution takes the form of an alternative ideology. He proposes St. Francis of Assisi as the patron saint of ecologists. St. Francis was a thirteenth-century Roman Catholic monk who held an unorthodox view of nature, one that did not involve any hierarchy in creation and in particular any dominion over nature by humanity. He is said to have preached to the birds and wolves. White's idea is that if we abandon the

29. White 1967, pp. 1203-04.

'axiom' that we have the function of ruling over nature, we won't want to dominate it.

The most common response to White has been to note that in Genesis the concepts of 'ruling' and 'dominion' are given not in terms of ownership but of stewardship. To return to our example, if a person for whom you have great respect lends you a book asks you take care of it, you would be less likely to write in it or tear out pages than you would if the book was yours. So also creation was entrusted to humanity not to mistreat but to look after on behalf of its maker.[30] This suggests that White's objection to the Baconian tradition should not be directed towards the Judeo-Christian ideology as such, but rather directed at a Judeo-Christian tradition that did not take its own ideology seriously enough.[31]

A second ecological objection to the Baconian vision focuses on the value of nature. According to so-called 'deep ecology' we need to abandon the assumption that nature was created for humanity. The answer to the ecological problem is to see that nature has intrinsic value, that is, that it has value in its own right, and not just instrumental value for the benefit of humans.[32]

However, defenders of the Baconian program have also argued that part of the Judeo-Christian tradition is the idea of 'the value of nature.'[33] So, in Genesis, every time something is created, the phrase "And God saw that it was good" is repeated, long before humanity appears on the scene. This implies that the objects of creation themselves have intrinsic value.

Another twentieth-century line of criticism of the Baconian vision expressed feminist concerns. In her influential book *The Death of Nature*,[34] Carolyn Merchant showed how thinking about women is connected to thinking about nature. In pagan religion in pre-Christian Europe, the earth was conceived of as feminine and to be respected. But deterioration of society's views about women, and increased attempts to keep them in their place — highlighted by the witch trials — brought the idea that na-

30. See, for example, Peacocke 1975, pp. 255-318.

31. Or alternatively, a post-Christian era that retains some but not all of its heritage. Merchant comments: "If eventually the religious framework providing for God's constant care . . . were removed, as it was in the eighteenth century, the possibilities for intellectual arrogance toward nature would be strengthened." (1980, p. 279).

32. Brennan 1988, p. 141.

33. Boltzer and Armstrong 1998, ch. 5.

34. Merchant 1980.

ture, as woman, was wild and disorderly and needed to be brought under control. Bacon himself is implicated in that in his public office he was close to the anti-woman practices of his patron, James I of England, and in that his views are given away by the feminine metaphors he sometimes uses to talk about nature, such as this:

> For like as a man's disposition is never well known or proved till he be crossed, nor Proteus ever changed shape till he was straitened and held fast, so nature exhibits herself more clearly under the trials and vexations of art than when left to herself.[35]

Thus Merchant concludes,

> This method [of Baconian domination], so readily applicable when nature is denoted by the female gender, degraded and made possible the exploitation of the natural environment.[36]

Whether the Baconian vision degraded nature and made possible its exploitation is a matter we have already considered. The concern here is the relevance of views about women. While Merchant's critique is in some respects justly damning, what needs to be shown for our purposes is that it is the Baconian vision itself that is damned.

One question is whether views about woman did in fact make a difference to attitudes to nature. We must note that while the pagan view of woman as described by Merchant is a serious religious metaphysic, the Baconian references are merely metaphorical, as the new religious metaphysic views nature as gender-neutral. Merchant's response to this is to point out that even metaphors that are officially harmless can have a profound influence on attitudes and practices, and that this is the case with seventeenth-century views about women and nature. Framed this way our question is a contingent historical matter. Philosophy can only tell us whether it is plausible that there is such a connection, and it certainly seems plausible that there could be.

Granting that views about women did influence people's attitudes towards nature, which in turn help explain subsequent ecological problems, we still need to ask whether this reflects on the Baconian vision itself

---

35. Cited by Merchant 1980, p. 169.
36. Merchant 1980, p. 169.

rather than on something extraneous to it. What is the connection between the cultural mandate together with Bacon's idea of experimental science on the one hand and negative views about women on the other?[37]

One response here has been to question whether the Genesis notion of a cultural mandate along with its accompanying theology is compatible with the negative views of women. The Genesis account places the man and woman together as equally made in the image of God, and equally subject to the cultural mandate:[38]

> So God created man in his own image, in the image of God created he him; male and female created he them. And God blessed them, and God said unto them, Be fruitful, and multiply, and replenish the earth, and subdue it. . . .

The question therefore is whether the seventeenth-century analogy of man:woman is as man:nature is tenable for a vision based on Genesis 1, given that the dualism explicit in the cultural mandate is of humanity (man and woman): nature. The argument is that the Genesis picture may be compatible with and even suggestive of a notion of non-exploitative joint male-female approach to the management of nature,[39] if such a thing is coherent. However, it must be admitted that the Genesis picture is also compatible with the Baconian view of women, since it is compatible with a picture where just as man exploits woman, so the man-(exploited)woman together exploit nature.

A second response draws on the point already discussed, according to which the cultural mandate implicitly involves an idea of responsible stewardship which excludes exploitation. If this is right, then it would seem that if belief in the cultural mandate together with exploitative views about women has helped produce the exploitation of nature — as we are supposing — then clearly what is to blame is the exploitative views of women rather than the cultural mandate. In fact Merchant's account can help explain why, in its exploitation of nature, the Western tradition came to ignore the stewardship aspect of its central mandate. In other words, it is

37. See Landau 1998.

38. Genesis 1:27-28.

39. Here the source is the biblical feminist revisionist readings of Genesis (e.g., Keller 1985; Merchant 1980). But as far as Genesis 1 is concerned, there doesn't seem to be much need of revision.

not the Baconian vision itself of dominion via experimentation which is implicated by Merchant's critique, but the exploitative view of woman, which when taken together with the Baconian vision distorts that vision into something which, by exploiting nature, actually runs counter to the original mandate.

Underlying objections of the sort we have just considered is often the idea that a pantheist conception of God would be a favorable one from an ecological point of view. According to pantheism God is not separate and independent of nature but a part or aspect of nature. The most celebrated pantheist of the seventeenth century, Baruch Spinoza (1632-1677), identified the essential nature of single existing substance as being 'God' and the changing attributes of that substance as being 'nature.'[40]

However, an examination of Spinoza's views on God and nature seems to put paid to the idea that a pantheistic rather than a theistic ideology would have engendered a more positive view of nature. Spinoza certainly denied the traditional Judeo-Christian concepts of God above nature, ruling it, and humanity — in the image of God — also above and ruling over nature.[41] But in the words of Genevieve Lloyd,

> [d]espite his rejection of any metaphysically privileged status for human beings in nature, Spinoza's philosophy continues to stress the appropriateness of human domination. His stress on a relation of integration rather than separateness between human beings and the rest of nature does not yield any repudiation of the exploitation of animals. He dismisses such concern as "unmanly" pity. In relation to animals, we should consider our own advantage, use them at our own pleasure, and treat them as is most convenient for us.[42]

Of course this is not to say that pantheism and non-exploitative views of nature are incompatible. But it does show that replacing the Genesis idea of dominion with a pantheistic axiom does not automatically lead to a non-exploitative attitude towards nature.

40. Spinoza 1982.
41. Lloyd 1994, pp. 154-60.
42. Lloyd 1994, pp. 155-56.

From God to Science and Back:
The Mutual Relevance of Science and Religion

We have already seen in an earlier chapter how thinkers in the seventeenth century saw the relationship between science and religion as one of harmony, guaranteed by the fact that the two books, Scripture and nature, have a single author, and by the fact that, for some such as Galileo, these books address different subject matter. But even if the two books address separate subject matter, this doesn't mean that science and religion are entirely independent. There are other sorts of interaction possible.

We have seen that the belief in the image of God in humanity, in two separate but related guises, provided a powerful impetus and motivation for the development of science in the seventeenth century. Someone who believes God has given us a mind like the divine mind therefore expects to understand the world that God has created. And someone who believes that we have a God-given responsibility to govern that world therefore believes that humanity has the capacity to control nature, and consequently also expects to understand the world. If this is so, then at least to some extent religion has provided the ideological underpinnings of the scientific optimism that accompanied the 'birth of modern science.' Then the relation between science and religion seems to be one of mutual relevance.

In particular, it is *theistic* religion that is significant. One argument that science would not have flourished without the particular religious context it had is due to the historian Joseph Needham,[43] in his work on the comparison between Western and Chinese science. He claims that even though science and technology in China were well developed early in history (for instance the invention of gunpowder five hundred years before it appeared in the West), science never really flourished in that context in the way it did in Europe. How are we to explain this phenomenon? According to Needham, the explanation is grounded in religious difference, in particular different views about human nature and our relation to the rest of nature.

But if this it true, then it suggests further connections between science and religion. In particular, if the relevant theistic beliefs justify optimism about human science, then by an inference to the best explanation any subsequent success of science justifies belief in the relevant theistic ideology. So let us suppose, as most do, that modern science is an outstanding success.

43. Needham 1954.

Take I to be the theistic doctrine that humanity is made in the image of God, and S to be the success of modern science. Then the truth of I makes S more likely. If our rational capacities match the rationality of the God who created the world, then it seems more likely that we could understand that world than it would be if, for example, there is no God. In other words, $P(S|I) \gg P(S)$, so theism qualifies as an explanation of the success of science.

Then, by inference to the best explanation, the success of science gives us reason to believe theism since $P(S|I) \gg P(S)$ entails[44] $P(I|S) \gg P(I)$. That science turned out to be successful confirms theism, compared to the alternative scenario in which science is unsuccessful, and the belief in nature's perspicuity turns out to be false.

If this reasoning is right then there is a two-way relevance between science and religion. Certain religious beliefs provide the motivation for doing science, and science's success confirms the truth of those beliefs.

This reasoning involves a number of assumptions — for example, that there are no better available explanations besides theism. But it would seem, for example, that naturalism (N) doesn't qualify as an explanation since $P(S|N) = P(S)$. Why should we expect to understand nature if we have no special rational capacity?

This reasoning also assumes a reasonable intrinsic probability of theism compared to naturalism, so the argument would be more likely to appeal in the seventeenth century than in later periods.

The argument also assumes that science really is successful. Some challenge this. According to constructivist accounts of science, scientific theories and the entities they describe are constructed by and constituted through social processes.[45] In other words, there is no world beyond the theories to which our theories, if true, correspond (or, on some versions, if there is such a world we have no access to it). The world described by the theory is a construction by that theory and the social and political forces which produce the theory. As one writer puts it,

> Rather than having "discovered" some "new world," akin to the discovery of America by Columbus and others, Newton's forebears in the scientific revolution had fabricated and constructed (heaped together) part of the man made synthesis about nature and its workings, to

44. Assuming certain other things are equal, this entailment is an expression of Bayes' Theroem. In particular, it assumes $P(I)$ is roughly equal to $P(S)$.

45. E.g., Latour and Woolgar 1979.

which Newton himself later made a contribution. Any 'new world' which came about was only in man-made accounts as Galileo and the others sought to write down what they could understand about the 'old world' around mankind.[46]

Then the 'success' of science is explained. The reason why we think that certain observations such as stellar parallax confirmed the theory that the earth moves has a social explanation. The theory is not true in the sense that it corresponds to the way things really are; it is true because we agree by certain social conventions to say that it is. It's no surprise that science is successful; we make it be so as we construct the world in our image. Then we have an alternative explanation, constructivism (C), which challenges the theist explanation of the success of science.

However, we need to distinguish between three kinds of success of science. The first is 'knowledge success', which is what we have so far meant by 'success.' Science provides success in this sense as it enables us to make predictions and to understand nature. We saw in the previous chapter that the instrumentalist account of science fails to explain this kind of success. The second sense is 'power success.' Science is successful in this sense when we gain power over nature; for example, if our aeroplanes fly or our cosmologically based navigation system brings us safely home. Thirdly, there is 'value success,' determined by our thinking that the consequences of science are intrinsically worth having.

It seems that both theism and constructivism are able to explain knowledge success. Further, theism can explain power success, since if we were placed in dominion over nature by its creator and ours, then it is not surprising that we do in fact have the capacity to successfully control it.

However, constructivism cannot explain the power success of science. Our theoretical commitments and social pressures may cause us to believe that we have a certain experimental result, but such factors cannot make aeroplanes fly. In fact, if social constructivism were true we would expect that things wouldn't work. It would seem a miracle that they do.[47] In other words, the power success (S_p) of science is explained by the theistic hypothesis, but not by constructivism. $P(S_p|I) \gg P(S_p)$, whereas $P(S_p|C) \ll P(S_p)$.

46. Fores 1984, p. 218.
47. Boyd 1984; Dowe 1996b.

CHAPTER 4

Miracles

Miracles, if they occur, challenge the naturalistic idea that the scientific domain of explanation is all-embracing. But even if we think of science and religion as separate domains, each legitimate, miracles seem to force a point of contact between the two. For this reason, the topic of miracles has always been one of the focal points in discussion of the relation between science and religion. The most penetrating analysis of miracles and their significance for religion that of Scottish philosopher David Hume (1711-1776).

In Chapter 10 of his *Enquiries Concerning Human Understanding*[1] Hume sets out the empiricist[2] challenge to the idea that miracles provide a rational underpinning for religion or some rational basis for belief in God.[3] In particular, Hume has in mind events such as the resurrection of Jesus Christ as a basis or rational underpinning for Christian faith.

Hume's discussion comes in two steps. The first step involves the probability of the occurrence of a miracle. Hume's 'first argument' leads to the conclusion that it is never rational to believe, on the strength of the testimony of others, that a miracle has occurred. The second step of Hume's argument addresses whether the occurrence of a miracle, if it could be established, could be evidence for the existence of God. Hume argues that it

---

1. Hume 1975b.

2. The empiricist believes experience is our only guide to the way things are.

3. There are, however, other sorts of attempts to provide a rational underpinning for religion, which Hume elsewhere (Hume 1951) tackles.

would not be, because such 'miracles' should rather be taken as as-yet un-explained natural events.

In a typical and delightfully ironic tone Hume ends his chapter with the following comment:

> Mere reason is insufficient to convince us of [a miracle's] veracity. And whoever is moved by Faith to assent to it is conscious of a continued miracle in his own person, which subverts all the principles of his understanding, and gives him a determination to believe what is most contrary to custom and experience.[4]

Hume means that given that we cannot ever rationally believe that a miracle has occurred on the basis of testimony, any person who does so actually witnesses a 'miracle' within themselves — that of being able to believe against the evidence!

In this chapter we examine the account given by Hume, and also responses from twentieth-century philosophers John Mackie and George Schlesinger. Mackie, whose book title *The Miracle of Theism*[5] alludes to Hume's ironic comment just quoted, defends Hume's conclusions, whereas Schlesinger defends the rationality of belief in miracles. Firstly, however, we need to understand Hume's account of rational belief, and in particular what the conditions are under which testimony can be accepted as grounds for believing something.

Hume's Theory of Rational Belief

Because Hume argues that belief in miracles violates the dictates of rational belief, we need to begin with Hume's views about what constitutes 'rational belief.' His fundamental principle about what makes belief rational is this:

> A wise man . . . proportions his belief to the evidence.[6]

Hume is not saying that people always proportion their belief to the evidence, but that only insofar as we proportion our belief to the available ev-

4. Hume 1975b, p. 131.
5. Mackie 1982.
6. Hume 1975a, p. 110.

idence are we wise or rational people. In other words, Hume is offering a normative definition of rationality or wisdom.

This in itself is controversial. It is roughly the view of Hume's predecessor John Locke (1632-1704), but it contrasts with the view expressed so graphically by Blaise Pascal (1623-1662), who argued in his famous Wager that, in view of the consequences, the only rational thing to do is believe in God even though evidence is entirely inconclusive. Since Hume, this view was developed most significantly by Søren Kierkegaard (1813-1855), who claimed that religious belief must not be based on evidence or else it is not genuine faith, and William James, who outlined further ways in which faith dependent on evidence might be taken as defective. Others, such as W. K. Clifford, have gone to the other extreme, claiming that it is immoral not to proportion one's belief to the evidence.

What does it mean to proportion belief to evidence? For a start, this requires that belief come in degrees, which seems reasonable. My belief that it will rain here today is not as strong as my belief that night will come at the usual time, but is stronger than my belief that it will snow here today.

Suppose there are dark gray clouds forming in the sky. On the strength of this we tend to believe that there will soon be rain. But what is the strength of that belief? One way is to rank all one's beliefs, say on a scale from one to ten, depending on their strength. I might give the number 7 to the belief that there will be rain here soon given that there are heavy gray clouds in the sky, the number 9.9 to the belief that night will come at the usual time, and the number 2 to the suggestion that it will snow today.

A less subjective way to measure degree of belief was suggested by twentieth-century philosopher Frank Ramsey (1903-30). He points out that we can measure someone's degree of belief by the shortest odds they would accept on the proposition in question. If I believe with degree five that there will be rain here soon then I should be willing to bet on rain at even odds (1-1). However, psychology has demonstrated that people do not generally act rationally, and so Ramsey's model is not a good model of how people actually behave.[7] So most philosophers take Ramsey's approach as normative, of what we should do if we are being rational — that is, as a measure of rational degrees of belief.

Hume would agree that people are generally not rational. His ac-

7. See Stich 1990.

count is normative too; his account of what makes degrees of belief rational is the 'maxim' that the degree of belief in P must correspond to the evidence that we have for P. Hume understands evidence in terms of experience. Roughly speaking, he treats the degree of evidence for P in terms of the proportion of times that we have had an experience of P, or have had the experience of others reported to us. How often does it rain when there are clouds on the horizon? If it rains seven times in ten when gray clouds appear, then my degree of belief should match that evidence.

According to Hume, complete agreement in the evidence amounts to a 'proof.' If in our experience it has always rained when gray clouds appear, and all records of the matter are in agreement, then this amounts to a 'proof,' which justifies us calling it a *law of nature*. The evidence for an event which does not happen all the time, but only a certain proportion of the time Hume calls a 'probability.' Either way, our strength of belief should correspond to the evidence. When confronted with a probability we should believe by degree; when presented with a proof, we should believe with certainty.[8] However, this can be misleading. As John Mackie has pointed out,[9] there is something unsatisfactory in the claim that a proof is constituted by a case in which 'all As are Bs,' and a probability is defined as a case in which 'some As are Bs.' We can argue deductively from the generalization — 'all As are Bs' to the conclusion that, in a particular case, — 'the next A that we encounter will be a B.' Similarly, if we have a law which states that 'ninety percent of As are Bs,' we can conclude that the truth of 'the next particular A will be a B,' roughly with 90 percent certainty.

However, this is different from arguing that because all observed As are Bs then in fact it is a law of nature that 'all As are Bs'. This is not a proof; it is an inductive step and under most circumstances is quite unjustified. My experience will count as evidence for a given law of nature, but it will never amount to a proof. Similarly, just because in ninety percent of my observations As have been Bs, this does not show that there is a law to the effect that 'ninety percent of As are Bs.' In other words, establishing the truth of a law of nature is not as straightforward as Hume apparently imagines. In fact, some 'uniform experiences' are strong evidence for a law of nature and others are not — depending, for example, on how extensive and representative our experience is.

8. Hume 1975a, pp. 101-111.
9. Mackie 1982.

This does not undermine the claim that we should proportion our belief to the evidence, nor as it turns out, does it undermine Hume's argument about miracles.

Testimonial Evidence

Testimonial evidence is evidence we learn about on the reports of other people. Philosophers often overlook it, yet the reasons that we have for our beliefs in many areas of life are testimonial in form. In giving a character or employment reference we hope someone will believe the testimony that is being presented. At school we mostly learn from the testimony of either textbooks or teachers. In a court of law much of the evidence that is presented comes in the form of testimonial evidence where witnesses are assessed as to their reliability. In science the dissemination and reporting of scientific results is a matter of testimony. And the rest of us tend to believe the testimony of those with the authority of being 'a scientist.' Mostly when we know something about science it is not that we have all had a uniform experience regarding some scientific discovery. Rather, the scientific evidence depends upon a few people carrying out experiments and then reporting their methods and findings in scientific journals. These findings are usually taken as reliable testimony.

Nevertheless, in general there is a difference between testimony given in a court of law and testimony delivered by scientists. Science requires repetition. Before any particular scientific result is accepted scientists require that their observations be repeated in different circumstances. And even once this is done we just have stronger testimonial evidence; it is still testimony that we are relying on.

Implicit in Hume's discussion is the idea that evaluation of testimony involves two considerations. One is how probable the event is in itself. If we are told that it will rain we should ask how likely that event is in itself. If that event is probable, we are inclined to believe the testimony. If, on the other hand, the event in question is highly unlikely, we might be less inclined to believe the testimony. The second consideration concerns the reliability of the witness who is responsible for the testimony. If the claim that it will rain comes from a meteorologist, we might be more inclined to believe it than if it came from a young child or from a salesman trying to sell drought-stricken pasture. So any evaluation of testimonial evidence must balance the inherent likelihood of the event in question and the reliability of the witness.

We must also account for cases in which two independent witnesses, say Jack and Jill, corroborate each other's testimonies.[10] Such a case would provide much stronger evidence for the event in question. If it is relatively unlikely that Jack is lying or mistaken, and it is also relatively unlikely that Jill is lying or mistaken, then the fact that both testimonies coincide becomes extremely unlikely. The strength of this compound testimony will be greater than the strength of the sum of the two testimonies. This is because in such cases we must not only explain how Jack came to be mistaken or lying, and how Jill came to be mistaken or lying, but also how it is that both Jack and Jill independently arrived at exactly the same story. This means that once the testimony of independent witnesses comes into play, the strength of that testimony increases dramatically.

Testimonial evidence is important in Hume's consideration of miracles because he has in mind the miracles in the Bible, and whether they can be regarded as proof of the veracity of claims made by Christianity. To believe that Jesus' resurrection actually occurred, for example, involves accepting the testimony of those who claimed they saw him die, that they saw an empty tomb, and that they saw him alive after he had died. It also involves accepting the testimony of those who wrote the record, and those who preserved it. Each of these aspects involves human testimony.

The Concept of a Miracle

If the definition of a miracle is just a 'very unlikely event,' then it would be quite plausible in Hume's scheme to believe that a miracle has occurred in cases where the testimonial evidence is sufficiently strong to counterbalance the inherent improbability of the event itself. We know that improbable events — sheer coincidences — do happen from time to time. Suppose the very day that John prayed for help, somebody anonymously left money in an envelope under his door. Certainly this sort of event can and does happen, but is it a miracle or mere coincidence? If by definition any improbable event is a miracle, then this occurrence should be classified as a miracle.

10. Mackie 1982.

However, if we define a miracle as an impossible event, then, depending on what we mean by 'impossible,' perhaps we can never rationally believe that a miracle has occurred. If by 'impossible' we mean something that can logically never happen, and therefore never will, then we cannot rationally believe a miracle has ever happened (assuming here that God cannot do what is logically impossible).

Hume himself defines a miracle as "a violation of the laws of nature." 'Laws of nature' are for him uniform regularities, such as 'all planets move in ellipses.' We think something is a law of nature if in our experience it is a uniform regularity. The evidence for the law 'all planets move in ellipses' is that all planets that we know about, or have discovered to date, have been observed to move in ellipses in every orbit, year after year, according to all observations in the entire history of astronomical observation and records. As something that has not admitted of any exceptions, this can be called a law of nature, since the evidence amounts to a full proof. The statements 'dead persons remain dead' and 'all metals expand when heated' are both taken to be laws of nature if in our experience there are no cases of persons rising from the dead or heated metals failing to expand.

But if we take a miracle to be a violation of a law of nature, and take a law of nature to be a universal regularity, then it follows very simply that a miracle simply cannot happen, as John Mackie has noted.[11] Under this definition of a law of nature it is logically impossible for a miracle to occur, if indeed this is a coherent concept of a miracle. For suppose that we did find a metal which did not expand when heated. This would mean that 'all metals expand when heated' is not a universal regularity and therefore not a law of nature after all. Suppose we have a case of a person rising from the dead. Then it follows that there is no regularity that all dead people stay dead, therefore it is no miracle. So, if a miracle is defined as a violation of a universal regularity, miracles are ruled out, out of hand. This leads Mackie to wonder if the notion of a miracle is a coherent one. If this is what we mean by a miracle, we cannot coherently ask whether we could ever have grounds for believing that one has occurred. One way for avoiding this problem that fits with Hume's argument is to define a miracle as a violation of 'an otherwise exceptionless regularity.'

However, there is another difficulty that Hume's account of laws faces. There are kinds of universal regularities that are not laws of nature,

11. Mackie 1982.

the so-called accidental regularities. For example, consider the fact that all of the coins in my pocket are gold — not a law of nature even though it may be a universal regularity. Or consider the universal regularity 'all balls of gold are less than two kilometers in diameter'. This regularity is universal in that nowhere in the entire history of the universe has there ever existed a gold ball greater than two kilometers in diameter. However, there is no law of nature that says there could not exist such a ball of gold. So philosophers say that this regularity, although universal, is accidental, and as such is not a law of nature. Contrast this with the regularity 'there are no balls of uranium of more than two kilometers in diameter.' This is a non-accidental law of nature because there is, in fact, a very good physical reason why balls of uranium of that size do not exist: pack too much uranium into a compact ball and it will trigger a nuclear reaction. There would seem to be nothing special about a violation of an otherwise exceptionless accidental regularity: such things can happen, even if they don't.

However, Mackie claims that a more adequate account of the concept of a law of nature can lead to a coherent concept of a miracle. For Mackie

> the laws of nature . . . describe the ways in which the world — including, of course, human beings — works when left to itself, when not interfered with.[12]

In order to discover 'the ways in which the world works,' we first need to discover the causal laws that underlie those workings. These causal laws will describe what will eventuate in the future, given an initial set of circumstances. Mackie calls these causal laws 'laws of working.'

Mackie claims that the idea of laws of working renders the concept of divine intervention coherent. Suppose an influence intrudes from the outside into an otherwise closed system (one that is isolated from its environment). The laws of working of that closed system tell us how that system would have evolved if it had continued to evolve in the absence of outside forces. If we now take the entire natural world to be a closed system, we can imagine the way in which it would evolve if it remained a closed system. Then the concept of miraculous intervention is simply the concept of something intruding into that closed system and changing the way that it evolves.

12. Mackie 1982, pp. 19-20.

If the laws of working are deterministic then there are fairly straight-forward conditions for the occurrence of a miracle. A system is deterministic if the particular state of that system at a given time, together with the laws of working of that system, fix the state of that system for all future times in the absence of intervention. We can then compare this with the way in which the universe will evolve if intruded upon, as in the case of a miracle.

If, however, the laws governing the system in question are probabilistic then things are not so clear, since in indeterministic systems there is always a chance that something will happen that is contrary to what has been predicted. But in the case of deterministic systems, at least, there is a very clear set of conditions that will tell us whether or not a miracle has occurred. So, Mackie concludes, the concept of 'divine intervention' does make sense and so we can reasonably ask whether we could ever have sufficient reason to think that such a thing has occurred.

In a footnote Hume also offers a "more accurate" definition of a miracle:

> A miracle may be accurately defined, a transgression of a law of nature by a particular volition of the Deity, or by the interposition of some invisible agent.[13]

This is a criterion that is even more difficult to meet. Not only must there be a violation of a law of nature, but we also have to know that it was done by the will of God.

There is another difficulty to be met here. To know that a particular event occurs by the volition of the Deity requires knowing the purpose or teleology of the event. As we will see in the next chapter, it is notoriously difficult to see what the objective purpose of such an event or object is. According to Mackie there is at least one solution to this difficulty. If someone is not only able to do a miracle but also to predict it in advance, then we might have reason to accept a claim that person has made about the purpose of the miracle. Take the case of Jesus' resurrection. If it is true that Jesus predicted his own death and resurrection, and told his disciples why it would happen, and then it did happen, then we have some reason to think that this was by the will of God.

13. Hume 1975a, p. 115.

So far we have considered the conceptual question, "what is a miracle?" We now turn to the epistemological question, "Can we ever know that one has occurred?"

Hume's First Argument against Miracles

Hume's main argument against miracles draws on his account of rational belief — that to be rational we must proportion our belief to the evidence — and his definition of a miracle as a violation of a law of nature. It follows from the latter that by definition, miracles must always have against them a 'full proof,' consisting of the uniform evidence that supports the law of nature.

Suppose that the testimonial evidence given in support of the occurrence of a miracle is as strong as it can possibly be, in fact so strong that it amounts to a full proof (if that is possible). In such a situation we would find ourselves with two full proofs, a full proof for the miracle and another full proof for the law of nature that it is supposed to violate. What are we to do in such a situation? Hume's theory of rational belief says that the two complete proofs, in effect, balance each other, so that to apportion our belief to the evidence is to remain agnostic as to whether or not the miracle really occurred. Hume concludes that in this case we cannot rationally believe that a miracle has occurred.

Alternatively, suppose that the testimonial evidence given in support of the miracle is not as strong as it could possibly be, and amounts to a probability rather than a full proof. In weighing the evidence in this case we find that we have a full proof in support of the law of nature on the one hand, and a mere probability in support of the miracle on the other, so on balance we should believe that a miracle has not occurred. So this, too, is a case in which we cannot rationally believe that a miracle has occurred.

Therefore, regardless of whether the testimonial evidence for a miracle amounts to a full proof or less than a full proof, we cannot rationally believe that a miracle has actually occurred. Thus Hume concludes that we can never rationally believe on the strength of testimony that a miracle has occurred. Since we can never rationally believe that a miracle has occurred, miracles cannot ever provide a rational foundation for religious belief. In Hume's words, we may establish it as a maxim, that no human testimony can have such force as to prove a miracle, and make it a just foundation for any such system of religion.[14]

It is important to emphasize that Hume is not claiming that miracles cannot happen. He is just claiming that we can never rationally believe on the strength of testimony that a miracle has happened. This is an epistemological matter, concerning what we can rationally or reasonably believe, not what can and cannot happen. In fact, according to Hume's empiricism no matter of fact is impossible. For Hume, nothing is necessary; even the laws of nature are contingent (that is, they did not have to be the way that they are). He notes,

> A miracle may either be discoverable by men or not. This alters not its nature and essence. The raising of a house or ship into the air is a visible miracle. The raising of a feather, when the wind wants ever so little of a force requisite for that purpose, is as real a miracle, though not so sensible with regard to us.[15]

Hume does not say anything about what we should believe if we personally witness a miracle. This issue is not taken up anywhere in *Of Miracles*. Nonetheless, the significance of Hume's argument for this kind of case would seem to be that if our senses are completely reliable and therefore their testimony amounts to a full proof, then this will be balanced by the full proof that supports the law of nature that the miracle is claimed to violate. In such a case we should suspend judgment and be agnostic about the occurrence of the miracle. On the other hand, if anything at all throws doubt upon the reliability of our senses, so that they amount to less than a full proof, then we should believe that the miracle has not happened. In other words, Hume's first argument applies equally to the case of miracles based on the testimony of others and to cases involving the personal experience of miracles. So, Hume should also conclude that we can never rationally believe, on the strength of our own observations, that a miracle has occurred.[16]

14. Hume 1975a, p. 127.
15. Hume 1975a, p. 115.
16. Hume does not advance this argument, but it is put forward by John Mackie in *The Miracle of Theism* (1982).

A Problem for Testimony

As we have seen, Hume's position is that the assessment of testimony must take two criteria into account: the internal probability of the event in itself, and the reliability of the witness delivering the testimony. In the case of miracles, Hume claims that the internal probability of the event itself is as low as it could possibly be. In fact, miracles fare so badly on Hume's first criterion that it appears not to matter how well they do on the second criterion. No matter how good the testimonial evidence is, or how reliable the witnesses are, the internal probability of a miracle is so low that its occurrence can never be rationally believed.

This approach to testimonial evidence has attracted an objection first noted by John Venn in 1888.[17] According to this objection, Hume's approach in assessing the validity of testimony is incorrect because it recommends withholding belief in many cases where we really feel we would be rational in accepting someone's testimony. Suppose Mary happens to come across Marge, an old acquaintance, when walking down the street in a large city that both, independently, happen to be visiting. The probability of this event occurring would be extremely low. Should we believe Mary when she says this happened? On Hume's first criteria for assessing testimony, we should not believe her, because the internal probability of the event in question is so low that it doesn't matter how reliable Mary is as a witness.

To take another example, on the five dollar bill I have in my hand I see the serial number BB 94809767. The probability of this exact number is, in fact, extremely low, so according to Hume's principles you should not believe me, no matter how reliable you might think that I am as a witness. In such cases as these we often do believe that the testimony is true, so it seems that Hume's system for assessing testimony is flawed.

However, there is one way in which Hume may reply to this objection. It seems that there is a relevant difference between these sorts of examples and the case of miracles. Both meeting someone and a five dollar note having a certain serial number, although improbable, are commonplace *kinds* of events. Every five-dollar bill has a serial number. But this is not true in the case of a miracle, such as rising from the dead, since that is the *kind* of event that never happens. So this suggests that the difference

17. Venn 1888.

between 'types' and 'tokens' is relevant. A token-event is a particular case, whereas a type-event is a class of events; 'getting cancer' is a type-event, and a token-event is a particular case of that type, such as 'Jane's getting cancer.' So one reply to Venn's objection may be that those cases outlined earlier, while improbable in themselves, are all tokens of type-events that are probable. However, rising from the dead is a case of an improbable type-event.

Can Hume's account of the testimony allow for this? There seems to be no reason why it cannot. The intrinsic likelihood of an event can be given in terms of the relevant kind of event. If someone tells me (a) that a lottery was won by someone, and (b) that John, who was in a lottery, won; all other things being equal I ought to attach similar credence to (a) and (b) as possible events, event though, in terms of the probability of the token events, (a) is virtually certain (depending on the kind of lottery) and (b) is virtually impossible.

Hume's 'Limitation'

Hume himself appears to allow another objection to his first argument. In Section 99 of *Of Miracles* he remarks,

> I beg the limitations here may be remarked, when I say, that a miracle can never be proved, so as to be the foundation of a system of religion. For I own, that otherwise, there may possibly be miracles, or violations of the usual course of nature, of such a kind as to admit of proof from human testimony; though, perhaps, it will be impossible to find any such in all the records of history.[18]

So Hume admits that there could be cases in which the testimonial evidence is so strong that we could believe that an observed uniform regularity had been violated and that a miracle had occurred. Hume offers the example of an eight-day darkness. Suppose in the year 1600 — more than one hundred years previous to the time of Hume's writing — it was reported that there had occurred a period of eight days of darkness that covered the whole earth. Being a violation of the usual course of nature this is,

---

18. Hume 1975a, p. 127.

by definition, a miracle. However, suppose that the testimony was extremely strong, and that many reliable witnesses from many different parts of the world reported the same phenomenon. Suppose that there is no disagreement amongst these reports, and that in every culture there is a lively memory of this event. This is a case, claims Hume, in which we would have to admit that a miracle has occurred.

But this appears to contradict Hume's first argument against miracles, according to which we never can have testimonial evidence strong enough to outweigh the full proof that supports a law of nature. At this point Hume seems to abandon his first argument.

Yet there seems to be a valid point here. Because our experience is limited, we may well come across a counterexample to what we thought was a law of nature. Hume's previous reasoning seems to imply that we should never believe a scientist who claims to have established a correction to what was previously considered to be a universal regularity. For example, suppose that we have never experienced an eclipse and then we hear of a report that an eclipse has occurred. Or, suppose that while performing an experiment a scientist discovers a kind of metal that does not expand when heated. Should we believe reports of this? Hume's first argument seems to entail that we, and the scientific community, should never accept the reports of these experiments because those results violate our prior uniform experience.

So the upshot of Hume's first argument seems to be that we can never really believe that novelties occur in the scientific arena. This leads to a kind of scientific dogmatism because new results that challenge the established paradigm can never be accepted. However, when we consider real science we see that from time to time new results do arise that challenge the established paradigm, sometimes requiring a complete overthrow of the previous understanding of the laws of nature.

Here Hume himself appears to be raising this objection against his previous argument. However John Mackie claims to find this latter point back in earlier sections, which if true somewhat relieves the sense of contradiction. Mackie notes that there is a hesitation in the first argument where Hume says

> The plain consequence is (and it is a general maxim worthy of our attention), "That no testimony is sufficient to establish a miracle, unless the testimony be of such a kind, that its falsehood would be more mi-

raculous, than the fact, which it endeavors to establish; and even in that case there is a mutual destruction of arguments, and the superior only gives us an assurance suitable to that degree of force, which remains, after deducting the inferior."[19]

Is this allowing that we could find testimonial evidence which outweighs the proof of the scientific law that the miracle is assumed to violate? Hume goes on to say that

> When anyone tells me that he saw a dead man restored to life, I immediately consider with myself, whether it be more probable, that this person should either deceive or be deceived, or that the fact, which he relates, should really have happened. I weigh the one miracle against the other; and according to the superiority, which I discover, I pronounce my decision, and always reject the greater miracle. If the falsehood of his testimony would be more miraculous, than the event which he relates; then, and not till then, can he pretend to command my belief or opinion.[20]

Mackie claims that Hume is countenancing the possibility of having testimonial evidence that is of greater strength than the evidence in favor of a law of nature. The case is one in which the falsehood of the testimony is more improbable than the falsehood of the law of nature in question, so that the falsehood of the testimony would be a greater miracle than the falsehood of the law of nature. This could be the same kind of case that Hume refers to later in his 'limitation.'

We must be careful to note that even in this case we must balance the probabilities and then deduct one from the other. Because of this, we are not going to be left with a strong sense of certainty either way. Nevertheless, if this is really what Hume is claiming, it does seem to refute his first conclusion, expressed in the 'maxim' that "no human testimony can have such force as to prove a miracle." However, he has a second argument.

19. Hume 1975a, pp. 115-116.
20. Hume 1975a, p. 116.

Hume's Second Argument against Miracles

In its place, Hume offers a second, quite different argument about miracles.[21] As we have seen, there are two steps involved in considering miracles.
First, we must ask whether the miracle in question has occurred, and second,
we must ask whether the miracle, supposing that it has occurred, constitutes
evidence for any religious claim, such as the existence of God. Hume's first
argument attacks the first of these issues and, because he argues that miracles never meet the first requirement, he can ignore the second.

But if there could be cases in which strong testimony leads us to believe
that a miracle has occurred, we need to ask whether this is any evidence for
religious claims, or whether miracles provide a rational basis for religion.

Hume argues that, in such cases, rather than inferring that the miracle
is an act of God capable of establishing religious belief, we should seek to
find the natural cause of this anomaly. We should suppose that the phenomenon is an as-yet-unexplained, but in principle explainable, natural event. So
in such cases we have discovered that what was thought to be a law of nature
is, in fact, not a law of nature. In this way scientific novelties are admitted.

In the case of the eight-day darkness, Hume says

> it is evident, that our present philosophers, instead of doubting the
> fact, ought to receive it as certain, and ought to search for the causes
> whence it might be derived.[22]

Hume does not appear to countenance, as few in the eighteenth century
would have, that there just is no explanation (see figure 5 below).

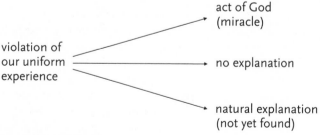

Figure 5: Explaining Miracles

21. Hume 1975a, pp. 127-129.
22. Hume 1975a, p. 128.

According to Hume's second, "more accurate" definition, a miracle is not simply a violation of a law of nature but a violation of a law of nature brought about by God. Under this second definition proof of the occurrence of what was deemed a miracle under Hume's first definition will not prove a miracle after all, since we should suppose it is an as-yet-unexplained natural occurrence.

How are we to assess Hume's second argument? Suppose that we have testimonial evidence that is strong enough to warrant the belief that a law of nature has been violated — for example, that someone has risen from the dead. On Hume's first definition, this event is a miracle, but on his second definition this is not established; rather, according to Hume's second argument, it is not a miracle because we should suppose that there is some natural explanation that we can't yet see. There must be some (rare) conditions under which people can come back to life. However, Hume does not advance any argument as to why we should pursue naturalistic explanations rather than divine explanations. For this reason his argument begs the question at hand.

On the other hand, we need to recall that Hume is attempting to show that miracles do not provide a rational underpinning for religious belief. Just as he needs some argument to support his preference for a naturalistic explanation, religious believers would need an argument in favor of a theistic explanation.

According to Mackie, Hume can be read as claiming that there are two burdens of proof on anyone who wishes to advance the miracle argument. The first is that the occurrence of the miracle must be established. For a miracle to be established, it must be the case that it would be a greater miracle for the testimony in support of that miracle to be false, than would be for the law of nature to be violated. Second, the theist must establish that the miracle in question is, in fact, from God and does not admit a natural explanation. Since it will be extremely hard to meet *both* these burdens, the miracle defender faces a dilemma. Mackie concludes,

> the intrinsic improbability of a genuine miracle, as defined above, is very great, and one or other of the alternative explanations in our fork will always be much more likely — that is, either that the alleged event is not miraculous, or that it did not occur, that the testimony is faulty in some way.[23]

23. Mackie 1982, p. 27.

Schlesinger's Defense of Miracles

George Schlesinger has addressed Hume's claim that we should always prefer the assessment that alleged miracles are unexplained natural events rather than acts of God. In his *Religion and Scientific Method*,[24] Schlesinger defends religion as a rational enterprise by utilizing inference to the best explanation, a kind of argument form found in science.

Schlesinger formulates 'Principle E' as

> When a given piece of evidence E is more probable on theory H than on theory H' then E confirms H more than H'

Or,

> $P(E|H) > P(E|H')$ entails that E confirms H more than H'

According to Schlesinger, Principle E (inference to the best explanation) is the basis of the scientific method.

Returning to an example from Chapter 2, suppose that a lecturer receives two identical essays (E), and contemplates two theories to explain this. One theory is that the essays were plagiarized or copied (H), and the other theory is that the students discussed the essay before the due date and any resemblance between the two is otherwise completely coincidental (H'). The first hypothesis makes it very likely that the lecturer would receive two identical essays. However, the probability that she would receive two identical essays given that two students talked about the topic is very low. Because $P(E|H) \gg P(E|H')$, the evidence confirms the first theory much more than the second.

Taking Schlesinger's example, suppose a healer claims to be able to heal a broken leg by laying his hands on a person's head. Now, let's suppose that we witness one particular case of such a healing (E). One theory (H) to explain this is that whenever the healer lays his hands on people they are miraculously healed of whatever illness they are suffering from. Another hypothesis (H') is that the healer is fabricating his story. Clearly, in this case the particular piece of evidence very much more confirms the healer's theory that he really is a healer than the rival hypothesis that he is a charlatan.

24. Schlesinger 1977.

Recall that the two main questions about miracles are "Did the miracle occur?" and "If the miracle did occur, can it provide evidence for the existence of God?" Schlesinger argues that in certain cases the answer to the second question is yes, a miracle can serve as evidence for the existence of God.

Schlesinger's main example is the biblical account of Moses turning the waters in Egypt into blood. In this narrative the Israelites are the slaves of Egypt and they are attempting to persuade the Egyptians to release them. Moses threatens to turn the water into blood if the Egyptians fail to comply. The Egyptians ignore him and the water does turn to blood.

Suppose that we have conclusive evidence that these events actually happened. Would the occurrence of such an event count as evidence for the existence of God? Schlesinger argues that most people would say that it would be evidence for the existence of God. We have

> H_1 — Theism. God grants Moses the power to turn the water into blood.
>
> H_2 — Naturalism. There is no God and there is nothing besides this universe as described by science.
>
> E — Conclusive evidence that water did turn to blood.

What is the probability that E would occur given theism (H_1)? Schlesinger claims that even if the exact probability concerned is debatable, whatever it is it will certainly be greater than the probability that this would occur given naturalism (H_2). So

$$P(E|H_1) \gg P(E|H_2)$$

In other words, this miracle confirms theism.

To see this, suppose a theist and a naturalist are present when Moses delivers his threat to turn the water into blood unless the Israelites are released. Which would give a higher credence to this event actually occurring? According to Schlesinger, it would be the former. If we apply Principle E to this kind of case, we would have to say that the occurrence of this event, (which occurs contrary to a law of nature), in fact confirms the theistic explanation rather than the naturalistic explanation.

Hume, in his second argument, claims that when faced with a contrary instance to a law of nature we should assume that the so-called 'miracle' is simply an unexplained natural event. But Schlesinger, on the other hand, is attempting to show that Principle E leads us to conclude that in this case at least the miracle is from God, and is therefore not a natural event. The evidence in the above case confirms theism rather than naturalism.

However, Schlesinger also notes that the use of Principle E is not sufficient to distinguish rival explanations, because of what is known as 'Jeffrey's Problem' (after the Princeton philosopher Richard Jeffrey). To see the problem, consider Galileo performing his experiment of dropping cannonballs from the top of the Tower of Pisa. Cannon balls dropped from differing heights yield different results, taking different amounts of time to reach the ground. So Galileo's evidence (E) is a collection of pairs of numbers, the time taken and the distance fallen of each cannonball. Suppose that we have a Galilean theory (H) of the form

$$s = 1/2gt^2 \qquad (H)$$

where 's' is the distance from the ground, 't' the time taken to fall, and 'g' the gravitational constant. Suppose that all the evidence collected so far fits this equation pretty closely. However, according to Schlesinger and Jeffrey, there could be any number of hypotheses that could explain such data. For example, there will be a function (f) that happens to be zero just in all the cases that we have observed to date. This would give us an equation like

$$s = 1/2gt^2 + f \qquad (H')$$

where f is some function equaling zero for the observations made so far, but with different values for future observations. The problem here is that

$$P(E|H) = P(E|H')$$

that is to say, H and H' equally predict the observational data. According to Schlesinger that we do not consider these hypotheses to be equally likely, shows that we need another principle to enable us to select between these sorts of hypotheses, which will allow us to conclude that H is more confirmed by the evidence than H'.

Schlesinger claims that we also need 'Principle A,' namely

When H and H′ are similarly related to all of the available evidence, H confirms the evidence more than H′ if and only if H is simpler or more 'parsimonious' than H′.

Schlesinger admits that the concept of simplicity is problematic but argues that in cases such as the one outlined above, it is clear that H is a simpler hypothesis than H′.

It is important to appreciate just how pervasive this problem can be. In fact any hypothesis that we consider is accompanied by a string of alternative hypotheses that will equally account for the data.

Yet the fact is that we do manage to decide between rival theories. Schlesinger argues that if we hold the view that nothing is needed over and above Principle E, then

> It would seem that I would not, for one further moment, remain inside this building since according to some of the hypotheses concerning the future state of the roof, it is just about to collapse. But I cannot stand on the ground outside the building either for it will melt beneath my feet according to some of the rivals to the generally held hypothesis postulating the continuing solidity of the ground. But then I cannot go anywhere or stay here, which is, of course, impossible without being destroyed. I would have to also stop breathing, since the hypothesis that the air will turn into poisonous gas the next moment is just as well confirmed as the one postulating that it will not.[25]

But can Principle A (simplicity) rather than, say complexity, be justified? Schlesinger defends Principle A as follows.

Suppose that rather than Principle A we decided to use a principle which demanded that we always choose the more complex of two equally confirmed hypotheses. Such a rule will not enable us to choose one unique hypothesis, because for any complex hypothesis there always exists some more complex hypothesis. So Principle A is the only rule that can provide us with a unique answer when choosing between equally adequate theories. Therefore, the most adequate theory is the one that is selected by the only useable guiding rule, namely Principle A.

Principle A is related to the other criteria of inference to the best explanation. Recall that the intrinsic probability of the preferred hypothesis

25. Schlesinger 1977, p. 162.

must be greater than the intrinsic probability of the alternative hypothesis. Schlesinger, and Richard Jeffrey himself, claim that the simplest hypothesis always is the most probable.

According to Schlesinger, Principle A is also needed in cases of miracles such as Moses turning water to blood. Although the available evidence confirms theism rather than naturalism, there could be other hypotheses which render the evidence equally probable, such as the hypothesis (H_3) that there is a malicious demon who gets pleasure from punishing people for sincerely believing in God and the afterlife. How likely is it given the evidence (Moses turning the water into blood), that H_3 is true? Given that this malicious demon actually prefers people to sincerely believe in God because he plans to punish them in the afterlife, it seems plausible that he would work toward this end. So, the malicious demon might be very keen for miracles to occur because miracles make people believe that God exists. It seems to be just as likely on H_3 that such a miracle would occur as it is on H_1 (theism). So, both H_1 and H_3 are equally confirmed by the evidence. Schlesinger claims that Principle A tells us to prefer theism to the 'demon hypothesis' because it is simpler and thereby intrinsically more probable. H_3 is "altogether too 'strange' a hypothesis to have an appeal."[26]

Schlesinger's approach raises important issues regarding the relation between science and religion. If, as Schlesinger holds, the methodology of science can be applied to religion, then there is overlap; a common rationality shared by religion and science. Again the method of inference to the best explanation, a method used widely in science (as we will see in the following chapter), also can be used to justify the rationality of belief in God.

26. Schlesinger 1977, p. 177.

CHAPTER 5

Creation and Evolution

The clash between evolution and creation is perhaps the best-known example of the interaction between science and religion. Mythology says Charles Darwin's theory of natural selection raised unanswerable implications for the Genesis account of creation. However, the fact is that in Darwin's day concern was focused more on the design argument for the existence of God, and questions of teleology and human dignity. Also, we have already seen in Chapter 1 how the relevant hermeneutical issues — such as the appropriate interpretation of Genesis — had been wrestled with long before Darwin's day. Further, the design argument had come into its own only in the eighteenth century, receiving its classic formulation at the hands of William Paley (1743-1805).

In this chapter we look at the notion of teleological explanation; Paley's argument; Darwin's theory of natural selection and his views on God; Darwin's interactions with Christian and botanist Asa Gray; and finally, the contemporary creation science movement.

Teleological and Mechanical Explanation

An account of the role of teleological explanation in science was originally provided by the Greek philosopher Aristotle. The term 'teleological' has its origins in the Greek word 'telos' which means 'end,' 'purpose,' or 'goal.' According to Aristotle, science seeks to answer four questions of any phenomenon: 'what is it?' 'what is it made of?' 'how did it come to exist?' and 'what is it for?' So, for Aristotle, a major aim of science is teleological, to discover the purpose of each observed phenomena. That purpose is a part of each thing's intrinsic nature, and in order to identify that purpose, we must fully understand a thing's intrinsic nature. For example, that the rain falls not of simple necessity but rather in order that plants may grow is part of the essence of rain.

The need for teleological explanations, which make reference to function or purpose, is most apparent in biology. Take the bodily organs, for example. The heart's purpose is to pump blood; the lungs' purpose is to facilitate breathing; the purpose of the eye is to see. In order to understand the biology of these organs we must understand their function and purpose. To characterize the heart as merely 'a large muscle through which blood passes' is unsatisfactory. For Aristotle every 'kind' has its own final cause. That final cause is that kind's intrinsic goal, driving its behavior. On an Aristotelian view of biology, a certain type of animal has sharp teeth because its purpose, or telos, is to eat meat.

Aristotle adopted this approach and applied it as a general methodological principle to science as a whole, offering teleological explanations not just for animate things and biological phenomena, but also for the behavior of inanimate objects in the realm of physics. In Aristotelian physics the heavenly bodies move in circles because it is the nature of heavenly things to tend toward circular motion. The reason that heavy bodies fall down to Earth is that it is part of the nature of earthly things to tend towards their natural resting place. All other motions are violent, not natural, and require some external interference.

Aristotle's notion of purpose is immanent in nature, within the form (or nature) of an object or being, and as such does not make reference to anything higher. But we might also want to ask how the thing in question comes to have that purpose. This issue was taken up systematically by the Christian theologian Thomas Aquinas (1225-1274) in the thirteenth century.

Aquinas starts from the Aristotelian notion of intrinsic purpose and asks how a thing comes to have a given purpose. The answer is that it was designed by God. The design argument was not original to Aquinas. It had been advanced by the Stoic philosopher Sextus Empiricus (A.D. 160-210) in the third century, and also by Cicero (106-43 B.C.). In his *The Nature of the Gods,* Cicero asks,

What could be more clear or obvious than when we look up to the sky and contemplate the heavens, that there is some divinity or superior intelligence?[1]

But Aquinas appeals explicitly to the notion of purpose. In the fifth of his famous Five Ways (arguments) for the existence of God, Aquinas says,

> The fifth way is taken from the governance of the world. We see that things which lack knowledge, such as natural bodies, act for an end, and this is evident from their acting always, or nearly always, in the same way, so as to obtain the best result. Hence it is plain that they achieve their end, not fortuitously, but designedly. Now whatever lacks knowledge cannot move towards an end, unless it be directed by some being endowed with knowledge and intelligence; as the arrow is directed by the archer.[2]

Heavenly bodies always move in circles, so we can see the purpose that is built into their motion. However, heavenly bodies do not have minds, and thus have no intentions, so their purpose cannot come from within themselves. We can deduce that their purpose has been endowed by some sort of intelligence. In other words, in order to explain the intrinsic purpose of an object we must appeal to a higher form of knowledge and intelligence. This leads Aquinas to conclude that "some intelligent being exists by whom all natural things are directed to their end; and this being we call God."[3] This is Aquinas' version of the design argument. It moves from a premise concerning purpose that appears to be in the world to the conclusion that there exists a designer responsible for that purpose.

However, the scientific revolution of the sixteenth and seventeenth centuries focused on the notion of 'mechanical explanation,' in deliberate contrast and reaction to 'teleological explanation.' Mechanical explanations appeal to prior states of the universe in order to explain why something behaves in the way it does. For example, during this period it was well known that water can be lifted using a cylinder and piston (see figure 6). It was also well known that using this method at sea level, water can be lifted to a height of thirty-two feet, but repeating it on a high mountain the water cannot be lifted as high.

1. Davies 1993, p. 94.
2. Aquinas 1973, p. 119.
3. Aquinas 1973, p. 119.

According to an Aristotelian explanation of this kind of phenomenon, nature has an inherent tendency to avoid a vacuum. So when the piston is raised, creating the possibility of a vacuum, nature will act to prevent this from occurring, in that the water will act to the end of avoiding a vacuum by rising up the column. But water by its nature tends towards Earth, so when the water rises within the column of the cylinder it is acting against its natural motion. So there are two tendencies involved here: the tendency of the water to move toward the Earth, and the tendency of nature itself to avoid a vacuum. These two principles are in conflict, and the motion of the water will be determined by the stronger of the two. When, at sea level, the water rises to a height of thirty-two feet, the two tendencies are balanced. On a high mountain the water rises to less than thirty-two feet because the tendency to avoid the vacuum is stronger than the tendency for water to tend toward the Earth, which is weaker since that water is further away its resting place.

But in the seventeenth century Galileo's student Torricelli (1608-1647) provided a mechanical explanation based on the fact that air possesses mass. At thirty feet above sea level, the weight of the water balances the weight of the air. On a mountain there is less air, and so less force due to the air, while the water has effectively the same weight. This is a completely mechanical explanation in that it is given purely in terms of mechanical concepts such as mass, motion, position, velocity, and force; and does not involve purposes or the ends to which things naturally move.

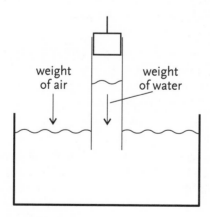

weight of air

weight of water

Figure 6: Torricelli's Mechanical Explanation

The attempt to explain all physical phenomena purely in terms of mechanical concepts, removing teleological explanation from physics, was a feature of the scientific revolution. Newtonian physics is a triumph of mechanical explanation.

However, even in the work of Isaac Newton (1642-1727) there remained room for the design argument for the existence of God. Newton's version of the argument from design differs significantly from that of Aquinas. In his famous letter to the theologian Richard Bentley, Newton wrote,

> To make this system, therefore, with all its motions, required a cause which understood, and compared together, the quantities of matter in the several bodies of the sun and the planets, and the gravitating powers resulting from thense; the several distances of the primary planets from the sun, and the secondary ones from Saturn, Jupiter, and the Earth; and the velocities, with which these planets could revolve about those quantities of matter in the central bodies; and to compare and adjust all these things together in so great a variety of bodies, argues that cause to be not blind and fortuitous, but well skilled in mechanicks and geometry.[4]

For Newton the purely mechanical operation of the solar system is so beautifully intricate and ordered that it simply could not have come about by chance. It must, therefore, have been the product of a mathematically minded designer. This version of the design argument does not appeal to the notion of intrinsic purpose, but rather to the order that is described by mathematical, mechanical explanations.

While mechanical explanation became the dominant methodology during the seventeenth century in most areas of science, it was not so successful in the area of biology. During the eighty years or so between the death of Newton and the birth of Charles Darwin it became increasingly apparent that removing teleological explanation from biology was not a simple matter. Aristotle had claimed that all areas of scientific endeavor should utilize the same method of explanation. Taking biology as his model, he applied the teleological method across the board. The new science took physics as the paradigm for science but was unable to unify all science in the way Aristotle had. Rather, the dominant view in the seven-

4. Quoted in Hurlbutt 1965, p. 7.

teenth and eighteenth centuries was that physics and biology are fundamentally different in the kinds of explanations that they require. Physics and chemistry are marked by mechanical modes of explanation, biology by teleological explanations. Physics makes appeal only to efficient causes, whereas biology appeals to function and purpose.

In this context a new version of the argument from design flourished. Its foremost promoter was William Paley.

Paley's Design Argument

William Paley (1743-1805) taught at Cambridge University and wrote three important works, all of which were very widely read as textbooks. *A View of the Evidences of Christianity*[5] contains an extremely detailed reply to Hume's argument against miracles. *Principles of Moral and Political Philosophy*[6] caused Paley a certain amount of trouble over his criticism of the notion of private property. His third book was *Natural Theology or Evidences of the Existence and Attributes of the Deity Collected from the Appearances of Nature*,[7] published in 1802. The fact that in 1831 the young Charles Darwin, then studying for his Bachelor of Arts degree at Cambridge University, was required to study all three of Paley's books indicates just how influential Paley was during this period.

Natural Theology appeals to a number of natural phenomena in an attempt to establish the existence of God. In his famous watchmaker analogy Paley imagines finding a stone while crossing a heath, and asking how the stone had come to be there. He says,

> I might possibly answer, that, for any thing I knew to the contrary, it had lain there for ever: nor would it perhaps be very easy to show the absurdity of this answer. But suppose I found a watch upon the ground, and it should be enquired how the watch came to be in that place, I should hardly think of the answer which I had before given, that, for any thing I knew, the watch might have always been there. Yet why should this answer serve for the watch as well as for the stone? . . . For this reason, and for no other, viz. that, when we come to inspect

5. Paley 1812.
6. Paley 1841.
7. Paley 1890b.

the watch, we perceive (what we could not discover in the stone) that its several parts are framed and put together for a purpose.[8]

The difference between the stone and the watch is that the watch has "parts framed and put together for a purpose," whereas the stone does not. In the case of the stone, we are unlikely to posit the existence of a designer, whereas in the case of the watch,

> the inference, we think is inevitable, that the watch must have had a maker: that there must have existed, at some time and at some place or other, an artificer or artificers who formed it for the purpose which we find it actually to answer; who comprehended its construction, and designed its use.[9]

The care with which the parts of the watch have been made and the fineness of their adjustment can only have one implication — that the watch had a maker who understood watches and who designed this one for its obvious purpose.

If then we can find natural cases that, like the watch, display obvious purpose, then we should likewise infer the existence of a designer of nature. The rest of the book describes numerous such cases, all of them biological.

Firstly, however, Paley answers three objections to the watchmaker argument. The conclusion, he says, would not be weakened had we never encountered a watch before, or could not conceive of how to make one — we would still conclude that the watch was built for a purpose. Nor would the conclusion be weakened if there existed parts of the watch whose purpose we could not understand. Finally, we would be very surprised to hear that the mechanism of the watch is no proof of design but only a motive to induce the mind to reach this conclusion. Nor would we be satisfied if we were told that the existence of the watch could be easily explained by an all pervading principle of order according to which the parts of the watch are disposed toward their present form and situation.

We can frame this last objection in terms of mechanical explanation. If we were told that the mechanical laws of nature could adequately explain the order that we perceive in the world, would we be satisfied? Paley thinks not. To say that a watch possesses an inner 'metallic nature' will not

8. Paley 1890a, pp. 9-10.
9. Paley 1890a, p. 11.

serve to explain why the watch is fitted together to tell the time. So there is a feature, purpose, which cannot be explained by mechanistic explanation. This much of biology requires a teleological explanation.

Paley goes on throughout the remainder of *Natural Theology* to provide a series of biological examples of purpose. For example, the bones and muscles of human beings, animals, and insects are of special interest — the fitting together of joints and the adaptation of muscles are powerful evidence for the existence of a designing intelligence.

However Paley's main example, which generated the most discussion in his day and since, is the eye. The various parts of the eye, the combination of those parts, and the adaptation to function as an instrument of sight, constitute for Paley most convincing evidence for design. He draws an analogy with the telescope:

> As far as the examination of the instrument goes, there is precisely the same proof that the eye was made for vision, as there is that the telescope was made for assisting it. They are made upon the same principles; both being adjusted to the laws by which the transmission and reflection of rays of light are regulated.[10]

Paley elaborates:

> Besides the conformity to optical principles which its internal constitution displays, . . . there is to be seen, in everything belonging to it and about it, an extraordinary degree of care, and anxiety for its preservation, due, if we may so speak, to its value and its tenderness. It is lodged in a strong, deep, bony socket, composed by the juncture of seven different bones, hollowed out at their edges. . . . Within this socket it is embedded in fat, of all animal substances the best adapted both to its response and motion. It is sheltered by the eyebrows; an arch of hair, which like a thatched penthouse, prevents the sweat and moisture of the forehead from running down into it. But it is still better protected by its lid. Of the superficial parts of the animal frame, I know none which, in its office and structure, is more deserving of attention than the eyelid. It defends the eye; it wipes it; it closes it in sleep. Are there, in all the work of art whatever, purposes more evident than those which this organ fulfils? In order to keep the eye moist and

10. Paley 1890a, p. 28.

clean (which qualities are necessary to its brightness and its use), a wash is constantly supplied by a secretion for the purpose; and the superfluous brine is conveyed to the nose through a perforation in the bone as large as a goose-quill. When once the fluid has entered the nose, it spreads itself upon the inside of the nostril, and is evaporated by the current of warm air, which, in the course of respiration, is continually passing over it. . . . [C]ould the want of the eye generate the gland which produces the tear, or bore the hole by which it is discharged — a hole through a bone?[11]

Paley's argument hinges on the use of analogical reasoning,[12] considered at the time an important mode of inductive reasoning. For example, J. S. Mill (1806-73) includes a chapter on analogy in his 1843 treatment of inductive logic, characterizing analogical reasoning in two propositions:

(1) Two things resemble each other in one or more respects; and
(2) A certain proposition is true of one, therefore it is true of the other.[13]

In the design argument we know, it is claimed, that both natural and artificial objects exhibit purpose, and that the purpose of artifacts is caused by an intelligent designer. So we infer, by analogy, that the purpose of natural objects is caused by a designer — God (see figure 7 on p. 113). Despite striking differences in scientific and philosophical context, the teleological arguments of Aquinas and Paley are remarkably similar. Like Aquinas', Paley's argument is an a posteriori argument, with a premise which is a contingent, (allegedly) empirical fact about the world, namely, cases of objective purpose. It is important for such design arguments that the purpose is objective, not subjective. Subjective purpose is purpose we choose to bestow on objects. The purpose of the eye is to see, but of course it could be given other 'purposes' — for example, it could be eaten. But such subjective purposes do not really belong to the eye itself. If the putative purpose in nature was merely subjective purpose, it could not be said to inhere in the natural objects themselves so as to require causal explanation. The argument from design requires purpose that is objective.

11. Paley 1890a, pp. 45-47.
12. As is particularly perspicuous in the version given by Hume (1951).
13. Mill 1843, p. 365. In fact, Mill goes so far as to say that all inductive reasoning is analogical.

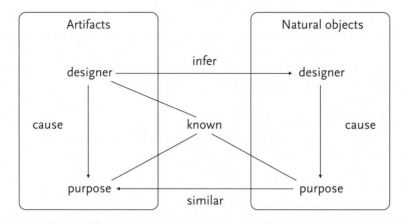

Figure 7: The Analogical Design Argument

Darwin's *The Origin of Species*

Paley's work exerted a strong influence on Darwin during his formative years. In his autobiography Darwin writes,

> In order to pass the BA examination, it was also necessary to get up Paley's evidence of Christianity. . . . The logic of this book, and as I may add, of his *Natural Theology* gave me as much delight. . . . Careful study of these works . . . was the only part of the academic course which . . . was of the least use to me in the education of my mind. I did not at that time trouble myself about Paley's premises and taking these on trust I was charmed and convinced by the long line of argumentation. By answering well the examination questions on Paley I gained a good place amongst the crowd of men who didn't go into honours.[14]

However, Darwin came to see that there was an alternative explanation: the theory of natural selection, which he first published in *The Origin of Species*[15] in 1859 (although as early as 1839 he had written several draft versions of his hypothesis, and in 1857 had sent a summary statement of his

14. Barlow 1958, pp. 58-59.
15. Darwin 1875.

theory to the American botanist Asa Gray).[16] Since Darwin takes his book to be 'one long argument,' we will take his points in the order that he presents them.

The first two chapters of *The Origin of the Species* are concerned with the issue of variation among living organisms. Darwin considers it an obvious empirical fact that organisms within a species vary. Dogs, for example, vary in size, color, proportion, and many other aspects. He also holds that the majority of this variation is produced in sexual reproduction and is inherited, that is, is passed on to the next generation. (Asexual reproduction leads to exact resemblance of offspring to parent and therefore no variation.) The first chapter deals with variation arising in domestic breeding of animals and plants, and the second chapter with that arising from 'breeding' in nature, an analogy Darwin draws on continually throughout *The Origin of Species*. A second feature of these early chapters is Darwin's argument against the traditional distinction between species and varieties within a species. The traditional system has its foundations in the science of Aristotle, which holds that to classify an organism we must assign it to a species; where certain characteristics define and fix the essential nature of a species. On this view a species — a natural kind — admits of no variation in essential characteristics. But Darwin attempts to blur the classical distinction between variation across a species and variation within a species. For Darwin, varieties are not fixed but, in fact, 'incipient species.'

The third chapter contains a discussion of the struggle for existence, or competition. In nature there is an almost universal tendency for organisms to increase in number geometrically, but there are also natural limitations upon resources that limit the rate of population increase. These two factors together produce the struggle for existence, as is evident not only among animals, but also plants, which compete for light and space. Generally speaking, every species produces many more offspring than can survive given certain limitations in resources. The competition is fiercest, Darwin says, between similar organisms that are competing for exactly the same resources.

---

16. In 1856 he had begun work on his *Natural Selection,* a large work which was never completed. In 1858 Darwin received a paper from an English naturalist living in the East Indies, called A. R. Wallace, which contained a basic outline of Darwin's as yet unpublished theory of natural selection. However the problem of priority was resolved by Lyell and Hooker, who uncovered some of Darwin's earlier writings, including his correspondence with Asa Gray, and published them alongside Wallace's article. Darwin himself responded, in 1859, by publishing a briefer version of *Natural Selection* entitled *The Origin of Species.*

Yet there is a balance in nature, in the complex network of inter-relations between various types of organisms and species. For example, the number of red clover plants growing in a given region might be proportional to the number of resident cats — if clover is pollinated by bees, bees are destroyed by mice, and mice are destroyed by cats. (We should note, however, that this balance is not a fine-tuned one, where some small disturbance is likely to destroy the entire system. Darwin is thinking of a highly stable equilibrium that can accommodate plenty of non-detrimental change.)

The concepts of variation and competition are directly related to Darwin's main thesis, natural selection, the subject of the fourth chapter. Here Darwin again draws on the analogy with breeding or artificial selection. Just as the difference between, say, a workhorse and a racehorse is the result of centuries of deliberate breeding, so the difference between a greyhound and a bloodhound is the result of prolonged natural breeding. Artificial selection is achieved by sometimes purposeful and sometimes unconscious accumulative selection processes whereby the breeder removes those young that are not suited to a particular purpose. If we apply this notion of selection to nature, we expect to find that competition will act on variations to produce stock better able to survive. Natural selection, then, is the preservation of favorable variations and the rejection of injurious or detrimental variations. An organism that carries injurious variations will simply not be preserved into successive generations precisely because it is not competitive. In Darwin's words,

> It may metaphorically be said that natural selection is daily and hourly scrutinizing, throughout the world, the slightest variations; rejecting those that are bad, preserving and adding up all that are good; silently and insensibly working, whenever and wherever opportunity offers, at the improvement of each organic being in relation to its organic and inorganic conditions of life. We see nothing of these slow changes in progress, until the hand of time has marked the long lapse of ages, and then so imperfect is our view into long past geological ages, that we only see that the forms of life are now different from what they formerly were.[17]

This brings us to the notion of divergence. In the case of artificial selection, we are able to produce two different breeds from a single stock

17. Darwin 1958, p. 90.

simply by selecting extreme forms and eliminating intermediate ones. For example, if we want workhorses we will breed for certain characteristics in order to produce horses that are strong, easy to handle, and good natured. If, on the other hand, we want racehorses we will breed for other characteristics, to produce attributes such as speed. Those horses which are intermediary to these purposes will, in all likelihood, be eliminated through the breeding process, so that, at the end of the process we are left with the two extreme forms only, with none of the intermediate forms.

Darwin argues that the same process occurs in nature, for two reasons. Because competition for resources is always fiercest between similar forms, there is a natural tendency towards divergence. Accordingly, varieties within a species diverge to extreme forms, such that all intermediary forms are eliminated. The extreme forms of a species will find different niches in which survival is assured, places where there is opportunity for different varieties to flourish. Divergence is important, then, since it is the mechanism whereby different species are produced.

Darwin offers numerous examples to support the claim that species tend to diverge. One of these is easily tested in an experiment. Suppose that we sowed two identical plots, the first with one particular species of grass, and the second with several different species with quite different characteristics. We expect to find a greater number of successful plants in the second plot; which is, in Darwin's view, evidence for nature's tendency toward divergence.

A second reason for divergence is geographical isolation. During his famous voyage on the H. M. S. *Beagle* Darwin took an interest in geographically isolated areas such as the Galapagos Islands and the two sides of the Andes. Within such isolated populations Darwin observed small variations between species, leading him to suggest that divergence occurs because the process of natural selection differs slightly from area to area. Even if environmental conditions are exactly the same in two isolated places, the process of natural selection will not necessarily operate in exactly the same way. In these cases we might expect divergence but, given those circumstances, there is no reason at all why there would be the intermediate forms.

In chapter four of *The Origin of Species* we also find the idea of the 'tree of life,' an ancient analogy that Darwin uses for his own purposes (see figure 8 on p. 117). In Darwin's tree of life there are on different branches of the tree organisms with very different characteristics and normally characterized as separate species, but which can be traced back to a common ancestor, that is, to the same node on the tree.

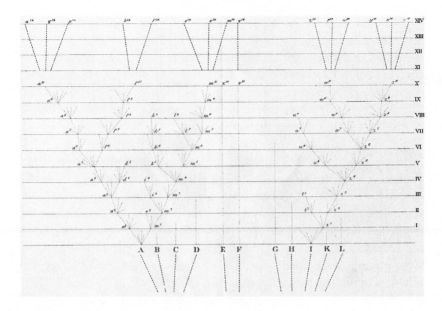

Figure 8: Darwin's Tree of Life[18]

In Chapters 7 and 8 Darwin argues that natural selection is based not only on structural but also behavioral characteristics. In the case of breeding dogs, for instance, we can intentionally breed for different sorts of traits, so that one dog may be adept at pointing while another is suited to retrieving. So if these innate tendencies or instincts can be intentionally bred, we might expect the same sort of process to occur in nature. Bumblebees are an example of just that. A bumblebee hive is a clumsy arrangement of cells compared to a domestic beehive, which is far more organized, with a more symmetric arrangement of cells. Since the bees' hive building is instinctual, bee instincts must change upon domestication. Natural selection provides an explanation of this. The environment of domestic bees requires much higher production, since the honeycomb is systematically depleted. The production of beeswax requires a large amount of sugar and pollen, and therefore any variation which leads to a more efficient use of sugar and pollen will be advantageous. Variations yielding instincts for more organized construction will therefore be selected for.

18. Taken From Darwin, *On the Origin of Species*, 1859.

In Chapter 14, "The Mutual Affinities of Organic Beings," Darwin offers a completely novel system of classification. The Aristotelian method of classification defines a species in terms of a straightforward comparison of characteristics. That task turns out to be very difficult in practice. Darwin's method of classification involves an appeal to descent rather than to essential characteristics, where species are classified according to their origins, or history. The first attempt to use this system was J. D. Hooker's 1860 work "Flora of Tasmania."[19]

We need to bear in mind that Darwinian natural selection is not equivalent to Lamarckianism, or the inheritance of acquired characteristics (a theory defended by J.-B. Lamarck, 1744-1829). According to the standard example of Lamarckianism, the giraffe acquired a longer neck because of daily stretching to reach high branches, and has then passed on this characteristic through inheritance. Darwin did not explicitly rule out the possibility of inheritance of acquired characteristics, but he did think that it could only be a minor mechanism in the process. Darwin's theory concerns natural selection acting upon variation produced in reproduction.[20]

Natural Selection or Special Creation?

If *The Origin of Species* is, in fact, 'one long argument,' it is worth thinking about exactly what form this argument takes. It is not enumerative induction, the argument form Francis Bacon claimed that science utilizes, since it is not an example of mere generalization from data. It is true that Darwin's theory arose out of the accumulation of a great deal of natural evidence; however, Darwin does not simply generalize from the available evidence. Nor does the argument operate by what is today called the 'hypothetico-deductive method,' according to which we first invent a theory and then deduce what sorts of facts we would expect to obtain if such a theory were true, and subsequently test for those facts.

In fact, it is best to think of Darwin's argument as an inference to the best explanation, as described in earlier chapters. Darwin's approach is to compare two rival explanations of the broad range of available evidence and to show how well each hypothesis can explain that evidence. The rival

19. Hooker 1860.
20. Darwin 1958, p. 128.

hypotheses are the theory of natural selection and the theory of special creation, the idea that each species was created in its final form. Darwin's 'long argument' shows that natural selection is a better explanation of the whole range of evidence. In particular, the probability of the range of biological evidence (E) given the theory of natural selection (H_1) is greater than the probability of that evidence given special creation (H_2). Or,

$$P(E/H_1) \gg P(E/H_2)$$

There are a number of features of biological systems that can only be explained on the hypothesis of natural selection, Darwin argues. One such feature is the widespread structural similarities of organs across species. If special creation were true, surely we would expect members of different species to be completely different in structure. Darwin comments,

> What can be more curious than that the hand of a man, formed for grasping, that of a mole for digging, the leg of the horse, paddle of the porpoise, and the wing of the bat, should all be constructed on the same pattern, and should include the same bones, in the same relative positions?[21]

Another feature is the existence of transitional grades between organs with distinct functions. In Chapter 6, 'Difficulties of the Theory,' Darwin concludes,

> Finally then, although in many cases it is most difficult even to conjecture by what transitions organs have arrived at their present state: yet, considering how small the proportion of living and known forms is to the extinct and unknown, I have been astonished how rarely an organ can be named, towards which no transitional grade is known to lead. It certainly is true, that new organs appearing as if created for some special purpose, rarely or never appear in any being: — . . . We meet with this admission in the writings of almost every experienced naturalist. . . . Nature is prodigal in variety but niggard in innovation. Why, on the theory of creation, should there be so much variety and so little real novelty? Why should all the parts and organs of so many independent beings, each supposed to have been created separately for its

21. Darwin 1958, p. 403.

proper place in nature, be so commonly linked together by graduated steps? Why should not Nature take a sudden leap from structure to structure? On the theory of natural selection, we can clearly understand why she should not; for natural selection acts only by taking advantage of slight successive variations; she can never take a great and sudden leap, but must advance by short and sure, though slow steps.[22]

In other words, if special creation were true we would not expect the existence of transitional grades. The evidence we have about these is improbable on the hypothesis of special creation.

Yet another feature of that natural world that seems to argue in favor of natural selection is disused characteristics — for example, the webbed feet of upland geese. The following passage nicely illustrates the general form that Darwin's argument takes:

He who believes that each being has been created as we now see it, must occasionally have felt surprise when he has met with an animal having habits and structure not in agreement. What can be plainer than that the webbed feet of ducks and geese are formed for swimming? Yet there are upland geese with webbed feet, which rarely go near the water; and no one except Audubon has seen the frigate-bird which has all of its four toes webbed, alight on the surface of the sea. On the other hand, grebes and coots are eminently aquatic, although their toes are only bordered by membrane. What seems plainer than that the long toes, not furnished with membrane of the grallatores are formed for walking over swamps and floating plants, yet the water-hen is nearly as aquatic as the coot; and landrail nearly as terrestrial as the quail or partridge. In such cases, and many others could be given, habits have changed without a corresponding change of structure. The webbed feet of the upland goose may be said to have become almost rudimentary in function, though not in structure. In the frigate-bird, the deeply scooped membrane between the toes shows that structure has begun to change.

He who believes in separate and innumerable acts of creation will say, that in these cases it has pleased the Creator to cause a being of one type to take the place of one belonging to another type; but this seems to me only restating the fact in dignified language. He who believes in

22. Darwin 1958, pp. 180-181.

the struggle for existence and in the principle of natural selection, will acknowledge that every organic being is constantly endeavoring to increase in numbers; and that if any one being varies ever so little, either in habits or structure, and thus gains an advantage over some other inhabitant of the country, it will seize on the place of that inhabitant, however different that may be from its own place. Hence it will cause him no surprise that there should be geese and frigate-birds with webbed feet, either living on the dry land and rarely alighting on the water; that there should be long-toed corncrakes, living in meadows instead of in swamps; that there should be woodpeckers where hardly a tree grows; that there should be diving thrushes and diving Hymenoptera, and petrels with the habits of auks.[23]

This argument clearly has the form of inference to the best explanation. We have the evidence of organs that serve no purpose in their current environment (E_D). On the hypothesis of special creation (H_2), this is a surprise, whereas on the hypothesis of natural selection (H_1), this will be no surprise. In other words,

$$P(E_D|H_1) \gg P(E_D|H_2)$$

But there are also features of biological systems that are prima facie problems for natural selection. Throughout *The Origin of Species* Darwin is candid about difficulties for the theory. One difficulty that receives extended treatment is the existence of complex organs that serve a well-defined function. The eye (which Paley had made good use of in his argument for design) is an example of this problem. The problem is that something like an eye is composed of many working parts, each of them useless to the goal of sight except when they are all working together. Given complex organisms that are the result of innumerable small variations, why should all of these earlier, smaller variations have been selected for? Darwin discusses this case in Chapter 6, "Difficulties of the Theory," in a section entitled "Organs of Extreme Perfection and Complication," admitting that the eye is the sort of thing that appears to have been formed in one act of design or creation:

To suppose that the eye, with all its inimitable contrivances for adjusting the focus to different distances, for admitting different amounts of

23. Darwin 1958, pp. 167-168.

light, and for the correction of spherical and chromatic aberration, could have been formed by natural selection seems, I freely confess, absurd in the highest degree.[24]

Darwin goes to lengths to attempt to show just how cases such as the eye can be explained by natural selection. There are two parts to his explanation. One part is that an organ or characteristic can serve different adaptive purposes, and nature produces structure out of whatever is at hand. This means that no organ has a single set objective purpose or function. Even an object such as the eye does not have a single objective purpose, although it is now used for seeing. But earlier on in the evolutionary process the eye may have served some other quite different purpose. Natural selection operates on the junk heap of its own past. Darwin provides many examples of the way in which particular organs have been used for one particular purpose in one context, but have subsequently come to be used for an entirely different purpose in a different context.

The second point is that function can be honed down over innumerable small variations. Darwin writes,

> Reason tells me, that if numerous graduations from a simple and imperfect eye to one complex and perfect can be shown to exist, each grade being useful to its possessor as is certainly the case; if further, the eye ever varies and the variations be inherited, as is likewise certainly the case; and if such variations should be useful to any animal under changing conditions of life, then the difficulty of believing that a perfect and complex eye could be formed by natural selection, though insuperable by our imagination, should not be considered subversive of the theory. How a nerve comes to be sensitive to light, hardly concerns us more than how life itself first originated; but I may remark that, as some of the lowest organisms in which nerves cannot be detected are capable of perceiving light, it does not seem impossible that certain sensitive elements of their sarcous should become aggregated and develop into nerves endowed with this special sensibility.[25]

So, according to Darwin, evolution through natural selection can explain how organs of extreme perfection can evolve by the operation of nat-

---

24. Darwin 1958, p. 168.
25. Darwin 1958, pp. 168-169.

ural selection in gradual steps. Darwin ends "Organs of Extreme Perfection and Complication" with a reference to Paley's analogy between the eye and the telescope. Darwin turns this on its head, claiming that the development of the telescope has undoubtedly involved a certain amount of trial and error, accident, improvement, and gradual variations. Telescope developers sometimes use materials developed for quite different purposes. The eye is like this, with natural selection in place of design.

There are other prima facie difficulties for natural selection. In Chapters 8 and 9 Darwin discusses hybridism. Hybrids, such as mules, are the result of crossing species (in this case a horse and a donkey), whereas mongrels, on the other hand, are the result of crossing different varieties within a species. It is well known that hybrids are infertile, whereas mongrels are highly fertile. Darwin takes this to be a challenge to natural selection. So did others. Samuel Wilberforce points out in his review of *Origin of Species* that since artificial selection has never been successful in producing fertile hybrids — that is, new species — the analogy between breeding and natural selection is suspect.[26] In reply, Darwin sets out evidence to show that there are some cases of fertile hybrids, especially among plants, arguing that this in itself is good evidence against the fixity of species and for his view that varieties within species are, in fact, incipient species.[27]

In Chapters 10 and 11 Darwin discusses the imperfections in the geological record made apparent by the study of fossils. The fossil records available in Darwin's time provided scant evidence for Darwinian natural selection, but Darwin pleads that the incompleteness of the geological record can explain this lack of empirical evidence.

A related problem is the age of the earth. The development of highly complex structures through natural selection would appear to require a very long time period. In the earliest version of *The Origin of Species* Darwin calculates the age of a certain valley in Kent to be three hundred million years, based on the time that it would have taken the sea to erode the valley to the form in which Darwin found it. Based on this estimate, Darwin's predicted age of the earth was very long, sufficient for the process of natural selection to occur. As it turned out, however, Darwin's estimate was completely ill-founded, because it was later determined that erosion

---

26. Wilberforce 1860.

27. He also offers an explanation as to why hybrids bred in captivity are infertile (Darwin 1958, ch. 15.).

actually occurred by other means in that valley, and Darwin subsequently withdrew that particular section from later editions. Some, such as the conservative Christian and renowned mathematical physicist William Thompson (or Lord Kelvin), argued that given the contemporary estimates of the heat loss of the earth, the earth could not be any more than approximately one hundred million years old, which is simply not a large enough time period for Darwinian evolution. (Current estimates of the age of the earth based on processes within the earth that generate heat from radioactive material, approximately 4.6 billion years, do predict sufficient time for evolution by natural selection.)

So Darwin does not deny that there are unexplained difficulties. He offers the theory of natural selection as a hypothesis which explains a lot of the evidence, and which does so a lot better than the rival hypothesis. As he comments in the last chapter of *The Origin of Species,*

> Any one whose disposition leads him to attach more weight to unexplained difficulties than to the explanation of a certain number of facts will certainly reject the theory.[28]

In a letter to the botanist George Bentham dated May 22, 1863, Darwin notes that,

> the change of species cannot be directly proved, and that the doctrine must sink or swim according as it groups and explains phenomena.[29]

So, to recap, Darwin presents *The Origin of Species* as 'one long argument' that natural selection fits the entire range of available evidence better than does special creation (the view that species were created in their final forms). There are a number of points that special creation struggles to explain, such as the existence of transitional grades and disused characteristics, and prima facie difficulties for natural selection, such as organs of extreme perfection, and hybrids, can be given a plausible explanation on the assumption of natural selection. Therefore natural selection is the best overall explanation.

28. Darwin 1958, p. 444.
29. Darwin 1887, vol. 3, p. 25.

Darwin and God

Early in life Darwin believed in God and, as we have seen, accepted Paley's design argument. Indeed, he entered Cambridge University planning to become a minister of the Anglican Church. By the end of his life, however, we find that he is very much more critical of religion and the idea of a deity. Thus Darwin reflects:

> In my most extreme fluctuations I have never been an atheist in the sense of denying the existence of a God. I think that generally, (and more and more as I grow older), but not always, that an agnostic would be the more correct description of my state of mind.[30]

The word 'agnostic,' newly coined by Thomas H. Huxley in 1869, means having no belief either for or against the existence of any God. We have already seen Darwin's argument against special creation. But the final words of *The Origin of Species* apparently leave room for God. (Being the final paragraph and the climax of the entire work, Darwin's style here becomes somewhat lyrical.) He writes,

> It is interesting to contemplate a tangled bank, clothed with many plants of many kinds, with birds singing on the bushes, with various insects flitting about, and with worms crawling through the damp earth, and to reflect that these elaborately constructed forms, so different from each other, and dependent upon each other in so complex a manner, have all been produced by laws acting around us. These laws, taken in the largest sense, being Growth with Reproduction; Inheritance which is almost implied by reproduction; Variability from the indirect and direct action of the conditions of life, and from use and disuse; a Ratio of Increase so high as to lead to a Struggle for Life, and as a consequence to Natural Selection, entailing Divergence of Character and the Extinction of less-improved forms. Thus, from the war of nature, from famine and death, the most exalted object which we are capable of conceiving, namely, the production of the higher animals, directly follows. There is grandeur in this view of life, with its several powers, having been originally breathed by the Creator into a few forms or into one; and that, whilst this planet has gone cycling on ac-

30. Quoted in Rachels 1991, p. 110.

cording to the fixed law of gravity, from so simple a beginning endless forms most beautiful and most wonderful have been, and are being, evolved.[31]

The idea that God is behind the process of natural selection as creator also appears earlier in *The Origin of Species*,

> I see no good reason why the views given in this volume should shock the religious feelings of any one. . . . A celebrated author and divine has written to me that "he has gradually learnt to see that it is just as noble a conception of the Deity to believe that He created a few original forms capable of self-development into other and needful forms, as to believe that He required a fresh act of creation to supply the voids caused by the action of His laws."[32]

Of course, Darwin had reason to placate people by allowing that natural selection was compatible with the existence of God. But while his reference to the Creator in the final sentence probably is not to be taken as indicating a firm belief in God's existence, it does seem that he sincerely held that natural selection and God's existence are compatible. In a letter to Asa Gray of 1860, Darwin comments concerning *The Origin of Species*,

> I had no intention to write atheistically. But I own that I cannot see as plainly as others do, and as I should wish to do, evidence of design and beneficence [God's goodness] on all sides of us. There seems too much misery in the world. . . . Not believing this, I see no necessity in the belief that the eye was expressly designed. On the other hand, I cannot anyhow be contented to view this wonderful universe, and especially the nature of man, and to conclude that everything is the result of brute force.[33]

It seems Darwin's view is that while the truth of natural selection does not prove that there is no designer, it does show that we cannot, as Paley did, infer the existence of a designer from the biological evidence concerning adaptation. Once we have the best explanation of certain evidence, that evidence cannot be grounds to infer to another explanation.

31. Darwin 1958, pp. 450
32. Darwin 1958, p. 443.
33. Quoted in Rachels 1991, p. 107.

Darwin himself, however, seems to have rejected belief in God on the philosophical grounds of the existence of suffering in the world. Right at the end of his life, in his autobiography, (which was not intended for general publication), he discusses various reasons why he is not a Christian. He claims that, in regard to the issues of evil and suffering, natural selection can provide a better explanation than theism; since under natural selection, we would expect to see a great deal of suffering and pain, whereas under theism we would not expect to see suffering and pain. All the same, he prefers to be called an agnostic rather than an atheist.

Darwin and Asa Gray

Darwin's friend and correspondent Asa Gray (1810-1888) was a professor of natural history at Harvard University, a leading botanist, and also a professing Christian. When Gray went to Harvard in 1842, he joined a conservative Calvinist church, going against a trend for academics to attend the much less conservative Unitarian Church. Gray and Darwin maintained regular correspondence, mostly about their current scientific work, but sometimes about religious issues also, especially in relation to the reception of natural selection, and the problem of design. Darwin often sent his work to Gray for comment before publication, and Gray in fact became Darwin's chief advocate in America, as Huxley was in Britain. In 1860 Gray wrote a series of three articles in which he argued that natural selection is not inconsistent with natural theology, which so impressed Darwin that he sponsored the publication of Gray's articles in England. Darwin also once made the comment that Gray never published a word that did not fully express his (Darwin's) meaning.

Gray was an active writer, defending Darwin against the negative reaction to his theory by various American reviewers. Many of Gray's articles are collected together in his book *Darwiniana*.[34] In *Darwiniana* Gray focuses the issue on two central hypotheses, fixity and derivation. Fixity is the hypothesis that all actual kinds (or species) are primordial in that they originated supernaturally and directly and have continued unchanged in the order of nature, like parallel lines. The alternative is that actual kinds are derivative, that is, that the kinds of species that we see today have arisen

34. Gray 1876.

due to some sort of genealogical connection with other species over many years, so that the parallelism between species is merely apparent, and in fact many species converge at some point in the past.

Gray claims that both of these doctrines must be seen as hypotheses as neither has any direct proof from experience. He also maintains that either hypothesis can be assumed to be true in order to account for natural phenomena; that is, either can be supported by indirect evidence. However, the indirect biological evidence that Darwin has presented supports the derivation of certain species. From this evidence Darwin inferred the general principle of evolution, that all species have come about by natural selection. On this latter point Gray maintains that we should suspend judgment and avoid jumping to conclusions.[35]

Gray was clearly disappointed by the general American reaction to Darwin's theory. He felt that people were not treating Darwin's theory as a scientific hypothesis, according to which evidence should be scrutinized and hasty conclusions avoided. He comments that,

> Even when the upholders of the former and more popular system [special creation] mix up revelation with scientific discussion — which we decline to do — they by no means thereby render their view other than hypothetical.[36]

Gray argued that appeal to Scripture, or 'revelation,' as he calls it, will not resolve the question of the status of Darwin's theory, and those who insist it does misunderstand Scripture or natural selection or both.

The main criticism made in the reviews that Gray considers is that natural selection is tantamount to atheism and the rejection of religion. One reason given is that natural selection in providing the mechanism by which species have evolved replaces creation.

Gray replies that creation by divine command does not preclude the idea of 'natural order' and 'secondary causes.' Here he appeals to the widely held view that God is the primary cause of everything, but that that does not rule out natural causes also operating, as secondary causes. Evo-

35. At the time of the publication of *The Origin of Species* Gray rejected the idea that humans could be part of Darwin's evolutionary scheme. However, on reading Darwin's *The Descent of Man* (Darwin 1874), which directly addresses the issue of the evolution of humanity, Gray accepted that humans are also subject to evolution.
36. Gray 1876, p. 107.

lution is a secondary cause, the physical mechanism through which God has created everything.

In the history of philosophy prior to Darwin the denial of secondary causes is a minority position. (The famous exception to this is the French philosopher Nicholas Malebranche, who holds that because everything that happens is directly caused by God, this leaves no room for secondary causation and entails that created things do not, strictly speaking, cause anything.) According to Gray, phrases in Genesis such as "let the earth bring forth the living creatures after its kind" imply secondary causes, although the fact that things were created 'after their kind' tells us nothing about what the original kinds could have been or the duration of this creation period. (But note that Gray is not claiming that we should glean our science from Genesis in this way.)

Gray rejects the idea that natural selection amounts to the denial of the manifestation of design. Gray replies that the theory of natural selection 'leaves everything as it is,' in that it has no relevance to the argument from design. In focusing on the fixity of species and the derivative hypothesis, Gray separates the question of the fixity of species from the issue of design. Taking both into account gives us three possible explanations:

1. derivation of species without God,
2. derivation of species with design, or
3. fixity of species with design.

There is really only one scientific issue here addressed by *The Origin of Species,* namely the status of the thesis of derivation of species, as opposed to the thesis of the fixity of species — in other words, 1-2 versus 3. The evidence is considered to indirectly and strongly support only one of these two hypotheses. Gray claims that there is nothing in *The Origin of Species* which addresses the question of design, that is, helps decide between 1 and 2. In support of this, Gray quotes a series of references in which Darwin seems to place a creator behind the whole process of evolution.

Gray himself offers an analogy, involving irrigation channels.

Streams flowing over a sloping plain by gravitation (here the counterpart of natural selection) may have worn their actual channels as they flowed; yet their particular courses may have been assigned; and where we see them forming definite and useful lines of irrigation, after a manner unaccountable on the laws of gravitation and dynamics, we should believe that the distribution was designed.[37]

Here Gray is thinking of a designer overlooking and channeling the entire evolutionary process, thus combining design with secondary causation. If this account is correct, the upshot of natural selection is that it does, in fact, leave everything as it is, as it has no implications for the question of the design. Gray even claims that there is a strong case to say that natural selection through design is, in fact, a better explanation of biological phenomena than special creation through design, due to the fact that waste and redundancy can be explained by natural selection but not by special creation.

However, in 1868, in *The Variation of Animals and Plants under Domestication*,[38] Darwin gave his own metaphor for natural selection, the stone house. Darwin asks us to imagine that we want to build a house out of stone, and so we go to the bottom of a cliff to collect pieces of stone for this purpose. Some fragments of stone are wedge-shaped for arches, whilst others are elongated for lintels, flat for the roof and so on. Darwin asks,

> can it be reasonably maintained that the creator intentionally ordered, if we use the words in any ordinary sense, that certain fragments of rock should assume certain shapes so that the builder might erect his edifice?[39]

Gray's immediate response to this is

> I found your stone house argument unanswerable in substance (for the notion of design must after all rest mostly on faith, and on accumulation of adaptations, etc.). . . . I understand your argument perfectly, and feel the might of it.[40]

So Gray seems to have changed his view that evolution 'leaves everything as it is.' He appears now to accept that particular instances of design, namely the adaptation of biological structure and function are explained by natural selection so that there is no longer a legitimate argument from adaptation to a designer.

37. Gray 1876, p. 122.
38. Darwin 1868.
39. Darwin 1885, p. 427.
40. Gray 1868, vol. II, p. 562.

Gray's final position seems to be something like this. Natural selection certainly operates and also explains the fit of biological structure to function. So Paley is wrong to say that we must infer the existence of a designer on the basis of particular instances of adaptation. However, this does not rule out design. By faith we can see the entire natural order as designed. It seems then that Darwin and Gray came to agreement on the significance of natural selection for religion. They did not agree on the existence of God, but for other reasons.

From the Monkey Jibe to the Monkey Trial

The religious response to Darwin was diverse and cannot be characterized as a war between biblical literalism and the scientific spirit. That characterization, common still in the late twentieth century,[41] mistakenly reads back into early critics of Darwin the literal interpretation of Genesis used by the much later 'creation science' movement. Early objections were generally of a scientific nature, and when they were theological, they appealed to more general concerns than a literal interpretation of Genesis: ones about the denial of design and human dignity.

The most famous opponent of Darwinism is Samuel Wilberforce, Bishop of Oxford, famous for his role in a debate that took place at a meeting of the British Association for the Advancement of Science in 1860 at Oxford. As we saw in the Introduction, according to popular mythology he asked his opponent, Thomas Huxley, whether it was his grandmother or grandfather who was descended from an ape; when Darwinian theory actually claims that humans and apes are descended from a common ancestor. Huxley replied that he would prefer to be descended from an ape than from someone like Wilberforce, who could ridicule science in such an ill-informed way.[42]

However, there is little grounds for casting this as a war between science and biblical literalism. James Moore refers to the "well-known fact that the bishop had, for the most part, simply served up scientific argu-

---

41. See Oldroyd 1980, pp. 244-245. Oldroyd does recognise the shortcomings of the warfare historiography of White (1960), his mistake is rather to think that the problem with evolution was that it challenged the literal reading of Genesis.

42. White 1960, vol. 1, p. 71.

ments learned from Owen, seasoned with his own acidulous wit."[43] There is no real record of Wilberforce's speech that day, but we do have his review of *The Origin of Species,* and in that review Wilberforce bases most of his critique of Darwinism on scientific grounds. He does say that "the principle of natural selection is absolutely incompatible with the word of God,"[44] but does not anywhere draw explicitly on, say, a literal interpretation of Genesis. In fact, it is clear from the review that Wilberforce himself believed the earth is very much older than a literal reading of Genesis allows.

According to some, Wilberforce's theological concern was with a perceived threat to the dignity of humanity.[45] The idea that humanity is the pinnacle of creation, unique in being made in the image of God and in moral capacity, seemed to Wilberforce to be undermined by natural selection.

The next most famous conflict between creation and evolution is the so-called 'monkey trial' in Tennessee in 1925.[46] A law had been passed that year outlawing the teaching of evolution in schools, and John Thomas Scopes was found guilty of breaking that law. The victorious lawyer for the prosecution, fundamentalist William Jennings Bryan, a thrice-unsuccessful candidate for president of the United States, based his defense on the Bible. Moral victory lay with the evolutionists, however, as Scopes's lawyer Clarence Darrow called Bryan as a witness and grilled him on the interpretation of Genesis and related issues. Bryan admitted ignorance on a number of points, and that he did indeed himself 'interpret' Genesis. When asked whether he thought the world was created in seven literal days Bryan replied that a day might be taken to mean a span of time much greater than one literal day. When he was asked how the serpent walked before it was told to crawl on its belly, and whether it had hopped along on its tail, the court erupted into chaos. Five days after the trial Bryan died in his sleep.

Yet we must not read such biblical literalism back into earlier responses to Darwin. Indeed, there was a wide range of responses, and biblical literalism rarely figured. Many religious spokespersons found that the idea of evolution fitted in quite well with their theology. So-called 'liberal

43. Moore 1979, p. 61. See also Oldroyd 1980, p. 247.
44. White 1960, vol. 1, p. 70.
45. Moore 1979, p. 219; Roberts 1997, p. 115.
46. de Camp 1968.

theology,' in opposition to 'conservative theology,' rejected the idea that the Bible was inerrant, especially with regard to what it says about science. It also rejected strong views of human sin and depravity, preferring more optimistic views of humanity and its capacity for progress. Thus certain versions of evolutionary theory fit in with the idea of human progress, which was part and parcel of the entire liberal view. One influential figure who held this kind of liberal, pro-Darwinian view was the American Henry Ward Beecher (1818-1887). Beecher was an American Congregational minister and a popular preacher from about 1853 to 1880, the height of his popularity coinciding with the publication of *The Origin of Species*. Beecher had given up conservative Calvinism as a fairly young man, and instead embraced liberalism. He saw evolution through natural selection as being the progression of God's creation towards moral perfection, a progression still under way. (In retrospect, perhaps what Beecher had in mind had more in common with cultural development in the Marxist sense rather than with Darwinian natural selection.) By stressing the design of the total system rather than particular parts he reconciled design with Darwinism. Beecher is responsible for the famous phrase, "Design by wholesale is grander than design by retail."[47]

However, biblical literalism in Darwin's day, like ours, was much more likely among conservatives than liberals. But even among conservatives there were many who accepted Darwin, and of those who did not, few argued on the basis of literal interpretations of Genesis. A good example of conservative anti-Darwinism is American Charles Hodge (1797-1878). A conservative Calvinist, Hodge influenced an entire generation through his Chair in Theology at Princeton Theological Seminary, which he held for fifty years, and through his 1872 three-volume work entitled *Systematic Theology*.[48]

In his chapter on "Creation," Hodge distinguishes immediate from mediate creation, arguing that Genesis teaches that after an initial creation of the world in a chaotic form from nothing[49] the rest of creation is progressive, by the power of God working in union with second causes, out of pre-existing substance.[50] This includes humanity: "The Lord God

47. Beecher 1885. Quoted in Moore 1979, p. 221.
48. Hodge 1872-3.
49. Described in Genesis, ch. 1, vs. 1-2.
50. Genesis, ch. 1, v. 3ff.

formed the man of the dust of the earth."[51] We can recognize this as a version of the theory of evolution given by Augustine, whom Hodge quotes approvingly.[52]

The big question is, how long did this evolution take? Hodge takes Genesis to be historical narrative rather than allegorical or mythical, so the obvious answer is that it took six days. But this interpretation "must be controlled not only by the laws of language, but by facts. . . . This is at present an open question."[53] Here Hodge refers to the Nebular Hypothesis that the solar system evolved out of gas, which, if true, indicated that the period of creation was very much longer than six days.

According to Hodge, "It is certain that there can be no conflict between the teachings of the Scriptures and the facts of science."[54] This Augustinian principle of hermeneutics leads him to explain the fact that Genesis assumes an earth-centered cosmology with solid heavens as an accommodation to everyday ways of thinking. In fact, because of the progress of science and the human tendency to read into Scripture the prejudices of our day, there will inevitably be struggles as people come to accept that a previously cherished interpretation is wrong.[55]

In the case of the interpretation of the 'days' of creation, Hodge notes that the "commonly received chronology" takes the days as literal twenty-four hour days and sets the age of the earth at a few thousand, but that geology shows that the creation process took much larger periods of time. Given this, we must either find a long gap between verses 2 and 3 of Genesis 1, or else read 'days' as longer periods of time. Hodge prefers the latter on the grounds that the word 'day' often refers to undefined periods of time throughout Scripture, for example in Genesis 2:4. He then quotes James Dana of Yale and Arnold Guyot of Princeton, who show how this approach harmonizes with geology.

The same does not apply to mere theories such as natural selection, however. In his 1874 book entitled *What Is Darwinism?* Hodge answers his own question in one word: 'atheism.' However, in his chapter on "The Origin of Man" in *Systematic Theology,* he admits there could be a theistic version of evolution, provided it proceeded according to physical law. One of

51. Genesis, ch. 2, v. 7.
52. Hodge 1872-3, vol. I, p. 557.
53. Hodge 1872-3, vol. I, p. 558.
54. Hodge 1872-3, vol. I, p. 573.
55. Hodge 1872-3, vol. I, p. 573.

Hodge's objections to Darwin, then, is its accidental progress. To say that God started it up but it develops on its own "is atheism to all intents and purposes."[56] Other objections are that it obliterates the evidences of God, and that it is a mere hypothesis, not inductively supported; it cannot be deduced from the available evidence.[57] Hodge also lists some of the objections that Darwin himself canvassed, arguing that Darwin hadn't answered the difficulties satisfactorily.[58]

So none of Hodge's objections are based on biblical literalism. His comments on the age of humanity illustrate this:

> The Scriptures do not teach us how long men have existed on the earth. Their tables of genealogy were intended to prove that Christ was the son of David and the seed of Abraham, and not how many years had elapsed between the creation and the advent.[59]

The idea that opposition to Darwinism was based on literal interpretations of Genesis is a Whiggish reading of later creation science themes back into the nineteenth century. This is so even for theologically conservative, Bible-believing opponents of Darwin.

This theme can be found repeated throughout Great Britain and America for the rest of the nineteenth century. According to James Moore's comprehensive *The Post-Darwinian Controversies*, biblical arguments were a relatively insignificant part of Christian anti-Darwinism on both sides of the Atlantic.[60] In Britain F. O. Morris, 'the most outspoken objector,' was a Bible-believer; however, he didn't base his arguments on the Bible, but rather on the inadequacy of Darwin's step from variation to transmutation. Likewise, C. R. Bree, a physician who wrote book-length refutations of Darwinism, asserted that "Scriptures are not scientific authorities, nor ever were intended to be,"[61] and based his opposition on fallacies in Darwin's reasoning, drawing replies from both Wallace and Darwin. T. R. Dawson, Professor of Moral Philosophy at Cambridge and 'foremost Evangelical anti-Darwinian,' did argue that Spencer and Darwin

56. Hodge 1872-3, vol. II, p. 16.
57. Hodge 1872-3, vol. II, pp. 16-22.
58. Hodge 1872-3, vol. II, pp. 27-32.
59. Hodge 1872-3, vol. II, p. 41.
60. Moore 1979, pp. 196-205.
61. Quoted in Moore 1979, p. 200.

contravened the plain teaching of Scripture, but even he offered many other arguments as well. In America, E. F. Bur, the 'most influential' U.S. writer, argued that special creation better explained the evidence than natural selection. G. T. Curtis believed the Bible but in his book *Creation or Evolution* ignored Genesis and its interpretation, claiming to show that Darwin's theory violated rules of inductive reasoning, while L. T. Townsend, a popular Evangelical apologist, argued Bellarmino-style that Darwinism should for the time being be treated as a 'mere working hypothesis' on the grounds that most scientists at that time rejected it. J. W. Dawson, Principal of McGill University and a 'Scottish Presbyterian' by conviction, held an Augustinian hermeneutical principle: as Moore comments, "If there was any possible way to preserve a literal reading Dawson was determined to follow it; only if this were clearly impossible did he search for other means of accommodation."[62] Yet his primary arguments were not from Scripture but focused on what he considered to be Darwin's inadequate inductions.

But not all conservative evangelicals opposed Darwin. Others were properly heirs of the tradition of Augustine, Calvin, and Galileo. A prominent example is James McCosh (1811-94), firstly a minister in the Church of Scotland, then from 1851 Chair of Logic and Metaphysics at Queen's College Belfast, and finally from 1868 President of the College of New Jersey (Princeton University). A conservative Presbyterian, McCosh accepted natural selection of living organisms and even human bodies, but held the soul requires special intervention. He saw the process of evolution as guided by God and did not think that it undermined the idea of design.[63]

Another prominent example is the theologian B. B. Warfield (1851-1921), who followed Hodge as professor of theology at Princeton Seminary. Warfield's theological views are mostly similar to those of Hodge: evangelical, conservative, and Calvinist, and holding a high view of Scripture as the infallible word of God. The similarity ends, however, on the issue of Darwinian evolution. According to Warfield, evolution might be "a tenable theory of the method of divine providence."[64]

62. Moore 1979, p. 205.
63. Moore 1979, pp. 245-250.
64. Quote in Moore 1979, p. 71.

Creation Science

In 1895 the Niagara Bible Conference issued a statement of the five essential beliefs of Christianity, in response to growing liberalism. These were: (1) The infallibility of the Bible; (2) the divinity of Jesus Christ; (3) the virgin birth; (4) the substitutionary atonement of Christ; and (5) the physical resurrection and eventual return of Christ. These formed the basis of a series of publications in the 1910 called 'The Fundamentals,' from which we get the term 'fundamentalism.' Interestingly, and as many deliberately overlook,[65] several of the contributors were Darwinists, most prominently, B. B. Warfield.

Something happened between 1910 and the 1925 Scopes trial, by which time biblical literalism was so clearly pitted against evolution. According to James Moore, "they panicked." Military language concerning creation and evolution began to abound. (After the First World War military language was also widely used in the Ku Klux Klan, anticommunism, and the prohibition movement.)[66] Whatever the reason for the change, the shape of the twentieth-century creation science movement had at last been formed.

Based on a literal reading of Genesis 1, creation science claims that the entire universe was created in a literal six-day period approximately six thousand years ago. On this view all species are forever fixed — the phrase 'after its kind' refers to species as we understand them today, thus proving the fixity of species. Similarly, a worldwide flood occurred literally as described in Genesis 6-8.

Creation science conflicts with modern science in a number of ways. Clearly it conflicts with the biological idea of the evolution of species. It also conflicts with geology regarding the age of the earth: on current estimates, the age of the earth is thought to be approximately four and a half billion years. It also conflicts with physics: according to most modern physicists the universe began with the big bang somewhere between ten and twenty billion years ago. For this reason creation science also necessarily conflicts with simpler and less theoretical facts about physics, such as the fact that light comes to us from distant stars — if the nearest galaxy is one or two million light years away, that means that the light from that galaxy has taken one or two million years to travel to the earth.

65. de Camp 1968, p. 18.
66. Moore 1979, pp. 74-76.

The modern creation science movement runs a two-pronged attack. On one front it attacks modern science, claiming that many aspects of modern science, such as evolutionary theory, are merely unproven theories. On the other it runs a campaign against any non-literal reading of Genesis.

The most prominent Creation Scientists are those affiliated with the Institute for Creation Research, established in 1970 in California under the leadership of Henry Morris, now President Emeritus of the Institute. If a war needs a distinct organization, we now have one.[67]

According to their manifesto:

All things in the universe were created and made by God in the six literal days of the creation week described in Genesis 1:1-2:3, and confirmed in Exodus 20:8-11. The creation record is factual, historical, and perspicuous; thus all theories of origins or development which involve evolution in any form are false.[68]

Research at the Institute for Creation Research involves, in their words:

Field Research. Example: measurements of selected isotopic ratios for 67 elements in Grand Canyon basalts.

Lab Research. Example: genetic analysis of inheritance of mammalian hair.

Educational Research. Example: analysis of textbooks and other teaching materials, development of creationist-based tests, development of instruments for understanding attitudes about creationist tenets.

Exploration. Example: search for Noah's Ark and other archaeological sites and artifacts.

Analytical Research. Example: analytical review of helium concentrations in the atmosphere as an indicator of a young earth.

Literature Research. Example: review and critical analysis of the Kettlewell studies of the English peppered moth.[69]

67. See Moore 1979, p. 85.
68. See http://www.icr.org/abouticr/tenets.htm.
69. See http://www.icr.org/abouticr/research.htm.

One of the common creation science arguments against evolution concerns the second law of thermodynamics. In his *Scientific Creationism*, Morris argues that evolution is a process of increasing complexity, and as such it requires a basic law of increasing complexity, a 'Principle of Naturalistic Innovation and Integration.'[70] But according to the theory of creation science, because God's creation is perfect we should expect there to exist an inbuilt principle of conservation which maintains this perfection, but that any change can be expected to be detrimental. It follows that the creationist view predicts the first two laws of thermodynamics, Morris argues. The first law of thermodynamics states that energy is conserved, while the second law states that amount of order (negative entropy) in the universe is always decreasing. But the theory of evolution is in conflict with the second law of thermodynamics since it leads to increasing complexity.

Entropy is simply a measure of the disorder of a system or the available useable energy of a system. The second law of thermodynamics says that the entropy of a closed system tends to increase. For example, heat will not flow spontaneously from a cold body to a hot body.

The standard reply to the creation science argument is, simply, that the second law does not apply to open systems such as the earth. The earth is not a closed system, since an enormous amount of energy comes to the earth from the sun, energy needed for evolution. The entropy of this total system — the sun and the earth together — will increase as the stores of energy are used up in the sun. Therefore, the second law does apply to evolution. Morris replies that all systems on earth are open to the sun in this sense, yet all of the other non-biological systems that we see here on earth do obey the second law of thermodynamics.[71]

A second creation science objection to evolutionary theory is the improbability argument. According to this objection, favorable variations are extremely rare, and most variations within species will be detrimental rather than favorable, so at every step of evolution there is a highly improbable event. If we add together all of the accumulative improbabilities of every step in the evolution of life we will find that result will be some enormous improbability. The probability of the evolutionary process is, in effect, zero. Morris puts it thus:

70. Morris 1974, pp. 37, 42, 45.
71. Morris 1974, p. 43.

It would seem obvious that if any one mutation is highly likely to be deleterious, then since a changed characteristic requires the combined effects of many genes, and therefore many concurrent mutations, the probability of harmful effects is multiplied manyfold. Conversely, the probability of simultaneous good mutations in all the genes which control a given character is reduced to practically zero.[72]

An analogy often used (although not by Morris) to make this point is the improbability that a monkey randomly hitting the keys of a typewriter would create the complete works of Shakespeare. It is so improbable that the hypothesis is not worth serious consideration.

The Darwinian answer is that the creation science objection overlooks the role that natural selection plays. If the objection were correct, we would be forced to also say that we cannot believe that people are able to breed racehorses or pigeons. But natural selection, like artificial breeding, singles out the rare, favorable variations and discards the common, deleterious variations. Then the appropriate analogy is not a monkey randomly typing the complete works of Shakespeare, but rather a monkey randomly typing on a computer that contains an inbuilt mechanism according to which if the wrong key is hit, the letter is deleted — so that we should expect the monkey to produce the complete works of Shakespeare, given a sufficient period of time.

Creation science also runs a campaign against alternative religious views. Their position is that theistic evolution, for example, is not a view that is possible for a sincere believer. One alternative Henry Morris calls the 'framework hypothesis,' according to which the creation narrative is a literary device, not actual history, variously seen as being allegorical, liturgical, poetic, or supra-historical. Morris maintains that

> This type of Biblical exegesis is out of the question for any real believer in the Bible . . . there is certainly no internal or exegetical reason for taking them in any other way.[73]

and Morris concludes that

> The "framework hypothesis" of Genesis, in any of its diverse forms, is nothing but neo-orthodox sophistry and inevitably leads eventually to

72. Morris 1974, p. 57.
73. Morris 1974, p. 244.

complete apostasy. It must be unequivocally rejected and opposed by Bible-believing Christians.[74]

For example, concerning the phrase 'after its kind,' Morris comments that "it is obvious that the word does have a definite and fixed meaning. One 'kind' could not transform itself into another 'kind.'"[75]

To label creation science a conflict view of the relation of science and religion, as I think we should, assumes a view of what 'science' is. If we take science to be what scientists do in mainstream universities and journals, then creation science is a conflict view. But that is not how they see it — they claim to be the true science, demonstrating the harmony between religion and true science.

But there is clearly something different here in comparison to religious responses in other cases of harmony we have looked at — such as those of Augustine, Galileo and the nineteenth century response to Darwin. Like Augustine and Galileo, creation science starts from the assumption of unity — that there is one God behind Scripture and nature, and that therefore Scripture is true. But unlike Augustine, Galileo, Asa Gray, and B. B. Warfield, they in addition do not allow any room for the reinterpretation of Scripture. This feature of committed literalism — for which they have earned the label 'fundamentalist' — is the unique feature that leads them into conflict.

74. Morris 1974, p. 247.
75. Morris 1974, p. 217.

CHAPTER 6

Big Bang Cosmology and God

The last ten to fifteen years of the twentieth century saw the phenomenon of 'popularizing physicists' — leading physicists authoring bestselling books. One of the themes of this trend was to discuss God as well as physics — apparently a surefire recipe for commercial success. The definitive blueprint for this genre was Cambridge theoretical physicist Stephen Hawking's bestselling book (and movie) *A Brief History of Time*.[1] In a now famous passage, Hawking writes,

> However, if we do discover a complete theory, it should in time be understandable in broad principle by everyone, not just a few scientists. Then we shall all, philosophers, scientists, and just ordinary people, be able to take part in the discussion of the question of why it is that we and the universe exist. If we find the answer to that, it would be a triumph of human reason — for then we would know the mind of God.[2]

However, despite the use of the word 'God,' this passage is quite scientistic. Although Hawking is not saying, as some take him to be, that physics has the answer to everything, he does seem to be at least implying that until we discover the so-called 'theory of everything' — the theory which unifies the four forces and hence the main physical theories — we cannot hope to answer questions about why we and the universe exist.

1. Hawking 1988.
2. Hawking 1988, p. 185.

142

Hawking's phrase to "know the mind of God" means simply to know the answers to those questions.

Stephen Hawking is just one example of a modern physicist whose writing touches on religious issues. Others include the particle physicist turned Anglican priest John C. Polkinghorne, and the physicist Frank Tipler. Tipler's contributions include the controversial book *The Physics of Immortality*,[3] in which he offers a theory of the evolution of mind and the universe and claims that, if proven, it shows that many parts of Christian theology are true (although Tipler is not himself a Christian).

But perhaps the most successful popularizing physicist is Paul Davies. In his *The Mind of God*,[4] Davies urges that although science does have the capacity to provide explanations for many phenomena, it is also the case that the more we learn about the order, complexity, and subtlety of the universe, the more we are struck by its majesty and wonder. Davies sees the universe as a marvelously ingenious and unified mathematical scheme, a unity that requires the sort of explanation that science itself cannot provide.

In this chapter we will consider the contributions by Hawking and Davies, and in particular examine the anthropic principle and its implication for the existence of God. As background we will consider the Kalām cosmological argument and some scientific developments concerning the age of the universe.

The Kalām Cosmological Argument
and the Infinite Universe

Between the time of Augustine and Aquinas lay the golden age of Islam, spanning the eighth through eleventh centuries. A major school in mature Islamic philosophy went by the name 'Kalām,' which literally means 'speech' but in this context means roughly 'natural theology.' The Mutakallim — philosophical theologians — built their philosophy on the Qur'an, believing they could know about God by reason. One of their major exponents was Abu Hamid Al-Ghazali (A.D. 1058-1111).

The Kalām cosmological argument as offered by Al-Ghazali and oth-

3. Tipler 1996.
4. Davies 1992.

ers is not to be confused with 'cosmological arguments' of Aquinas and Leibniz, which are arguments from contingency (and require no commitment to a finite-in-time universe). The Kalām cosmological argument goes as follows:

1. Everything that begins to exist has a cause of its existence.
2. The universe began to exist.
3. Therefore the universe has a cause of its existence. That cause we may call 'God.'

The first premise, that everything that begins to exist has a cause of its existence (a version of the Law of Causality), was taken to be a self-evident principle of reasoning. Al-Ghazali defended the second premise as follows. There cannot be an infinite sequence of temporal events because it is possible to derive a contradiction from the supposition that there is. For example, Jupiter revolves around the sun once every twelve years, Saturn once every thirty years. If the solar system existed for an infinite time back into the past, then the total number of revolutions of both Saturn and Jupiter would be infinite, but Jupiter also orbits twice as many times as Saturn, and it's absurd to have infinities of different sizes (this is equivalent to one of Cantor's paradoxes).[5] Therefore the universe has a beginning in time, a result which fits nicely with Genesis and the teachings of the Qur'an.

The notion of a temporally finite, static world fitted comfortably with the medieval worldview. However, the scientific revolution challenged people's thinking about the age of the universe. Early developments such as the Copernican hypothesis and Galileo's discovery of new stars forced the realization that the universe is very much larger than had been imagined. At first this did not flow through to encompass the age of the universe as well; Newton himself used the Bible to calculate the age of the earth at around six thousand years.

However, beginning in the eighteenth century, developmental hypotheses contributed to the acceptance of a temporally infinite universe. According to the Nebular Hypothesis of Kant (1724-1804) and LaPlace (1749-1827), stars are not fixed, having existed always as we now see them, but rather evolved from an original chaotic cloud of gas that, under gravity, gradually formed into the stellar arrangements we see now. These and

5. For a reply to this see Mackie 1982, pp. 92-95.

other developmental theses — such as Buffon's (1707-1788) age-of-the-earth calculation based on the cooling of the earth in analogy with cooling rates of iron balls — challenged the young-universe thesis. By the eighteenth century most geologists set the age of the earth at millions of years. "Creation is not the work of a moment," as Kant famously remarked.

Other hypotheses even suggested an infinite age. Uniformitarians claimed that geological explanations need only appeal to processes that we see around us now, such as erosion, which work slowly by innumerable similar small changes, never in leaps and bounds. According to Hutton (1726-97) there is no scientific value in the idea of a beginning or an end of the universe, so for scientific purposes the universe can be considered in effect infinite in time. Development operated by the principle of 'parsimony of force and prodigality of time,' according to Uniformitarians like Sir Charles Lyell (1797-1875).[6] Similarly Darwinian evolution, as we saw, demands a very old earth.

But if the universe is infinitely old, there seems no place for the Kalām argument for the existence of God. If it is simply that there is no evidence for a beginning, then belief in creation is a matter of faith. But if indeed there were conclusive scientific evidence that the material universe has always existed then there seems no place for creation at all.

In the mid-twentieth century many cosmologists favored an infinite 'steady state' model of the universe. According to the so-called 'Perfect Cosmological Principle,' the universe looks the same from any direction at any time and place. Within infinite time arise the birth, degeneration, and dissipation of galaxies, with a constant average density of matter. That the universe is expanding was already accepted since the 1920s on the basis of Einstein's general theory of relativity together with the evidence of red-shifted galaxies (far-distant galaxies that recede very quickly). But the old age of some galaxies led proponents of the steady state cosmology to claim that the universe is eternally expanding, and consequently that matter is continuously created to sustain constant average density.

However, as evidence mounted in favor of big bang cosmology, some cosmologists continued to support the steady state universe on metaphysical grounds. Sir Fred Hoyle (b. 1915), for example, objected to the idea of a beginning which itself had no scientific explanation.[7] In 1975 he wrote,

6. Gillispie 1959.
7. Jaki 1974, p. 247; Craig and Smith 1995, pp. 44-47.

The abrupt beginning is regarded as *meta*physical — i.e., *outside* physics. The physical laws are therefore considered to break down at t = 0, *and to do so inherently.* To many people this thought process seems highly satisfactorily because a 'something' outside physics can then be introduced at t = 0. By a semantic manoeuvre, the word 'something' is then replaced by 'god,' except that the first letter becomes a capital, God, in order to warn us that we must not carry the enquiry any further.[8]

Nevertheless, despite this warning, the day was won by big bang cosmology, to which we now turn.

Big Bang Cosmology

The standard picture of the universe in the second half of the twentieth century was that the universe began as a point-sized, infinitely high-density and high-temperature singularity about ten to twenty billion years ago, then expanded rapidly, cooling until gravitational forces clumped matter together into the galaxies that we see today. On the inflationary version, the universe underwent rapid expansion early on, which accounts for its current large size and uniformity. The evidence that won widespread acceptance of the big bang model was the cosmic background radiation predicted by George Gamow and discovered accidentally in 1965 by Arno Penzias and Robert Wilson, who at first thought it was just the interference of birds. This radiation, at a temperature of 3K, can be seen in every direction and is taken to be the heat remaining from the initial explosion of the big bang.

Some, most notably philosopher William Lane Craig,[9] have used the evidence for the big bang as a way to resurrect the Kalām argument. Stephen Hawking seems to accept this view, or at least, its plausibility. He writes in *A Brief History of Time* that if the initial boundary conditions of the universe occur in a singularity where the laws of physics break down, then there is no way that we can know how it began. Something outside the universe is needed.[10]

8. Hoyle 1975, pp. 684-85.
9. See Craig and Smith 1995.
10. Hawking 1988, p. 143.

However, Hawking offers his own proposal, the 'Hartle-Hawking no-boundary condition,' according to which the universe can be pictured as a having a spherical shape without the conventional singularity at t = o. Hawking's universe is finite in size but has no boundary or edge, so there are no initial conditions to be specified, and the laws apply to everything. To be more precise, the universe is represented as a smooth, finite, three-dimensional surface in four-dimensional space (not space-time). An analogy is the surface of a ball — a two-dimensional surface in three dimensional space — which has finite surface area but no boundaries. The no-boundary proposal removes any need to suppose there is a creator who started the universe, Hawking claims.[11] In another famous passage in *A Brief History of Time* in which he mentions God, Hawking writes,

> The idea that space and time may form a closed surface without boundary also has profound implications for the role of God in the affairs of the universe. With the success of scientific theories in describing events, most people have come to believe that God allows the universe to evolve according to a set of laws and does not intervene in the universe to break these laws. However, the laws do not tell us what the universe should have looked like when it started — it would still be up to God to wind up the clockwork and choose how to start it off. So long as the universe had a beginning, we could suppose it had a creator. But if the universe is really completely self-contained, having no boundary or edge, it would have neither beginning nor end: it would simply be. What place, then, for a creator?[12]

In other words, if we accepted the standard big bang theory of the origin of the universe, we might conclude that there is a need to postulate the existence of God as creator, as in the Kalām argument, but if the 'no boundary' cosmological model is adopted, there is no need to postulate the existence of a creator. Indeed, reading *A Brief History of Time* (as opposed to Hawking's technical writings), one gets the distinct impression that the whole rationale for the no-boundary model is to avoid the conclusion that there is a God.

One problem with Hawking's response is that it is only in imaginary

11. Hawking 1988, pp. 143-49.
12. Hawking 1988, p. 149.

time that the singularity disappears — in real time singularities and black holes are still there. The most natural way to interpret this is to take real time as the real universe, and the Hawking model as a useful model for making predictions, rather than taking the no-boundary model as real and the real time model as simply a mathematical device. Hawking's response to this fact is to argue that all cosmological models are simply mathematical devices, and to ask which corresponds to reality is meaningless.[13] Here Hawking is articulating an antirealism of an extreme, positivist kind, which sits rather uneasily with his other claims about discovering the mind of God and so on.

But if we allow that there are boundary conditions that need explaining, how exactly might this lead to postulating the existence of God? One response is the Kalām Cosmological Argument. Another independent response is the anthropic principle.

The Anthropic Principle

The term 'anthropic principle' refers to the remarkable connection between the initial conditions and constants of the universe, and the fact that life has arisen in the universe. This remarkable connection requires explanation. Why is our universe fine-tuned for life? Why didn't it have any of the much more likely configurations that would not have produced life? In subsequent sections we will examine three attempts to explain this connection: that it is due to intelligent design, that there is a pantheistic explanation, and that it is explained by the existence of multiple universes. In this section, however, we look more closely at the anthropic principle itself.

In this context the word 'anthropic' simply means human-centered. In the sixteenth and seventeenth centuries there was a move away from an anthropocentric view of the universe. For example, there was the move from the Aristotelian system, in which the earth was the center of a fairly small, young universe, with humanity the focal point, to the Newtonian system with its infinite universe in which the earth was not at the center of the solar system, much less at the centre of the universe. The anthropic principle involves a reversal of this trend.

13. Hawking 1988, pp. 147-48.

One of the first scientists to employ anthropic reasoning was Fred Hoyle. Hoyle was interested in how carbon is produced inside stars, and how sufficient carbon was produced for life to evolve. For life to be produced, elements such as carbon and oxygen must be present in the right quantities. We know that hydrogen and helium were produced in the big bang, but elements such as carbon and oxygen are produced through the process of nuclear fusion, which occurs only inside stars. Carbon is produced through the process of nuclear fusion, in which three helium nuclei come together at high speed. The energy involved must be great enough to overcome the mutually repellent electric forces between the three colliding nuclei, and the only place in which energy levels ever get this high is in the interior of stars. However, even inside a star these triple-nuclei encounters are extremely rare, because the fusing of two helium nuclei produces beryllium, which is extremely unstable. This instability makes it highly improbable that beryllium will fuse with a third helium nucleus before it decays back to helium.

Hoyle realized that the entire process is so improbable that it is overwhelmingly unlikely that there can have been enough carbon produced since the Big Bang for carbon-based life to have evolved. The fact remains however, that sufficient carbon was produced. How can we explain this improbable good fortune? Hoyle responded by reasoning anthropically. Given that we exist, we know there is enough carbon in the universe, so there must have been something about the conditions involved that made this fact sufficiently probable. Hoyle therefore predicted that there must be a characteristic energy level of carbon — 'resonance' — to which the typical energy level of helium nuclei within stars correlates. Hoyle was thereby able to predict a previously unknown resonance energy level of carbon. His prediction was later tested and shown to be correct.

It's hard to exaggerate how fortuitous this is. If the energy levels involved in this process had been any higher or lower there would be no carbon, and therefore no life in this universe. It appears as if carbon itself was designed so that sufficient carbon would be produced for life to evolved. It is as though the universe has the conditions for life built into its very laws. Paul Davies reports on the reaction of Hoyle (an atheist) in these terms:

Hoyle was so impressed by this "monstrous series of accidents," he was prompted to comment that it was as if "the laws of nuclear physics

149

have been deliberately designed with regard to the consequences they produce inside stars." Later he was to expound the view that the universe looks like a "put-up job," as though somebody had been "monkeying" with the laws of physics.[14]

This phenomenon is not limited to carbon production. Good fortune seems to abound in our universe. In particular, the state of the emerging universe (at about one second after the big bang), involved many features which have life 'built into them,' in the sense that if these characteristics had been any different, life could not possibly have evolved. *The Anthropic Cosmological Principle*,[15] by physicists John Barrow and Frank Tipler, contains numerous examples of the amazing coincidences that are necessary in order for life to evolve. For example, the exact excess of quarks over anti-quarks (the so-called 'baryon asymmetry'): if the difference had been less, the present matter density would have been too small for galaxies to have formed; if it had been greater virtually the entire universe would have burnt to helium long before life could have formed. Another example is the initial rate of expansion of the universe. Had the expansion rate had been slightly more rapid, stars and heavier elements would never have formed. Had it been slightly slower, the universe would have collapsed long before life could have developed.

In addition to these critical boundary conditions, for life to have developed certain fundamental constants had to have values very close to the ones they in fact do have. The electron to proton mass ratio and the fine structure constant could not have been any larger or else the chains of molecules essential for biochemistry would not have formed. On the other hand, they could not have been any smaller or there would not have been any stable atoms.

There are various forms of the anthropic principle, and there are no agreed definitions. The following usage follows that in Barrow and Tipler's book.[16] According to the weak anthropic principle (WAP),

> The observed values of all physical and cosmological quantities are not equally probable but they take on values restricted by the requirement that there exist sites where carbon-based life can evolve and by the re-

14. Davies 1992, p. 199.
15. Barrow and Tipler 1986.
16. We will attempt to clarify what these definitions might mean below.

quirement that the Universe be old enough for it to have already done so.[17]

The argument advanced by Hoyle in regard to carbon is an example of the use of the weak anthropic principle. The strong anthropic principle (SAP) states that

> The Universe must have those properties which allow life to develop within it at some stage in its history.[18]

The participatory anthropic principle (PAP) of the physicist John Wheeler states that

> Observers are necessary to bring the Universe into being.[19]

The final anthropic principle (FAP) states that

> Intelligent information-processing must come into existence in the Universe and once it comes into existence, it will never die out.[20]

It should be noted that the last three of these definitions are controversial. Indeed, Martin Gardener has commented that a more apt name for any of them would be the completely ridiculous anthropic principle (CRAP).[21]

The essential challenge the anthropic principle presents is, of course, to explain the remarkable coincidences. Can it be just a coincidence, just chance, that the universe is set up this way? Normally we are very suspicious of uncanny coincidences.

To borrow an illustration from John Leslie,[22] imagine that you are blindfolded and face a row of twenty rifles. The command comes to fire, but miraculously every single rifle misfires. You might want to ask why it is that all the guns misfired. Was your survival due to chance, or is there some explanation as to why all of the twenty rifles misfired? Perhaps the misfiring, or fine-tuning of the situation can be explained; for, example, a

---

17. Barrow and Tipler 1986, p. 16.
18. Barrow and Tipler 1986, p. 21.
19. Barrow and Tipler 1986, p. 22.
20. Barrow and Tipler 1986, p. 23.
21. Cited in Earman 1987.
22. Leslie 1989.

friend in the rifle department, or God, or a guardian angel, has adjusted the mechanisms of the rifles to ensure that you survived.

Or suppose there is major large-scale bomb attack on the city in which you live, such that every building is razed to the ground, with the highly improbable exception of the building where you are. You may conclude that your survival is due to chance — or that an explanation lies in the exceptional structure or foundations of your particular building, or in the deliberate planning of the bomber pilots.

So what explanation can be found for the seemingly fortuitous fine-tuning of our universe? If we accept SAP (that the universe must have those properties which allow life to develop within it at some stage in its history) or for that matter FAP (that intelligent information-processing must come into existence in the universe), then no further explanation of the coincidences is required. For once the principle is accepted the necessity of the tuning is guaranteed. Being necessary, it requires no explanation. The problem is why we should accept such strong principles in the first place.

There is in fact no reason to accept them, and the reason why people have found these principles at all plausible is due to a confusion of prediction and explanation.

There is an important difference between use of the anthropic principle for prediction and for explanation. WAP (that the observed values of all physical and cosmological quantities are not equally probable but take on values restricted by the requirement that there exist sites where carbon-based life can evolve), when taken in the plausible sense, involves just prediction, whereas SAP purports in addition to provide an explanation. The claim about prediction is valid, but the claim about explanation is not.

Consider the following fallacious line of reasoning: If we follow strictly the method of inference to the best explanation, as described in Chapter 2, we would conclude that since the probability of the fine-tuning given that we are here is far greater than the probability of the fine-tuning alone, the fact that we are here explains the fine-tuning of the universe. The probability of the fine-tuning of the universe is very low, but given that we are here, the probability of the fine-tuning of the universe is one. We can express this argument in symbols, with 'F' for fine-tuning and 'us' for the fact that there is now intelligent, carbon-based life in the universe:

P(F) = negligible,
P(F|us) = 1
Therefore, P(F|us) >> P(FT)

In other words, the probability of the fine-tuning of the universe given that we are here is far greater than the simple probability of the fine-tuning of the universe. So according to inference to the best explanation, our existence explains the fine-tuning. But clearly there must be something wrong with this line of reasoning.

The problem is partly that it uses something in the future to explain something in the past. For example, you could ask why you were born, an intrinsically improbable event. Perhaps your parents wanted a second child, or perhaps their contraceptives failed. You could reason: I am here now, and the probability that I was born, given this fact, is one. But there seems to be something wrong with this as an explanation. You cannot explain the past by reference to the future. You can validly 'predict' your birth by reference to your later existence, but you cannot explain it. So a requirement should be added according to which the explanans (the event doing the explaining) must occur before the explanandum (the event being explained).[23] (More generally, the requirement should be that causes explain their effects, but effects do not explain their causes.)[24] Such a requirement will rule out the SAP.

Recall our firing squad example. The probability of all twenty guns misfiring is extremely low, but given that you are alive the probability of that coincidence is about one. Does this mean that the fact that you are alive explains the misfiring of the rifles? Certainly not in any normal, direct sense. A later event cannot explain earlier events. The misfiring could be explained in terms of somebody's desire that you survive at a later time, but this explanation makes no appeal to a later event.

On the other hand, backward anthropic prediction is perfectly acceptable. We can predict — or more accurately, 'retrodict' — states of affairs that must have obtained given the present state of the universe. We can infer from the fact that we are here now that the universe was fine-

---

23. Better still, we should require that the explanans is the cause of the explanandum, and not vice versa. Then if there is backwards in time causation, backwards explanation is allowed.

24. Horwich 1987; Salmon 1984.

tuned in certain ways at some time in the past (WAP). This is what Hoyle is doing when he claims that the resonance state of carbon had to be a certain way due to the fact that we know how much carbon exists in the universe today. This is not an attempt to explain past events by recourse to events in the present. In fact, the weaker version of the anthropic principle amounts to the trivial and rather obvious claim that since we are here now, the universe must have been such as to allow us to be here. The stronger versions differ from that in that they entail that because we are here, the universe had to be in a certain state, that is, they attempt explanation, not just prediction.

God as an Explanation

So how could the anthropic principle be explained by theism or pantheism? Classical theism is the view that we find in conventional Judaism, Christianity, and Islam. According to classical theism, first, God is not dependent on the world in any way, but rather, the world is entirely dependent on God; and second, God is a person with personal qualities, very much like human persons. For example, God speaks, has intentions, likes and dislikes, loves certain things, sees some things as good and others as not good, and so on. Many of the great Western philosophers have been classical theists, among them Augustine, Aquinas, Descartes, Locke, Leibniz, Bacon, Galileo, and Berkeley.

Pantheism, on the other hand, is the view that God is not a person distinct from the world, but is immanent in the world, to be in some sense identified with the world. According to one version of pantheism, the whole of reality is united into, or is an aspect of, a single being. Baruch Spinoza, perhaps the most famous advocate of pantheism in Western philosophy, argues that since substance is completely self-sufficient, and only God is self-sufficient, God is therefore the only substance. God is, in fact, everything. Other Western pantheists include Hegel, Schopenhauer, and Emerson. Pantheism also underlies some Eastern religions, such as certain types of Buddhism and Hinduism. According to the Vedic tradition in Indian philosophy, the multiplicity of reality that we see around us is an illusion whereas the true reality is the single being (Brahma) that underlies the multiplicity of appearances. Again in this case God is not independent of the world but is identified with it.

The way that God is used as an explanation for fine-tuning is in fact a version of the design argument. Taking theism first, if the personal God of classical theism exists, then quite plausibly that God would want to create persons — that is intelligent, conscious beings. Therefore it is highly probable that God would create a world that allowed for the development of life. In other words, according to this argument the universe is fine-tuned for life because it was created by God for the deliberate purpose of allowing life. We should infer the truth of theism (leaving aside considerations from other areas of inquiry), since the probability of the fine-tuning of the universe given that theism is true is far greater than the probability of the fine-tuning of the universe alone, following the method of inference to the best explanation.[25]

Thus the design argument hinges on the method of inference to the best explanation, where the key requirement is that the hypothesis raises the probability of the evidence. In the case of the anthropic design argument the relevant hypothesis is the existence of a designer-God — and the relevant evidence is the fine-tuning F of the universe. So,

$$P(F|God) \gg P(F).$$

Or, the probability of there existing a universe which is fine-tuned for life, conditional on the existence of God, is greater than the probability of there existing a universe which is fine-tuned for life. It follows from this that

$$P(God|F) \gg P(God)$$

That is, the probability that God exists, conditional on the evidence that this universe is fine-tuned for life, is greater than the probability that God exists. In other words, since the hypothesis raises the probability of the evidence, it follows that the evidence confirms the hypothesis.

Of course, when using the method of inference to the best explanation, we must always compare the available hypotheses. If there are several hypotheses that explain the available evidence, we must ask which raises the probability of the evidence to the greatest degree, or, at the very least, check each hypothesis against a criterion of satisfactory explanatory power. In this and the following sections we compare alternative putative explanations.

25. Swinburne 1991, app. B.

As we saw in previous chapters, Paley's explanation of biological adaptation is not the only type of design argument, although it is the most famous. Newton, for example, employs the design argument to explain the universe as a whole, especially its ordered laws and regularities. Paley's version of the argument is undermined by Darwin's theory of evolution by natural selection. But natural selection does not undermine Newton's design argument, since the latter does not appeal to biological adaptation. And further, since we would not expect some fact to be discovered which could explain the overall structure, regularity, and beauty of the universe as a whole, more general versions of the argument from design — such as Newton's — appear to be immune from refutation by subsequent scientific developments.

According to one objection the anthropic design argument is not similarly immune to scientific refutation because it is possible that further developments in science will uncover a physical explanation of the fine-tuning. According to the objection, this raises a problem known as the 'god of the gaps' — an objection often put by theologians.[26]

The god of the gaps story goes like this: The ancient Greeks explained lightning in terms of Zeus throwing objects around in the heavens, an explanation which was superseded by scientific developments. Newton explained the fact that the solar system does not run down, as earthly systems do, by the hypothesis that God introduces comets into the solar system at the right moments to maintain the energy levels. But within one hundred and fifty years Newton's explanation had been superseded by the articulation of the distinction between the first and second laws of thermodynamics. Paley claimed that when we observe natural phenomena such as the human eye, we are forced to conclude that there must be a designer. But Darwin explained adaptation in terms of natural selection. So, the march of science has gradually explained these features, and God has less and less of an explanatory role to play. In addition, our concept of God becomes smaller and smaller as science progresses. God is no longer the designer of life, the sustainer of the solar system, or the source of lightning. The objection (which usually comes from religious sources) is that this is not the way in which God should be conceived. It is dangerous to introduce God in order to account for only those things that science fails to explain, because we may soon find that the gaps which we are invoking God

26. E.g., McMullin 1993.

to explain are closed by the progress of scientific explanation. Similarly, goes the objection, the anthropic version of the design argument is defective because it may soon be superseded by scientific developments.

Let's now turn to pantheism. This option is discussed by Paul Davies in his book *The Mind of God*.[27] Davies is impressed by the underlying unity of the universe, including what he calls the "felicitous dovetailing of the large and small," and claims that we cannot deny that the universe appears to be designed. But does this mean classical theism is true? Here Davies follows the philosopher John Leslie, who thinks not.[28] Leslie maintains that the universe exists as a result of what he calls an 'ethical requirement' or 'ethical need.' According to this view, this is an objective, non-physical quality of the universe that existed there before humans did. This ethical requirement is a teleological property of the universe, which demands and therefore leads to the creation of ethical features in the universe. So, according to Leslie, human beings are a manifestation of that ethical feature, and as conscious, intelligent beings we have the capacity for morality. He explains the fine-tuning of the universe by the hypothesis that this ethical quality, in needing to be instantiated, has somehow brought about these requisite conditions.[29]

Paul Davies takes a slightly different view. Davies is interested in qualities such as ingenuity, economy, and beauty, which he considers to possess genuine transcendent reality, in that they exist objectively in the universe. These qualities are reflected in the structure of the natural world and are responsible, or at least partly responsible, for bringing the universe into existence. This, Davies claims, explains the fine-tuning of the universe. Because human life best expresses these qualities, which want to maximize themselves in the universe, the qualities force the universe into the unlikely state of being fine-tuned for life. The universe is designing itself according to a blueprint into which these qualities are written. These qualities are teleological, immanent in the world — which suggests pantheism — and genuinely causally efficacious. According to Davies we can call the personification of these qualities 'God' if we so wish.

However, in response to this option, philosophers such as Swinburne

27. Davies 1992.
28. See Hacking 1987, p. 331, n. 2.
29. See also Leslie 1989, especially Chapter 8, where Leslie expands his notion of a 'Neo-platonic God'.

have argued that pantheism does not provide a clear explanation of the fine-tuning. According to theism, the world is fine-tuned because God wanted conscious life in the universe and so created the world with the intention that such life would be possible. This is a well-known and understood explanation of apparent teleology. Often things are suited to an obvious function precisely because a person (usually human) set it up with the deliberate intention of having something to fulfill that function. The alternative well-known form of explanation, mechanical explanation, explains function only in terms of chance. However, Leslie's and Davies' pantheism claims that God or the universe developed itself in order to bring about conscious life. This hypothesis fits neither of our familiar models of explanation.

We may therefore legitimately ask whether an unexplained immanent teleological principle qualifies as an adequate explanation. Pantheism retains the word 'God' but removes the key feature of the theist explanation, namely that God is a person who has particular thoughts, desires, and intentions. It is not clear how the properties that this God/universe is left with can explain why the universe's physical properties were appropriately fine-tuned in the big bang.

Chance and Many Worlds Explanations

We turn now to the hypothesis that chance might provide an alternative to the design argument. According to Stephen Jay Gould,

> The central fallacy in this newly touted but historically moth-eaten [design] argument lies in the nature of history itself. Any complex historical outcome — intelligent life on earth, for example — represents a summation of improbabilities and becomes thereby absurdly improbable. But something had to happen, even if any particular 'something' must stun us by its improbability. We could look at any outcome and say "Ain't it amazing. If the laws of nature had been set up just a tad differently, we wouldn't have this kind of universe at all."[30]

In other words, when it comes to the fine-tuning of the universe for life, there is really nothing to explain. The world had to be some way or another.

30. Gould 1985, p. 183.

For example, if you win the lottery, even though it is a highly improbable outcome, there is no need to explain why you rather than some other ticket holder won, because someone had to win. The fact is that whoever won would have been in exactly the same position, faced with the same overwhelming improbability.

Or suppose that you select five cards at random from a 52-card pack. What is the chance of you having selected exactly those five cards that you did? The answer is $\frac{1}{52} \times \frac{1}{51} \times \frac{1}{50} \times \frac{1}{49} \times \frac{1}{48}$, an extremely small number (about one in three hundred million). But we don't think that this highly improbable event requires explanation, even though the chances of it happening are so small. Some highly improbable outcome or other had to happen.

Another more elaborate attempt to deny the need for explanation is the multi-world hypothesis — that there are many universes, besides ours, strung out in hyperspace, instantiating different combinations of values. There are several versions of this hypothesis.

The basic version is the hypothesis M that there is a large but finite number of universes, with values randomly distributed across the possible combinations of values, as produced by some kind of randomly generating mechanism. Because there exists a very large number of these universes the existence of a world fine-tuned for life is very likely. The vast majority of these worlds will not support life, but probably at least one will.

Another version involves oscillating universes — also called 'Wheeler worlds' (M_W) after physicist and popular author John Wheeler — something like a string of sausages. Suppose our Big Bang arose out of a previous Big Crunch of a previous universe, which in turn arose from an 'earlier' Big Bang, and so on ad infinitum. Each universe is a random configuration, so some will be short lived, others not. Because this mechanism is random, we can expect the instantiation of all kinds of possible universes. This hypothesis differs from M in that rather than involving many universes spread out across hyperspace, these universes are connected to one another like sausages, although we can never have any evidence of the characteristics of previous or future universes because each universe is completely independent.

Another version is the 'Carter worlds,' named after Brandon Carter. According to the Carter worlds hypothesis M_C, there exists a string of infinitely many worlds in which every possibility or configuration is, in fact, instantiated in the sequence. This means that the probability that one of these worlds is fine-tuned for life is one. This idea is sometimes called the principle of plenitude, and is similar to the "ultimate ensemble" theory of

Mark Tegwell[31] and the possible world realism of Princeton philosopher David Lewis.[32]

According to the many worlds argument in its most general form, if there are many such worlds the fine-tuning of our particular universe is explained because it is highly likely (or better), in this scenario, that some world will be fine-tuned for life. It follows from this that it is very likely that this world is fine-tuned.[33]

Paul Davies objects to multi-world explanations on the grounds of Ockham's razor, according to which metaphysical entities must not be multiplied beyond necessity. Davies claims that explanations of fine-tuning which appeal to a designer are simpler than multi-world explanations. But in reply to Davies it could be noted that Ockham's razor refers not to how many entities of a certain kind there are, but how many kinds of entities there are. From this perspective, the multi-world hypothesis is superior because it postulates more of the same kind of thing, whereas the design argument postulates a different kind of entity.

The Inverse Gambler's Fallacy

A more serious objection is that of the atheist philosopher Ian Hacking, who in his article 'The Inverse Gambler's Fallacy'[34] claims that the multi-world explanation commits the so-called Inverse Gambler's Fallacy. Suppose that there is a random mechanism for rolling a pair of dice. On any one trial the chance that the device will throw a double six is one in thirty six. Hacking considers three possible chains of reasoning.

(1) Reasoning R: The more times the dice are thrown, the greater is the chance of getting at least one double six in the sequence of throws. This reasoning, says Hacking, is valid.

(2) Gambler's Fallacy: Suppose that the device has thrown the dice thirty-five times and has not got one double six. Since we know that in thirty-six throws the chance of getting at least one double six somewhere in the sequence is two-thirds, we might be willing to bet that the device

31. See Chown 1998.
32. Lewis 1986.
33. Smith (1986) discusses this kind of multi-world hypothesis.
34. Hacking 1987.

will throw a double six on the thirty-sixth trial. This reasoning is known as the Gambler's Fallacy. The fact that the device has been 'unlucky' so far does not make it any more likely that the very next throw will be 'lucky.' In fact, the probability that the device will throw a double six on the thirty-sixth throw is exactly the same as it was on every other throw — one in thirty-six. A string of unfavorable outcomes does not make a favorable outcome more likely.

(3) Inverse Gambler's Fallacy: Thirdly, imagine that a gambler walks into a casino and witnesses one trial, which results in a double six, and infers from this that the device has previously thrown many non-double six trials, because this would make it more likely that a double six should be thrown this time. This is what Hacking calls the Inverse Gambler's Fallacy. According to this reasoning, we infer that 'good luck' or a favorable outcome was preceded by a string of 'bad luck' or unfavorable outcomes.

It will be instructive to have a spatial example. Suppose that a coin is tossed ten times and that the coin lands heads on all ten tosses, against all probability ($\frac{1}{1024}$). How should we explain such an unlikely outcome? Should we infer that there are many rooms in which people are tossing coins ten times in a row? After all, in a large enough sequence of rooms, the chance that somebody somewhere will throw ten heads in a row is quite high. But this would be an example of the Inverse Gambler's Fallacy. It's clearly fallacious to think that the probability that I throw ten heads in a row is somehow greater given the multi-room hypothesis. Of course, the probability of throwing ten heads in a row is exactly the same no matter how many rooms there are. What does follow from the multi-room hypothesis is that if the number of rooms in which people are tossing coins is large enough, then it is probable that at least one person will throw ten heads in a row. That is 'reasoning R.' However, it does not follow from the 'multi-room hypothesis' that any particular person is more likely to throw ten heads in a row. The probability that any one person in particular should throw ten heads in a row remains the same, that is, $\frac{1}{1024}$.

Let's see how the Inverse Gambler's Fallacy applies to M, the multi-worlds hypothesis. Hacking claims that in attempting to explain the fine-tuning of the universe, the multi-world hypothesis commits the Inverse Gambler's Fallacy as follows: According to the multi-world hypothesis, the probability that our universe should be fine-tuned for life F, given that the multi-world hypothesis is true, is much greater than the probability of fine-tuning alone. That is,

$$P(F|M) \gg P(F).$$

This is not the case, however. Even if there exists a multitude of worlds, this does not make it any more probable that our world is tuned as it is, any more than the fact that there many rooms in which people toss coins makes it more probable that a particular person will throw ten heads in a row. The truth is that the probability that our universe should be fine-tuned for life, given that the multi-world hypothesis is true, is equal to the probability of fine-tuning alone. That is,

$$P(F|M) = P(F).$$

On the theory of explanation that says that the hypothesis must raise the probability of the evidence, the multi-world explanation does not explain why our world is fine-tuned for life.

What role does 'reasoning R' play here? According to reasoning R, if there are many worlds it is very probable that some world or other will be fine-tuned for life. Reasoning R tells us that some world or other will be fine-tuned on the multi-world hypothesis. However there is a difference between assertions about this world and assertions about some world. Our evidence is not just that *some* world is fine-tuned, but that *this* world is, and that's what requires explanation.

We have considered the multi-world hypothesis M as an alternative to the hypothesis of the existence of a designer — God. The basic idea that we have been considering is that if we can appeal to M, the fine-tuning of this universe is adequately explained because given M, it is highly probable that our world is fine-tuned. As we have seen, this commits the Inverse Gambler's Fallacy. Hypothesis M in fact does not render the evidence (the fine-tuning of this universe) any more probable. What it does do is make it more likely that there is some world somewhere that is fine-tuned for life. It follows from this that if we had independent evidence that these worlds existed, then we could conclude that (as in the lottery example) the fine-tuning of the universe does not require explanation but can be put down to chance.[35]

Hacking claims that the hypothesis of the Wheeler worlds also com-

---

35. Smith (1986) discusses several possible physical reasons that we may have for countenancing the existence of many worlds.

mits the Inverse Gambler's Fallacy in its attempt to explain the fine-tuning of the universe. But in fact, the existence of Wheeler worlds does not make the fine-tuning of this universe more probable, because

$$P(F|W_W) = P(F).$$

The hypothesis of Wheeler worlds does make it more probable that some world or other in the chain should be fine-tuned for life. But this is not the same as saying that this world is likely to be fine-tuned. So the Wheeler version of the multi-world hypothesis also does not explain the fine-tuning of this universe.

But when it comes to the Carter worlds hypothesis (there exists a string of infinitely many worlds in which every possibility or configuration is, in fact, instantiated) Hacking comes to a different conclusion, because it involves a deductive line of reasoning. It is not a matter of probability that there be a fine-tuned world, but rather this follows deductively from the Carter worlds hypothesis. Because this step is deductive, this hypothesis does not commit the Inverse Gambler's Fallacy (which is a fallacy of probabilistic reasoning).[36] Therefore Hacking concludes that Carter worlds can explain the fine-tuning of the universe and are therefore a viable alternative to the design argument.

However, there is a problem with this argument. The existence of Carter worlds does not entail that that finely tuned world will be our world. Hacking appears to be thinking that if there did exist a finely tuned universe somewhere in the sequence, it would be us. But who is the 'us' to whom Hacking refers? A collection of disembodied souls, hovering over the universes, waiting to be instantiated in an appropriately tuned world (as John Leslie puts it)? The mistake is not exactly the Inverse Gambler's Fallacy, but it is similar in an important respect.

This point can be illustrated by returning to the firing squad example. Suppose there exists a string of executions, rather than just one. In this sequence every possible combination of events is instantiated. We can ask whether or not the existence of the infinite sequence of executions makes it any more likely that one particular person should survive. If we think that it does, we are committing the Inverse Gambler's Fallacy or, at least, something related to it.

36. Hacking 1987, p. 339.

The Observer Selection Effect

A standard reply to Hacking's argument is that it overlooks the importance of the observer selection effect.[37] F is explained by the existence of multiple universes which make it probable that some world is fine-tuned, *together with* the fact that we know we are here now, which means that our universe is that fine-tuned world.[38] For example, Ernan McMullin writes,

> If one adopts a many-universe model, where a multiplicity of actual universes co-exist, each realizing a different set of initial conditions and (perhaps) a different relationship between the physical constants, then the fact that we find ourselves in a universe apparently 'fine-tuned' for our existence requires no further explanation. All (or many) of the other universes *have* been realized, and we, of course, are in the one that permits (it need not necessitate) our existence. Provided the other universes are actual and not just possible, the improbability has been removed.[39]

Unless the explanandum has changed, the idea seems to be that a two-step inference is needed:

> Step 1: The multiple universes hypothesis M makes it more probable that there is some world that is fine-tuned.
>
> Step 2. The observer selection effect (OS) shows us why the existence of some fine-tuned universe entails F, that this universe is fine-tuned.

The rationale of the two step strategy seems to be that M by itself falls short of raising the probability of F, so that OS is needed to go the rest of the distance; and that OS doesn't work by itself, it needs something else to get it going (or else M would be superfluous).

Step 1 is valid, but does not explain F, as we have seen. Step 2, however, violates the requirement that effects don't explain their causes. In an earlier section we saw that the reasoning 'that we are here now explains F' violates this requirement. The difference with OS is that we appeal to our

37. See, for example, Leslie 1988.
38. Leslie 1988.
39. McMullin 1993, p. 380.

existence to 'select' the fine tuned universe out of many universes. But OS contains as a crucial part of the explanans a feature — the existence of observers — that is the effect of rather than the cause of the explanandum F. And since OS commits that fallacy then so too does OS plus M, since that must also appeal to an effect of F, where the effect — the existence of observers — is essential to the explanation (because M is not sufficient on its own).

Suppose gangsters force you into this game: you are to draw three balls, with replacement, from a box containing 99 black balls and one red ball. If you draw the red ball three times you will be allowed to live, but otherwise you will be shot dead. Suppose, with a probability of one in a million, you draw three red balls and live. It's no explanation of this outcome to hypothesize that there are innumerable gangster games going on around the world, the vast majority of which end in the victims' death, because the existence of such gangster games makes it no more likely than otherwise that you will draw three red balls and live. That probability remains exactly as it was without the many games hypothesis — one in a million.

This example involves an observer selection effect. If there are very many games, then probably someone gets three reds and lives. Then, given that someone survived the gangster game, since you are here now you must be that someone. Clearly this does not explain why you drew three reds.

A different kind of example is commonly offered[40] in defense of the view that multiple universes plus observer selection explains the fine-tuning of this universe. These examples are of the following form. In a second gangster game, the gangsters put you in a cell and tell you that over the next week they will play a sequence of at least one game (three ball draw with replacement from the box with 99 black and 1 red), and maybe more, and instead of killing the participant(s) they make a record of the result. At the end of the week they will free you if someone got three reds, otherwise they will shoot you. As it happens, at the end of the week they free you.

In this case you should infer that many games were played, because on the hypothesis of one game your probability of release is one in a mil-

---

40. Leslie 1988, p. 270; McGrath 1988, p. 265; Whitaker 1988. (Note, however, that Leslie appears to reject the assumption that explanans must raise the probability of the explanadum, so this point does not apply to him.)

lion, of two games two in a million, and so on; on the hypothesis of a very large sequence your release is quite probable. The existence of many games makes it more probable that someone will get three reds.

But this is not the observer selection effect. OS says that since you are alive, then you must be the one who survived the gangster game. But this example brings in a *mechanism* by which any success in the sequence brings about my success.[41] You don't need to assume that you are here; you deduce that you are here from the fact that someone drew three reds. For this reason it does not violate the requirement that effects don't explain their causes.

The key question is, does the multiple worlds scenario resemble the first gangster game or the second? The answer is clearly the first. There is no mechanism by which success somewhere in the sequence results in our success. To have an analogy with the second gangster case we need something like the supposition noted above that 'we' are disembodied souls floating through the ethereal regions of hyperspace seeking a world which is fine-tuned, in which we can find a home. That scenario is not part of the standard multiple universes hypotheses.

But fallacies are not just mistakes; they are seductive mistakes. They have some feature that tempts people to fall for them, so an account of a fallacy needs not only to show the error, it also needs to explain why it is seductive. The inverse gambler's fallacy confuses the probability of X on any trial with the probability of X on a particular trial, when the trials are independent. We need to explain why people might make such an elementary error.

It cannot be an exact inverse of the lure of the Gambler's Fallacy, that is, the repeated failure to get a successful outcome. It would not have that lure had there been an occasional success already. So since multi-world hypotheses do not appear to insist that there is not more than one fine-tuned universe, it seems that their lure is not the inverse of that of the gambler's fallacy. So why is it seductive?

I offer the following possibly-why explanation. In the case of the gangster game no one is tempted to commit the fallacy. The temptation comes only when we are dealing with universes. The reason may be that gangster games are situated in a spatiotemporal, and causal, context so that no one is tempted to confuse the fact that *someone* drew three reds with the

41. Roger White calls this the 'converse selection effect.'

fact that *you* drew three reds. The 'someone' could be in any number of easily imagined contexts, which almost certainly differ from your context. In the case of universes, there is no spatiotemporal or causal context to help us distinguish the fact that some world is fine-tuned from the fact that this world is fine-tuned. We are tempted for this reason then to think that if some world is fine-tuned, then this world is that world.

Denial of the Need for Explanation

Does this mean that the multi-world hypothesis has no role to play in explaining the fine-tuning of the universe? Perhaps not.

Let's return to the lottery example. There is no need to explain the fact that a certain person won the lottery since somebody had to win and the outcome that a certain person won is just as improbable as any other person winning. So if we know there is a random mechanism at work then we don't think there is a need for explanation.

But the difference between the lottery and the multi-world hypothesis is that in the case of the lottery we already know that there is a random mechanism at work, which is why it is no surprise that someone or other wins the lottery. However, in the case of the multi-world hypothesis, an improbable event occurs and we infer from this a multi-world hypothesis in order to explain that improbable event. But we do not know, prior to the occurrence of that improbable event, that there exists a multitude of worlds.

However, it could be argued, in the case of the fine-tuning of the universe, that if we already knew on independent grounds that there did exist many universes, then although the fact that our universe is fine-tuned for life remains improbable it is no longer surprising. The fine-tuning has not been explained, but the need for explanation has been removed. Just as the demand for explanation is removed in the lottery case (because after all, someone had to win), it is also removed in the fine-tuning case (because after all, some world was likely to be fine-tuned). If we have independent grounds to believe that our world is part of a random mechanism, the need for explanation of fine-tuning disappears.

If we accept this, what should we conclude about the anthropic design argument for the existence of God? It seems that if an independent case can be made for the existence of multiple worlds then, as in the lottery case, the fine-tuning of the universe would not stand in need of explanation. Further, even if the anthropic design argument is successful, it will always be left open to the possibility of being superseded by the advance of science. This means that the anthropic version of the design argument is open to the god of the gaps objection.

In fact, there does seem to be an increasing weight of theoretical reasons for supposing our universe is one of many random trails. The inflationary model of the big bang in effect shows how a quantum fluctuation (in which large amounts of mass can be produced from nothing when there is a corresponding amount of negative energy in the form of a gravitational field) can produce a universe as large as ours by rapid expansion in the first fraction of a second of the big bang — by a factor of 10^{25} in 10^{-30} seconds.[42] In the chaotic version of Andre Linde in 1983,[43] 'bubbles' arising randomly separate to form disconnected mini-universes of different configurations.[44] If this kind of model is right, then our universe is produced by a lottery-style mechanism, and then we may need to say that there is no need to explain the fine-tuning of our universe.

This conclusion assumes that all possible outcomes for a world are to be treated equally. But are all outcomes equal, so that no matter which outcome we get, no explanation is required? It would seem not. If you draw a royal flush randomly from a fair deck of cards you might not look for any explanation, after all, you had to get some sequence of five cards, and any particular sequence is as improbable as any other. But you probably would start to look for an explanation if that happened several times in a row. As James Bond said, "Once is chance; twice happenstance; three times is enemy action!" Or if the lottery proprietor's daughter won the lottery twice, people might demand an explanation. So it seems that some improbable states of affairs do require explanation, whilst others do not.

How do we decide which improbable event require explanation? Suppose that you arrive in an uninhabited country, and come across a group of apple trees on a hill. It just so happens that the apple trees are in a perfect ten by ten grid. Does this state of affairs require explanation? There is nothing about the nature of apple trees or hills that entails that the trees should be in such a formation. Should we say that the apple seeds had to

42. Guth 1998, p. 14.
43. Linde 1987.
44. See Hawking 1988, ch. 8; Guth 1998.

fall in some pattern or other, and a ten by ten grid is no more improbable than any other distribution? Or should we think that this state of affairs does stand in need of explanation, that the country is not uninhabited after all, or something?

Take the case of a monkey, randomly hitting the keys of a typewriter. Imagine that at the end of an extended period of typing the monkey produces a complete Shakespearean sonnet. We could calculate the probability of this state of affairs (which would be extremely small). Should we attribute this to chance? After all, the monkey had to strike the keys in some improbable order or other. Or should we conclude that this state of affairs does require explanation, and examine the mechanism of the typewriter for monkey business? It seems that in this case, most people would demand some kind of explanation. It seems that it is in cases where there is something special about the outcome that sets it apart from others, that we think that an explanation is required.

It would seem that our universe with its fine-tuning for life is a perfect example of this of sort of special outcome. For example unlike any other world, it exhibits consciousness and intelligence. Here we have an objection to Gould's claim. Recall that Gould maintains that because the universe had to be some way or other, the fine-tuning of the universe is entirely due to chance, and therefore does not require explanation. The fact is however that sometimes we are simply dissatisfied with this kind of appeal to chance. There is something unsatisfactory about putting a world like ours down to chance. According to this view there is something special about our universe that sets it apart from other universes. Design explains this.

CHAPTER 7

God and Chance

This chapter considers a final area of putative conflict between science and religion, namely, the 'chance worldview.' It is thought by some that the existence of chance, allegedly proved in quantum physics, refutes the classical theist doctrine of providence. So in this chapter we consider the implications of Bell's Theorem for the relation between divine and natural causation.

The Chance Worldview

The French scientist Charles Ruhla concludes his book *The Physics of Chance* with the words, "this book will have achieved its aim if it can help the reader make the conceptual leap from commonsense to the wisdom of physics, and from determinism to chance."[1] But more probably, for better or worse, the conceptual leap has already been taken in our culture, and the chance worldview has already taken hold of the popular mind, partly through the recent popularizing physicists mentioned in the previous chapter.

The essential element of the chance worldview is a metaphysical claim, namely, that our universe is intrinsically chaotic in the sense that its development from moment to moment is sometimes a matter of chance. In other words, the world does not know in full detail where it is going

1. Ruhla 1992, p. 214.

170

next. This is a metaphysical claim in the sense that it is a broad question about the nature of reality, although not in the sense that it is not an empirical question, since it does contend that contemporary science indeed provides justification for this central metaphysical claim.

The chance worldview, being a worldview, involves other dimensions in addition to its central metaphysical claim. It also embodies attitudes towards knowledge, power, purpose, and human decision making. Concerning knowledge, it involves a skepticism about our ability to predict the future: If the world itself doesn't know where it's going, then neither can we humans. Further, if the world to some extent is unpredictable, then it's also to some extent uncontrollable, and not amenable to our having power over it. If taking a certain medicine will either cure me or have a side effect and the difference is a genuine matter of chance, then I don't have power to use the medicine to control the outcome. Thus chance limits humanity's capacity to exercise power over nature. Concerning purpose, it is thought that if there was no reason why something occurred the way it did, then that occurrence had no purpose, and therefore chance events have no purpose. Random events can't be random and at the same time be deliberate. Decision-making also is necessarily affected. If there are inbuilt limits to our ability to predict and control the future, then we need to learn to make the most of this situation and follow decision strategies that allow for genuine chance. Special navigation strategies may be called for. Philosophers, economists, and social scientists working on what is known as 'game theory' have indeed developed such strategies.

The chance worldview is not new to humanity; the concept of chaos in the cosmos can be found in ancient Greek and Babylonian cultures, while many others have viewed the world as intrinsically mysterious and unpredictable. However, the chance worldview, in our intellectual history, stands in quite stark contrast to the 'rational worldview,' which has dominated Western thought since the seventeenth century. The seventeenth-century philosopher Leibniz, for example, held that the world is a designed product of God, with every part fitting in for a purpose. Leibniz' philosophy is built on the Principle of Sufficient Reason, according to which everything has a reason why it is the way it is rather than some other way.[2] According to Leibniz, God created the world in the beginning with its entire purpose in mind, and then the world developed according to the natu-

2. Leibniz 1975b.

ral deterministic laws that God had set for it. A deterministic view of the world has held sway until fairly recently.

The nineteenth century witnessed the rise of probability in science, but this is not necessarily a blow to determinism, because probability can be interpreted as a matter of ignorance — meaning just that we don't know what the underlying reasons and causes are. So, we know that there's a 50% chance that if I'm a heavy smoker I'm going to die of some smoking-related disease, but we don't think that that's a matter of our world being chancy. We think, rather, that there are certain factors that we simply don't know about, which is why we invest money into research to find out what those factors are. Just because there is probability in science does not mean that we have moved away from a rational worldview.

By contrast, the twentieth century saw the rise of something philosophers call 'objective single-case chance.' This is where the state of a system together with all the laws of nature fail to fix what the subsequent state will be. Objective single-case chance is a probability that can't be interpreted as being just a matter of our ignorance and as having underlying causes. It was widely held that quantum mechanical probabilities are objective single case chances. So, for example, if this particular atom has a 50 percent chance of decaying in the next sixty seconds, then that is an objective chance, because there are no underlying factors about that atom that determine exactly when it will decay. If it decays after thirty seconds, then there's no reason why it decayed then rather than a bit earlier, or rather than a bit later. The probability is the full story; there are no further factors underlying it, according to the standard view on quantum physics. Then chance is inherent in the basic nature of microscopic processes.[3]

How does a theist respond to this kind of development? Arthur Koestler, not a theist, said, "As long as chance rules, God is an anachronism."[4] And R. C. Sproul, a Christian, writes in his 1994 book *Not a Chance,*

> The mere existence of chance is enough to rip God from his cosmic throne. . . . If chance existed, it would destroy God's sovereignty. If God is not sovereign, he is not God. If he is not God, he simply *is* not. If chance is, God is not. If God is, chance is not. The two cannot coexist by reason of the impossibility of the contrary.[5]

3. See Dowe unpublished ms.
4. In Sproul 1994.
5. Sproul 1994, p. 3.

Clearly what's at issue here, to Sproul, is God's sovereignty, and in particular, God's work of providence. If he is right and if quantum mechanics is true, then modern science refutes the providence of God. Then providence and chance are mutually exclusive. So we now turn to the issue of providence.

Providence

Providence is a theological concept concerned with the continuing action whereby God preserves and directs the world. At least since John Calvin it has been common for theologians to distinguish, under the heading of 'providence,' the preservation of the world, whereby God upholds all things, from its government, whereby God directs and rules over creation. Government is not just a statement of God's power and the fact that there is no one to rival or to usurp it. It is a statement that God actually exercises control over all areas of creation — over the forces of nature, over the animal world, over the destiny of nations and of governments, over the circumstances of our lives, and even over our inner thoughts, beliefs, and desires.

According to Calvin, providence is absolute in the sense that it extends to every single detail of the universe. In the *Institutes* Calvin writes, "Single events are so regulated by God and all events so proceed from his determinate counsel, that nothing can happen fortuitously."[6] Calvin has a pastoral reason for this that he develops at length: we human beings get important comfort from the knowledge of God's sovereignty.

An absolute or completely deterministic providence means that every event and every aspect of every event is directed by God. This involves at least three claims. The first is that God is the necessary cause of every event and every aspect of every event. If A is the necessary cause of B, then without A, B wouldn't have happened. On this view, no event in our universe would happen if it weren't for God. This is part of the idea of God being the sustainer of the world. If God sustains the world at every instant, then that means that every event that happens wouldn't happen without God. If God withdrew from the world, none of it would happen.

The second claim is that God is a sufficient cause of every event and every aspect of every event. If A is the sufficient cause of B, then if A occurs

6. Calvin 1949, p. 176.

B will occur. A sufficient cause is the full cause, or the active cause — the thing which, when it happens, will ensure that the effect will happen. This doesn't make it a necessary cause, as there may be alternative ways to ensure that something happens. A sufficient cause is a kind of motor cause, the thing that actually directs the event and makes it happen.

The third claim, which is sometimes overlooked in modern discussions (although it was very well understood in premodern times), is that God provides the complete reason. This is not something that can be understood in terms of a motor cause, or a mechanical reason, or a causal chain. Sufficient reason in this sense concerns the purpose for something, which involves intentionality — somebody has a specific intention or purpose for the event. To say that God is the complete reason for every event and every aspect of every event in our universe is to say that God has a special purpose for everything, a special reason in mind for bringing about this particular event.[7] This is to be contrasted with the idea of an accident or chance event in Aristotle's sense, that is, an event that doesn't have a purpose.

There is certainly more to absolute providence than just these three things, but these are the elements that are relevant here. It is usual to contrast providence with deism, and in particular the idea that God created a world but one way or another does not have continued involvement in it. For example, one version of deism we might dub 'uncaring deism,' according to which God is the creator but not the sustainer of the world (creating a world at the start that will survive left by itself) and does not necessarily have a complete reason for creating things the way they are. On this view God may well be a sufficient cause of the present state of the universe, because the universe is thought by deists to be deterministic; God's having created it a certain way and given it certain laws ensures that it evolves in a certain way. But God created it without much caring what was going to happen later on. According to uncaring deism, God may have had some purposes in creating the world but didn't have a particular interest in some of the things that are going to happen in it — for example, the events and circumstances in our individual lives. So it is untrue, according to uncaring deism, that there is a complete reason for everything that happens.

This view can be contrasted with what could be called 'caring deism.'

---

7. This is not to be taken to mean that God does not observe the distinction between means and ends. I thank an anonymous referee for pointing this out.

Like its counterpart, caring deism holds that God is (in a deterministic universe) the sufficient cause of everything that happens but not the necessary cause, because the universe has its own power to continue to exist by itself. But caring deism holds that God does actually have a complete reason for everything. So, in creating the world, God looked forward to see what was going to happen, and created it so as to ensure that it came out a certain way. Having set it up like that, with that concern for what was going to happen in the future, God is able just to let it go and it will run on its own. Thus it is 'caring' because God has a concern about what is going to happen; but it is still deism because God is able to withdraw and doesn't have to sustain the world.

I mention both versions to bring out the point that what is at issue in deism is whether God has to sustain the world — that is, whether it can exist and have its being independently of God. The theologian M. J. Erickson gives the analogy of a power tool.[8] Some power tools are such that when you let go of the trigger they continue to run; others are such that when you let go, they stop, so you can't put them down and walk away and expect them to continue going. The tool that keeps going is like the universe according to deism, and the tool that stops when you leave it is like the universe according to providence.

Three Models of Providence

In philosophy there are at least three models of absolute providence, or divine determinism (all of which are rivals to deism): occasionalism, concurrence, and a third model devised by Leibniz. One of the key issues depends on the difference between a direct and indirect cause. An indirect cause is one in which there is an intermediate link between a cause and its effect. If I tread on Tim's toe and he yells out, and Derek drops his glass because he is startled, then when I trod on Tim's toe I caused Derek's dropping the glass and breaking it. I am not the direct cause, because there are a number of links in between, but I am the indirect cause. This distinction helps us to see that there are different ways to think about God's absolute providence.

The first position is occasionalism, proposed most famously by

8. Erickson 1983.

Nicolas Malebranche, the seventeenth-century French philosopher.[9] According to Malebranche, God does everything directly. God is the direct, not indirect, cause of every event that ever happens in the universe. Strictly speaking, created things don't ever actually cause anything. When a billiard ball hits another one, it is not that the billiard ball had the power to make something happen; it is actually God that makes it happen every time. Likewise, it's not that I'm actually making this book fall if I give it a shove; really what's happened is that God made the shove happen, and God made the book fall. Nature has no real power — everything is due only to God. What we call causes are really just the occasions of God's action.

The second alternative is called concurrence; it was promoted by scholastic philosophers and by more recent theologians such as Louis Berkhof.[10] Concurrence is the idea that every event has two concurrent, sufficient, direct causes: a divine, or primary, direct cause — that is, God, who is the primary cause of everything that happens; and also a real, natural, or secondary direct cause, such as my decision, or the billiard ball moving. So any event has two direct concurrent causes. This leads to a number of problems; for example, over-determination — that an event has two sufficient causes, which raises the problem that if God is a necessary cause then natural cause can't be sufficient, or, conversely, if the natural cause is sufficient then God is not a direct necessary cause.

The third view, which I want to focus on, is due to Leibniz.[11] According to Leibniz, God created the world at the beginning complete with all of its causal powers and laws of nature. Since then, the world has evolved deterministically, but not independently of God because God sustains everything in its being and in its causal power. The world has its own power, given and sustained by God, and God doesn't need to make every step happen directly. So God is not the direct cause of every event, but rather the indirect sufficient cause of every event.

9. Malebranche 1980. See Dowe unpublished.

10. Berkhof 1938, p. 56; and Mascall 1956, pp. 195-202.

11. See, for example, Leibniz 1975a; Dowe 1996c. This approach to providence was not original to Leibniz; it can be found in various guises in Medieval philosophy; for example, the Molinists held that God controls free actions in that God knows ('middle knowledge') what free agents will do in given circumstances, although those acts are not dependent on God's will; and therefore God can plan and direct the universe accordingly. Whether this counts as absolute providence in my sense depends on what counts as 'causation' and 'sufficient reason.'

On this view God also has a sufficient reason for everything. Before creation, God considered all the possibilities that could happen for the entire history of the universe. On the strength of that, God created the world such that the universe, considered over its entire history, would turn out to be the best of all possible worlds, the best of all the possibilities. So God created the universe looking forward to the details of its future development, creating everything exactly the way it is for specific reasons. In this way God has an intimate interest in everything that happens in the universe from beginning to end.

Yet some people harbor concerns that providence defined in this way is ultimately a veiled form of deism.[12] One problem is that there seems to be a kind of temporal distance — God is supposed to be involved in my life at every step, but appears on this model to be distant in time. But Leibniz is no deist; on this theory God *is* involved in individuals' lives. Despite seeming removed, God has considered every last detail and has designed the world out of concern about exactly what happens. As an analogy, suppose God did something from a spatial distance. Imagine, for example, that you are lying in the bush having a snooze. A tiger snake slithers up and is about to bite you, when suddenly a neutrino arrives from outer space, just at the right time, and enters the brain of the snake and zaps something there that makes the snake turn away and go off. Now, virtually all conventional theists will agree that this is an example of absolute and special providence — an example of God having orchestrated things so that a particular neutrino would arrive from a star right across the other side of the universe.

If God can organize things from a spatial distance, then God can organize things from a temporal distance as well (as indeed must have been the case with the neutrino). The key idea is that God is interested in what is happening to you and has arranged things so that they will happen in the way that they are intended to happen for you at each moment of your life.[13]

---

12. van Inwagen 1988, p. 215, n. 4.

13. And if you think about God as outside time, which is the classical way to think that goes back to Augustine, then it doesn't really seem to be relevant. We don't think God is over there at that side of the universe just because God sent that neutrino, any more than to believe in providence you have to think that God is located right here. God is everywhere, outside of space rather than in it, and if you think about time like that, that God is outside of time and time is simply part of creation, then it doesn't really seem to matter much at what point God came into it.

The subsequent argument about chance will not depend on which of these three views is right; it will work for any of them. I will draw on the Leibnizian story later in this chapter, but any of them will do. So if you prefer one of the others, then just translate the argument into the terms of that other account.

Quantum Chance

'Chance,' as it is used here, refers to single-case objective chance — for example, the probability of an atom decaying in the next minute. If there is a genuine chance, then the state of the system right now does not fix what it will be in a minute's time. It could either have decayed or not decayed, and all the facts about it right now, together with all the laws of nature, do not fix which of those two states it will be in.

Determinism is connected to chance. Determinism is the view that the state of the universe right now, together with the laws of nature, fixes what the state of the universe will be at any subsequent time.[14] So if determinism is true, there is no chance in our universe. Conversely, if there is any chance in our universe then our universe is not deterministic. If there is quantum chance, then we live in an indeterministic world.

A common reaction to quantum chance is to say, "Well, look, it's got to be ignorance, it's got to be just that you don't know exactly what the full cause is. The scientists haven't found out what the causes are. But how could they prove that there really aren't any causes? That's ridiculous!" But there is a surprising and very powerful physical argument to say that it is not ignorance but genuine chance, and it has to do with a result in physics known as Bell's Theorem.

In physics one uses a state function to describe a system. A state function is a piece of mathematics that enables one to predict the results of measurements with a probability; for example that the probability of an atom decaying over one minute is one half. Many quantum physicists since Niels Bohr[15] say that the state function is complete — meaning that there are no relevant factors, apart from those described by the state function, that would give a deterministic account. If a state function that gives only

14. Earman 1986.
15. Bohr 1935.

178

probabilities is complete, then there must be genuine chance involved. Other physicists, among them Albert Einstein, rejected the claim that the state function is complete. In a famous paper called the Einstein-Podolsky-Rosen Paper,[16] written in 1935, Einstein argued that there must be other factors, called hidden variables, underlying the state function. "God," he famously noted, "does not play dice with the universe." For example, if the quantum mechanical state function gives a certain probability of a certain atom decaying in the next minute, and that atom does decay in that amount of time, there must be further factors which are going to tell you why, in this particular case, it did so. There must be hidden variables that we don't know about. So the state function is not complete.

But in 1964 the Scottish physicist John Bell published a result known as Bell's Theorem, which provided a way to test experimentally whether the hidden variable theories, or quantum mechanics, is correct.[17] He showed that the assumption that there are hidden variables underlying the statistical predictions of quantum mechanics that do not interact in a way that violates special relativity leads in certain cases to predictions different to those derived from the quantum mechanical state function. Experimental testing has conclusively shown that the predictions of the hidden variable theories are wrong. Thus it is argued that determinism has been proved to be false.

It may be a little difficult at first to conceive just how it could be proved that a certain description is the full story, and that there are no further factors to account for. This brings us to the central puzzle in the interpretation of quantum mechanics, which lies at the heart of the so-called Bell phenomenon. Instead of discussing the physics of this remarkable phenomenon, I propose to illustrate the central puzzle by giving an analogy concerning identical twins. This analogy is imperfect; I've deliberately simplified things in order to focus on the central puzzle. However, I hope to show that one does not need to know anything about physics in order to understand the really puzzling feature of Bell's Theorem.

Suppose there are identical twins from Sydney, Steve and Mark. One of these twins, Steve, moves to Hobart, where he falls foul of a mysterious disease and dies. It is reported that this disease is triggered by excessively cold weather, and a person with the condition will almost certainly die if

16. Einstein et al. 1935.
17. Bell 1964.

he or she is subjected to, say, about two or three days of continuous cold. This exotic disease has become known as "freezerphobia." The other twin, Mark, stays in Sydney, where he is hit by a bus and dies.

Let's call putting a person in Hobart "the cold test." Now, we've heard rumors from scientists that when a pair of twins go to Hobart then often they both die. In fact, it is reported that there is a one to one correlation, namely, that if two identical twins are both cold-tested, one dies if and only if the other dies. On this evidence it's reasonable to think that this disease is genetic, and that's why we get this correlation between identical twins. This means, for any pair of identical twins, if we subject both twins to the cold test — that is, take them both to Hobart — then if one dies from freezerphobia then the other will too, simply because the disease is genetic and identical twins share the same genetic makeup. Therefore, we might reason, given what we know about Steve, we can infer that Mark also had freezerphobia, even though we can't actually test that, since he's dead, having been hit by a bus.

So we have formed a kind of theory, a mechanistic theory. We think the correlation is due to an underlying mechanism — genetic, probably — which can be traced back to a condition of the unsplit egg from which both twins were produced. That is, we suppose that the correlation has what philosophers call a common cause explanation.[18] It's a reasonable hypothesis, and the reasoning seems to be common sense.

Let's move now from this particular case of our friends Steve and Mark, and look instead at what the scientists are doing about this. In fact, we find already established at St. Vincent's Hospital in Sydney the so-called 'Freezerphobia Register Of Scientific Terminations' or 'FROST' for short. (The significance of the terms 'Scientific Terminations' will become clear shortly.) We find that the scientists have set up an experiment, and also that many of them already had formed a theory similar to our own commonsense idea of an underlying genetic mechanism, but of course they wanted to wait and see how the experiments turned out before they formed any firm beliefs about the matter.

Let's look at the experiment under four headings: the setup, the method, the results, and the interpretation. First, the experimental setup involves attracting pairs of identical twins from the general population to volunteer as participants. This is done by offering participants free trips

18. See Salmon 1984.

either to Hobart or to Dunedin in New Zealand. Two planes have been chartered, and observation cells have been set up in Hobart, Dunedin, and Sydney.

Second, the method has four steps. (1) A pair of identical twins are taken to Sydney airport. One twin is put on the Hobart plane, and one on the Dunedin plane, and when measures have been taken to ensure that there can be no further communication between the twins, both planes take off. (2) Once in the air, the Dunedin pilot tosses a coin; if it comes up heads she heads for Dunedin, but if it is tails she does a big loop and lands back at Sydney Airport. (3) On arrival at whatever destination, the subjects are locked up in the observation cells and are carefully monitored. (4) The scientists simply record whether the participants die. These four steps are followed for large numbers of identical twins.

The results of the experiment are divided into two groups, because there are two possible experiments done on a pair: they could end up in Hobart and Dunedin, or in Hobart and Sydney. Remember that it a matter of chance which of these two experiments is performed on a particular pair of twins. For the Hobart-Dunedin pairs, it is found that 62 percent of those who get to Hobart die, and 62 percent of those who get to Dunedin die. In each case the other 38 percent survive with no ill effects apart from occasional non-fatal cases of frostbite, flu, and chilblains. Further, it is noted that there is a one-to-one correlation among the ones who died: the 62 percent who died in Hobart were the siblings of the 62 percent who died in Dunedin (the result I referred to earlier). We should note here that the results so far are regarded by most of the scientists (but not all) as confirming the Genetic Mechanism Theory, because that theory predicts this one to one correlation. So far so good.

But for the Hobart-Sydney pairs, the results stun everyone. The scientists found that 45 percent of those who end up in Hobart died, while none of those who ended up in Sydney died. What's puzzling about that? What's puzzling is that 45 percent is not the expected result. One would have expected that figure to be about 62 percent, because that's what the genetic mechanism theory predicts. It should not make any difference to those heading for Hobart whether their twin goes to Dunedin or Sydney. If it is already set by your genes that you will die if cold-tested, then it is irrelevant whether your twin is cold-tested. These results are very puzzling, and this feature is parallel to the central puzzle in Bell phenomena.

So let's turn to the scientific interpretation of these freezerphobia results. First, let's look again at the Genetic Mechanism Theory. This theory is a deterministic, hidden variable theory. It says that there is a factor l that, if one identical twin has it, then the other does as well; and if a twin has factor l, then if she is subjected to the cold test, she will certainly die. Thus the condition of the twins back at the time of conception sets the results of the measurement, were it to be performed, and this condition is "hidden" in the sense that it does not manifest itself directly in the measurements. But the experimental results are a major setback for the Genetic Mechanism Theory, at least in its present form. In fact, the scientists all agree that the Genetic Mechanism Theory in its present from is refuted by these data, and so they abandon that theory. But with what can it be replaced?

Well, when the dust settles there are numerous differing views among the scientists. But the dominant group focuses on the mathematical description of the results of the various measurements. They hold that we should simply figure out the mathematical formula, called the state function, that describes all the results of all the measurements, both actual and possible. But we should not ask how to explain it. The state function should be regarded as a mathematical tool for making predictions about the results of measurements, and not as a pointer to underlying mechanisms. 'The state function is complete,' becomes their slogan. The truth is they had not been pleased with the way most scientists had interpreted the first part of the experiment and are feeling pretty smug about the way the second part has gone. In fact, they now claim that the results prove that the state function is complete.

The situation in quantum mechanics is analogous to this parable in a number of important ways. In particular, the situation in Bell setups seems to be such that the predictions of 'local realist' theories[19] run into conflict with the predictions of the quantum mechanical state function. Experiments conclusively support quantum mechanics over the local realist theories. But the local realist theories can be derived from very plausible assumptions. This difficulty, which Bell first articulated in 1964, is perhaps one the most startling conceptual problems in twentieth-century science. As one prominent scientist has said, "Anyone who's not bothered by Bell's Theorem has to have rocks in his head."[20]

If the state function really has been proved to be complete, then de-

19. See the influential presentation in d'Espagnat (1979).
20. Cited in Mermin 1991, p. 504.

terminism has been disproved. And if determinism is false then there is genuine chance in the world.

Chance and Providence

So what are the implications of the idea of chance for providence? Calvin said, "The providence of God as taught in Scripture is opposed to fortune and fortuitous causes."[21] But as we will see, it is a knee-jerk reaction simply to deny the no-hidden variables proof — as, for example, R. C. Sproul does in *Not A Chance*. His argument is that quantum mechanics is refuted because the idea of a quantum jump implies that a particle goes out of existence and comes back into existence, and that's a contradiction; therefore quantum physics is just nonsense.[22] But it seems that Sproul fails to come to grips at all with the force of the relevant physical argument — his appears to be little more than an automatic response.[23] Rather than a knee-jerk reaction, what is required here is a more careful consideration of the relationship between theology and science.

On the other hand, the judgment of William Brown in dismissing the problem altogether is too hasty: "The findings of the new physics," he claims, "do nothing to alter a biblical perspective of the world."[24] The first question that needs addressing is this: When we talk about chance, or indeterminism in the physical world, is this a claim restricted to the physical world, or does it apply to the action of God, as well? In the case of quantum chance, are we saying that the exact moment of decay is not caused by anything physical, or that it is not caused by anything including God? This is a question that has to be answered before one can draw any conclusions about the significance of chance for theology.

So, from the perspective of quantum physics, is it possible that God brings about the events that quantum mechanics deems to be the results of chance? There are two possible answers to this question — either it is possible or it isn't. Either it is possible both that an event is a matter of chance

21. Calvin 1949 pp. 172-73.
22. Sproul 1994, p. 44.
23. Actually, I believe there is a loophole in the no-hidden variables argument, and it has to do with backwards-in-time causation. But this is beyond the scope of this discussion, and in any case it's very controversial (see Dowe 1996a and Dowe forthcoming).
24. Brown 1990, p. 485.

and that God causes it, or it is the case that if an event is a matter of chance then it cannot be caused by God.

If the latter is true, then God does not cause any event caused by chance. Then the no hidden variable proof entails that God doesn't cause the quantum chance events. By proving there are no hidden variables we have proved that it's not the case that God has made it that the atom will decay now rather than at another time. Then chance refutes providence.

If the former is true, then we are allowing that God produces what, physically speaking, we call chance. On this alternative, the atom decays after twenty seconds and there's no physical reason, but it is possible that God brought it about that it would decay just at that time rather than at some other time. A further question then arises: does God *in fact* bring about the results of chance events? Donald Mackay for example, takes the view that not only is it possible that God causes chance events, but that this always happens. He holds that God is sovereign and directs all things and is the sufficient cause over all natural things, including chance events.[25]

Physical Chance, Divine Cause

According to John Polkinghorne, the fact that the chancy universe is what he calls 'open' is theologically significant, because it shows that (contra Leibniz) God allows the universe to have a degree of independence and maturity in itself.[26] Like children who, in order to grow up, must be allowed to make their own decisions, so also the universe is given a certain amount of independence. Secondly, Polkinghorne holds that an open universe allows creativity, and that it is actually God that is being creative. God acts in the quantum gaps, the open bits, creatively responding to the world somewhat like a chess grandmaster,[27] able to think very quickly about events and react to those developments, thus influencing the world to go a certain way. Polkinghorne's idea is that in the quantum gaps there is information transferring from God to the physical system, although energy doesn't flow. Thus chance becomes God's steering wheel.

But Polkinghorne's idea seems to involve a contradiction: God con-

25. MacKay 1988, pp. 197-211.
26. Polkinghorne 1986, p. 69. See also the review by Doye and others (1995).
27. Cited in Doye and others 1995, p. 136.

trols the chancy bits, he argues — but didn't the chancy bits bring independence to the world? If God is controlling them as well as the fixed bits, then there's no independence for the world. And, further, since God caused the fixed bits by his initial creation and ordering of the laws of nature, why is any further steering required? So in what sense is God guiding a world with its own independence? (Perhaps Polkinghorne means that some of the chancy bits are independent, and some of the chancy bits are used by God to turn things back again.)

These difficulties aside, if God directs the chancy developments in the universe, then chance is no affront to providence. If God directs the chancy bits in the way Polkinghorne envisages, then chance is just a causation that is hidden from us, as opposed to the more open direction that we can see in the laws of nature. This is not a new idea; it has been urged by theists throughout the twentieth century.[28]

But is this steering wheel model of chance possible in the light of quantum mechanics? In particular, does the no hidden variable proof prove that 'God didn't do it' — that quantum chance effects have no cause, physical or divine? If quantum mechanics proves that God is not the hidden variable, then it seems that science refutes absolute providence. So is science incompatible with absolute providence?

The answer is no. The reason is that there's an assumption in the Bell proof that is called 'locality.' Locality assumes that two separated things cannot signal to each other faster than the speed of light, which follows from Einstein's special theory of relativity. And so, in the freezerphobia case, if the twins are separated far enough and the decision whether to go to Dunedin is made late enough, then one may assume that the Hobart twin's chances of dying are not being influenced by that choice. For example, one suggestion that might come to mind is that there is some kind of telepathy going on, so that the twin who has gone to Hobart knows by (not entirely reliable) telepathy whether her sibling has gone to Dunedin and is squealing in pain, or whether she is in Sydney enjoying herself. Locality rules this out.

But the locality requirement wouldn't apply to God. If God really were involved in bringing about events in the way that we are considering in this suggestion about absolute providence, then it would be incoherent to suppose that God is going to be subject to the locality restriction. The reason is simply that God is not located in space. If God knows what hap-

28. See Mascall 1956, pp. 200-02.

pens in the world, and can act at locations in this world, then we can suppose that God deliberately brings about one event knowing instantaneously of the occurrence of another, distant to the first, without requiring a locality-violating physical signal. So the proof simply doesn't apply in the case of God. It only applies to physical causes, which are subject to the locality condition. So, the evidence for quantum mechanical chance is not evidence against absolute providence, because of this locality loophole.

But another question arises here, namely, why does God produce the strange correlations uncovered by Bell? Why would God want to do that? It's one thing to use chance as a steering wheel, but that doesn't explain why the weird correlations uncovered by Bell phenomena are necessary.

One possible answer is that they are there in order to leave a trace — a trace of God's existence, indeed of God's providence. Firstly, recall the Kalām Cosmological Argument: Everything that comes into existence has a cause of its coming into existence; the universe had a beginning in time; therefore there has to be something which is not part of the universe which is the creator of the universe, which brings about that first cause. By analogy with the Kalām Cosmological Argument, consider what we might call the Quantum Cosmological Argument (to my knowledge this has never been seriously proposed). The first premise is the Law of Causality — everything has to have a sufficient cause. The second premise is that there are genuine objective chances in quantum physics — there are things in our world that don't have a sufficient physical cause. So the conclusion is that there must be a non-physical cause — God — to bring about these events. Thus Bell's Theorem proves God.

I am not seriously proposing this argument, because the Law of Causality itself is very hard to offer any argument for; it's one of those fundamental assumptions that can't really be proved. It is commonly held that quantum chance shows that it is false. I merely point out an alternative: that the Law of Causality is true because there is a non-physical cause.

Physical Chance, No Divine Cause

Suppose now that where there is objective chance, there is no cause, physical or divine. It then follows from the existence of chance that God is not in complete control of the universe. How serious is this theologically?

Here we can consider a model proposed by the American philosopher Peter van Inwagen[29] that is similar to the model of Leibniz, but with the addition of objective chance (an addition, of course, which Leibniz himself would not have accepted).

According to van Inwagen, God's purposes for the universe are achieved by controlling less than everything. The purposes that God has for the universe do not extend to absolutely every fine detail. So, at the beginning God sets up the laws and initial conditions — and possibly the laws involve probability — and then God sustains things in their causal powers. But because chance is involved, not everything has sufficient cause; God merely uses the initial conditions to ensure that certain things obtain. So, for example, van Inwagen thinks that God wants to ensure that there are people but doesn't need to ensure that there are particular people doing particular kinds of things. So he sets up a universe which will ensure that there will be conscious beings, but he doesn't need to do much more than that because his purpose is just to have conscious life one way or another.

This is limited providence, not absolute providence. It would certainly conflict with the kind of providence that I described earlier, in which God is involved in every last part of individuals' lives. But if you take a weaker version of van Inwagen's model and you limit providence to a lesser extent, then van Inwagen's idea can closely approximate a theologically adequate providence while including chance. To see this we turn briefly to the idea of coincidence.

Meaningless Coincidences

A coincidence as I will here understand it is a situation in which two or more events occur together against all probability and with no apparent reason why they have done so. For example, philosophers often tell a story about a mother who had a dream one night about a chandelier falling on her baby. Despite her husband's skepticism, she went into the child's room and moved his crib. Later that night there was a violent storm and the chandelier fell down, right where the baby would have been. If the conjunction of these two events — the woman's dream and the light falling —

29. van Inwagen 1988.

has no explanation then it is just a coincidence. If there is some explanation then it is not a coincidence at all.

Another example is the case in which a father watches in despair as his little daughter runs out onto a train track just as train is due to come around the corner — but then, for some reason, the train just stops. It couldn't have stopped because the engineer saw the child because it would have had to begin to stop before it turned the corner. What happened, it turns out, was that the driver had died suddenly of a heart attack and by chance had slumped onto the brake.

This is a coincidence only if there is no reason why the driver died at just the same time that the child wandered on to the track. Leibniz' Principle of Sufficient Reason and absolute providence both say that there are no accidents. Every event and every aspect of every event has a reason, so there are no coincidences. It is no coincidence that the train driver slumped just then — this is part of the world that God had set up from the beginning to be the best possible world, and part of that world was that that child would not die that way.

Coincidences aren't explained just if the two separate events each have a sufficient explanation. There may be a sufficient reason why the train stopped right then, in terms of the driver's condition and the way he was sitting. There also may be a sufficient reason why the child ran onto the track, in terms of the child's routine, character, and desires. But that each of the individual events has a sufficient reason does not mean that the coincidence has a reason. This requires a reason why the two things happen at the same time.

Consider now meaningless coincidences. The examples just considered both were meaningful, very important in the lives of the people concerned. But think of meaningless coincidences, such as a leaf falling from the tree outside my window just at the very instant I wrote the word 'baby' a few minutes ago. That's a coincidence — it's just as improbable as the train driver and the child. But it's also quite meaningless — who cares if a leaf falls just as I write 'baby'? Such meaningless coincidences occur all the time.

What, in the doctrine of special providence, requires that God has complete reasons for these kinds of coincidences? What reason is there in the Bible for thinking God has reasons for meaningless coincidence? For example, in the texts that Calvin adduces to prove the importance of this doctrine for comforting believers, none are about meaningless coincidences.[30] This suggests that the doctrine of absolute providence could be relaxed so that it does not apply to meaningless coincidences without affecting the theological significance of the doctrine. God controls all things that are of importance, but may not control all things that are of no importance to anyone. Then some things, such as the timing of the leaf's fall relative to my writing 'baby,' have no reason in God's mind. They are just accidents, coincidences. If this is true, chance events could occur where God does not determine the outcome, providing the outcome is not meaningful to anyone.

Then there is no reason theologically or biblically to assert that God does have complete reasons for absolutely every aspect of every event. Why should God have purposes for meaningless coincidences? But if this is the case, then, strictly speaking, absolute providence is false.

If quantum chance doesn't lead to meaningful happenings, God may choose not to control the outcome. So, there could be room for chance in an exactly analogous way to meaningless coincidences. If these chances — such as those about atom decays, for example — make no meaningful difference to anybody, then God has no need to control their outcomes in order to ensure the divine purpose is fulfilled. So, providing it doesn't impinge on meaningful things in people's lives, then it doesn't seem to be that chance without divine causation refutes providence. Absolute providence is relaxed, but not to any theologically significant degree.

However, some quantum chance may be humanly meaningful. For example, if chaos theory can amplify the quantum chances and affect our weather, maybe the results of atoms decaying will turn out to be humanly meaningful. This is an empirical matter that has yet to be properly settled. But if this is so, then some chances are humanly meaningful and that would mean that, given a strong view of providence, then one should have to infer that God at least causes some of the objective chances in the world.

Conclusion

So should theists be bothered by the chance worldview? Does chance refute providence? No. If chance exists then either it is caused by God (and that is allowed by Bell's Theorem) and this is no problem for providence

30. Calvin 1949, pp. 171-81.

and there's no conflict with science; or chance is not caused by God, in which case it's compatible with strong Calvinist providence providing it doesn't lead to meaningful consequences. Insofar as chance does lead to meaningful consequences, strong providence entails that God causes that chance.

CHAPTER 8

The Interaction of Science and Religion

It is now time to draw the threads of our discussion together, and to express some conclusions a little more explicitly. In my view the best way to make sense philosophically of the relation between science and religion in Western history is in terms of harmony. Although there are points at which, politically or socially, religious elements have impeded the progress of science, philosophically there is no strong reason to see religious belief as an intellectual impediment to science.

However, I have rejected strong forms of the independence account, according to which harmony between science and religion is achieved at the cost of interpreting either the scientific or religious project antirealistically. This leaves some form of an interaction account: that science and religion are to at least some extent mutually dependent.

Mutual Interaction

One way we have seen this mutual dependence is in the continuity of rationality and methodology. Inference to the best explanation, arguably a widespread, high-level tool in science, also operates in theorizing in the religious realm. We have seen it at work not only in the scientific arguments of Galileo and Darwin, but also in the arguments against antirealism, in the argument for theism based on the success of science, in the discussion of miracles, and in design arguments both biological and cosmological.

Thus we see not only a continuity of method, but also mutual points of relevance. Science informs us about the religious domain — how to interpret Scripture, evidence for the existence of God, and so on; and religion informs us about the scientific domain: that we can expect to understand the world, that we are designed to rule it, and so on.

To see this, it has been important to distinguish philosophical conflict from social conflict. We defined 'philosophical conflict' as a clash of beliefs or ideologies and 'social conflict' as an explicit and heated clash of interests within society. With this distinction firmly in mind we find remarkably little philosophical conflict in our case studies.

The social conflict in Galileo's case was not spurred by an intellectual problem in the religious tradition; the problem had already been resolved. In the case of Darwin the major intellectual issue concerned not biblical literalism but the design argument from biological adaptation. This was not a longstanding religious belief, but rather an eighteenth-century product of the development of biological science. Paley's *Natural Theology* was not a defense of traditional theology in anything but the broadest sense; rather, it was a scientific textbook with a philosophical emphasis. In any case, its argument did not hinder science, but in Darwin's case, proved to be an important factor in his arriving at the theory of natural selection: the design argument had helped to clarify what needed to be explained. The same can be said for Stephen Hawking. In the worse-case scenario for religion, in which history judges him to have successfully answered arguments for God from cosmology, then it still will be the case that such arguments spurred him on in his work, rather than hindered him.

But if the relationship between science and religion is one of harmony, there is still the question of what kind of harmony: independence or mutual interaction? I have argued that there is considerable interaction. For example, we saw in Chapter Three that belief in the image of God in humanity provided a powerful motivation and impetus for the development of science in the seventeenth century. If we were created with minds like God's we should therefore expect to understand the world which God has created. And if we have a God-given responsibility to govern that world we should therefore believe that humanity has the capacity to control nature, and consequently also expect to understand the world. Still further, if it turns out that we were right to expect to understand and control nature, as indeed it has, then that gives us a strong reason to believe that the original theological assumption of the image of God in humanity is correct.

This is but one example of the way science and religion interact, but it suffices to show that a complete independence view of the relation between science and religion cannot be right. Because of these kinds of considerations I conclude that the appropriate account of the relation is one of mutual interaction.

There is also another dimension to the interaction that has been prominent in our discussion, which concerns continuity in methodology — an issue to which we now turn.

Defeasibility and the God of the Gaps Objection

One of the marks of scientific knowledge is that it is defeasible, that is, open to revision. No scientific theory can be regarded as the final word, no matter how well confirmed and established it is today. There may yet be a different, even more accurate and successful theory to take its place at some time in the future. This is all the more true for the more speculative and tentative results of many arguments to the best explanation.

To some extent the same must be said in the religious area, if there is to be any continuity between the scientific and religious domains. But this is exactly what we have seen. Paley was right (rational) to infer the existence of a divine designer, for that was the best explanation available. However, once Darwin had articulated his theory of natural selection, and it became clear that it was a better explanation of biological adaptation, it was no longer rational to infer the existence of a designer just from adaptation.

The same can be said for the anthropic design argument. Provided there is no independent evidence for multiple worlds, we should infer the existence of a designer. However, once there is such independent evidence, then we need to face the question of whether there is a need for explanation.

This approach is open to the god of the gaps objection. According to this way of thinking, it is a mistake to believe in God on the grounds that doing so will explain some particular fact about nature, because such reasoning is open to refutation the moment subsequent scientific development uncovers perfectly good natural explanations for the facts in question (see Chapter Six). For example, if one's reason for believing in God had been the Paley argument, and one's conception of God had included the notion of a designer necessary to explain the phenomena, then when that reason is removed one's reason for belief is removed and one's conception of God is reduced.

However, this objection is faulty. It is true that further developments in cosmology may force us to rethink the argument from the fine-tuning, and indeed abandon it. But that is no reason to ignore it now. We must draw conclusions based on the evidence we have. All scientific reasoning works like that — it is by its nature defeasible. That it is defeasible is no reason to ignore the conclusions as we now see them. The same may sometimes be true of reasons for God. If the reason is removed at a later time, then unless that was our only evidence for God, that is no reason to think God does not exist, and should, logically, be no reason to doubt. On the other hand, if that reason were the only reason we had to believe in God, then where would we be if we ignored that reason? Certainly not with stronger faith. If the only reason we have for believing in God is removed, then why should we continue to believe? In my view we should follow Hume — if there is no evidence for the existence of God then it is not rational to believe in it.[1]

We should note, by the way, that in neither of these particular cases is there a traditional belief under attack from the progress of science. In both cases the design argument in question arose in its relevant form only because of recent developments in science. Paley's argument is a characteristically late eighteenth-century argument; the fine-tuning argument is a characteristically late twentieth-century argument. But traditional belief also falls under the same methodology, at least according to Augustine in his 'relevance' moments, because scientific progress also may throw light on how to interpret Scripture, including — in theory — traditional religious beliefs. But this does not seem to be what in fact occurred in the famous cases of the 'conflict' of science and religion.

A related objection is the view that such arguments as we have considered in this book are irreligious or irreverent. It leads us to trust human reason rather than have faith in God. Behind this objection lies a view that reason and faith are incompatible, that reason destroys faith necessarily. Frankly, I do not understand this idea of faith. If God does exist and did create the world, then it is most plausible that there might be reasons for thinking so. Why should it destroy anyone's faith to think about reasons?

Another version of this line of thought objects to the argument be-

1. For a contrary view see the papers in Plantinga and Wolterstorff 1983.

cause it establishes only the existence of a designer rather than the triune God revealed in the Christian Scriptures. The god of the argument is the wrong god, it is thought. But this thought also is based on an error. That the argument proves only the existence of a designer and not that the designer is, in fact, triune does not mean that the argument proves that the designer is not triune. In fact, the designer revealed by science is perfectly compatible with the God revealed by the Bible, who is powerful enough to fashion the entire world, and did so according to particular purposes, and whose purposes involved to some extent a special interest in the human race. That the heavens declare the glory of God does not mean that the heavens declare that God is to be worshiped a certain way; but we should not infer from this that the God whose glory the heavens declare is the wrong god. It is true that the anthropic argument will not settle, for example, whether Christianity or Islam is correct, but if correct it does show that one of these or something similar is right, and that atheism is not.

Conclusion

Throughout this book we have considered some major cases of alleged conflict between science and religion. We have also considered proponents of a range of positions on the relationship between science and religion. I have argued that an open-minded look at these case studies shows that the best account of the relation between science and religion is that they are in harmony, with a considerable amount of fruitful interaction. I have argued that in Western history religious belief as given in the Judeo-Christian tradition is neither incompatible with nor a hindrance to science; there is no philosophical conflict between the two. At very least, this is so in the cases of Galileo, Darwin, and Hawking.

Bibliography

Aquinas, T. 1973: "The Classic Cosmological Argument." In *Philosophy of Religion: Selected Readings,* edited by W. Rowe and W. Wainwright. New York: Harcourt, Brace, Jovanovich, pp. 117-123.

Armstrong, D. 1980: "Naturalism, Materialism and First Philosophy." In *The Nature of Mind and Other Essays,* edited by D. Armstrong. St Lucia: University of Queensland Press, pp. 149-165.

Augustine. 1961: *Confessions.* Middlesex: Penguin.

————. 1972: *City of God.* Harmondsworth: Penguin.

————. 1982: "The Literal Meaning of Genesis." In *Ancient Christian Writers: the Works of the Fathers in Translation,* edited by J. Quasten, W. Burghardt, and T. Comerford Lawler, T. New York: Newman Press, pp.xx-xx.

Ayer, A. 1936: *Language, Truth, and Logic.* Harmondsworth: Penguin.

Bacon, F. 1905: "The Great Instauration and The New Organon." In *The Philosophical Works of Francis Bacon,* edited by J. Robertson. London: Routledge, pp. 243, 386-87.

Barbour, I. G. 1966: *Issues in Science and Religion.* London: SCM.

Barlow, N., ed. 1958: *The Autobiography of Charles Darwin.* New York: Norton.

Barrow, J. and F. Tipler. 1986: *The Anthropic Cosmological Principle.* Oxford: Clarendon.

Beecher, H. 1885: *Evolution and Religion.* New York: Howard and Hulbert.

Bell, J. 1964: "On the Einstein Podolsky Rosen Paradox." *Physics* 1: 195-200.

Bellarmino, R. 1955: "Letter to Foscarini." In *The Crime of Galileo,* edited by G. de Santillana. Chicago: University of Chicago Press, pp. 98-100.

Berkhof, L. 1938: *A Summary of Christian Doctrine.* Edinburgh: Banner of Truth Trust.

196

Bibliography

Bohr, N. 1935: "Can Quantum Mechanical Description of Physical Reality be Considered Complete?" *Physics Review* 48: 696.

Boltzer, R. and S. Armstrong, eds. 1998: *Environmental Ethics: Divergence and Convergence,* Boston: McGraw Hill.

Boyd, R. N. 1984: "The Current Status of Scientific Realism." In *Scientific Realism,* edited by J. Leplin. Berkeley: University of California Press, pp. 41-82.

Brennan, A. 1988: *Thinking About Nature: An Investigation of Nature, Value and Ecology.* Athens: University of Georgia Press.

Briggs, J. C. 1996: "Bacon's Science and Religion," in *The Cambridge Companion to Bacon,* edited by M. Peltonen. Cambridge: Cambridge University Press, pp. 172-99.

Brown, W. 1990: "Quantum Theology: Christianity and the New Physics." *Journal of the Evangelical Theological Society* 33: 477-87.

Butterfield, H. 1931: *The Whig Interpretation of History,* London: G. Bell.

Calvin, J. 1846: *Commentary on the Book of Psalms,* Volume II. Edited by J. Anderson. Edinburgh: Calvin Translation Society.

―――. 1847: *Commentary on the Book of Genesis,* Volume I. Edited by J. Anderson. Edinburgh: Calvin Translation Society.

―――. 1949: *Institutes of the Christian Religion,* Volume I. London: James Clarke.

Chown, M. 1998: "Anything Goes (Theory of the Existence of Several Universes)." *New Scientist,* pp. 26-31.

Copernicus, N. 1939: *On the Revolutions of the Celestial Spheres.* Translated by C. Wallace. Annapolis: The St John's Bookstore.

Cottingham, J. 1986: *Descartes.* Oxford: Blackwell.

Craig, E. 1987: *The Mind of God and the Works of Man.* Oxford: Clarendon.

Craig, W. and Q. Smith. 1995: *Theism, Atheism, and Big Bang Cosmology.* Oxford: Clarendon.

d'Espagnat, B. 1979: "The Quantum Theory and Reality." *Scientific American* 241: 128-140.

Darwin, C. 1868: *The Variation of Animals and Plants Under Domestication,* Volume 1. London: John Murray.

―――. 1874: *The Descent of Man and Selection in Relation to Sex.* London: John Murray.

―――. 1875: *The Origin of the Species by Means of Natural Selection.* 6th ed. London: John Murray.

―――. 1885: *The Variation of Animals and Plants Under Domestication,* Volume 2. London: John Murray.

―――. 1958: *The Origin of the Species.* New York: Mentor.

Darwin, F. 1887: *The Life and Letters of Charles Darwin.* London: John Murray.

Davies, B. 1993: *An Introduction to the Philosophy of Religion.* Oxford: Oxford University Press.

Davies, P. 1992: *The Mind of God.* London: Simon and Schuster.

de Camp, L. 1968: *The Great Monkey Trial.* New York: Doubleday.

Descartes, R. 1984: "Discourse on the Method." In *The Philosophical Writings of Descartes,* Volume I. Edited by J. Cottingham, R. Stoothoff, and D. Murdoch. Cambridge: Cambridge University Press, pp. 111-51.

————. 1986: *Meditations on First Philosophy with Selections from the Objections and Replies.* Cambridge: Cambridge University Press.

Dowe, P. 1996a: "Backwards Causation and the Direction of Causal Processes." *Mind* 105: 227-48.

————. 1996b: "J.J.C. Smart and the Rise of Scientific Realism," in *Australian Philosophers.* Edited by P. Dowe, M. Nicholls, and L. Shotton, L. Hobart: Pyrrho Press, pp. 25-37.

————. 1996c: "Recent Work on Leibniz on Miracles," *Leibniz Society Review* 6: 160-163.

————. 1996d: "Leibniz on Causation." Paper presented at Australasian Association of Philosophy Conference, University of Queensland, July.

————. n.d.: *Chance, Coincidence, and Accident.* Unpublished manuscript.

Doye, J., I. Goldby, C. Line, S. Lloyd, P. Shellard, and D. Tricker. 1995: "Contemporary Perspectives on Chance, Providence and Free Will." *Science and Christian Belief* 7: 117-39.

Duhem, P. 1954: *The Aim and Structure of Physical Theory.* Translated by P. Werner. Princeton: Princeton University Press.

————. 1969: *To Save the Phenomena.* Chicago: University of Chicago Press.

Earman, J. 1986: *A Primer on Determinism.* Dordrecht: Reidel.

————. 1987: "The Sap Also Rises: A Critical Examination of the Anthropic Principle." *American Philosophical Quarterly* 24: 307-17.

Einstein, A., B. Podolsky, and N. Rosen. 1935: "Can Quantum-Mechanical Description of Physical Reality Be Considered Complete?" *Physical Review* 47: 777-80.

Erickson, M. J. 1983: *Christian Theology,* Volume I. Grand Rapids: Baker.

Euclid. 1926: *The Thirteen Books of Euclid's Elements: Translated From the Text of Heiberg,* 2d ed. Edited by T. Heath. Cambridge: Cambridge University Press.

Fores, M. 1984: "Constructed Science and the Seventeenth Century 'Revolution.'" *History of Science* 22: 217-44.

Frazer, J. 1911-1913: *The Golden Bough: A Study in Magic & Religion,* 3d ed. London: Macmillan.

Galileo, G. 1937a: *Discoveries and Opinions of Galileo,* 1st ed. Translated and edited by Stillman Drake. New York: Doubleday.

————. 1937b: "Letter to the Grand Duchess Christina." In *Discoveries and Opinions of Galileo,* edited by Stillman Drake. New York: Doubleday, pp. 176-216.

————. 1967: *Dialogue Concerning the Two Chief World Systems*, 2d ed. Berkeley: University of California Press.

Gellner, E. 1992: *Postmodernism, Reason, and Religion*. London: Routledge.

Gillispie, C. 1959: *Genesis and Geology*. New York: Harper and Row.

Gould, S. 1985: *The Flamingo's Smile: Reflections on Natural History*. New York: Norton.

Gray, A. 1876: *Darwiniana: Essays and Reviews Pertaining to Darwinism*. New York: Appleton.

Gray, J., ed. 1868: *The Letters of Asa Gray*, Volume II. Boston: Houghton, Mifflin.

Guth, A. 1998: *The Inflationary Universe*. London: Vintage.

Hacking, I. 1987: "The Inverse Gambler's Fallacy: the Argument from Design. The Anthropic Principle Applied to Wheeler Universes." *Mind* 96: 331-40.

Hawking, S. 1988: *A Brief History of Time*. New York: Bantam.

Heidel, A, trans. 1954: *The Babylonian Genesis: The Story of Creation*. Chicago: Chicago University Press.

Hilgevoord, J., ed. 1994: *Physics and our View of the World*. Cambridge: Cambridge University Press.

Hodge, C. 1872-3: *Systematic Theology*. New York: Scribner, Armstrong.

Hooker, J., ed. 1860: "Flora Tasmaniae." In *The Botany of the Antarctic Voyage of H.M. Discovery Ships Erebus and Terror, in the Years 1839-1843, Under the Command of Captain Sir James Clark Ross*, London: Reeve.

Hooykaas, R. 1974: "The Impact of the Copernican Transformation." In *The 'Conflict Thesis' and Cosmology*, edited by C. Russell. Milton Keynes: The Open University Press.

Horwich, P. 1987: *Asymmetries in Time*. Cambridge, Mass.: MIT Press.

Hoyle, F. 1975: *Astronomy and Cosmology*. San Francisco: Freeman.

Hume, D. 1951: *Dialogues Concerning Natural Religion*. New York: Hafner.

————. 1975a: *An Enquiry Concerning Human Understanding*, 3d ed. Edited by L. Selby-Bigge and P. Nidditch. Oxford: Clarendon.

————. 1975b: "Of Miracles." In *An Enquiry Concerning Human Understanding*, edited by L. Selby-Bigge and P. Nidditch. Oxford: Clarendon, pp. 109-31.

————. 1976: *The Natural History of Religion*. Edited by A. Colver. Oxford: Clarendon.

Hurlbutt, R. 1965: *Hume, Newton and the Design Argument*, Lincoln: University of Nebraska Press.

Jacobsen, T. 1987: "Mesopotamian Religions." In *The Encyclopedia of Religion*, edited by M. Eliade. New York: Macmillan, pp. 447-69.

Jaki, S. 1974: *Science and Creation*. Edinburgh: Scottish Academic Press.

Keller, E. 1985: *Reflections on Gender and Science*. New Haven: Yale University Press.

Koestler, A. 1959: *The Sleepwalkers*. London: Hutchinson.

Landau, I. 1998: "Feminist Criticisms of Metaphors in Bacon's Philosophy of Science." *Philosophy* 73: 47-61.

Latour, B., and S. Woolgar. 1979: *Laboratory Life.* London: Sage.

Leibniz, G. 1975a: "Discourse on Metaphysics." In *Philosophical Writings,* edited by G. Parkinson. Totowa: Rowman and Littlefield, pp. 18-47.

———. 1975b: *Philosophical Writings.* Edited by G. Parkinson. Totowa: Rowman and Littlefield.

Leplin, J., ed. 1984: *Scientific Realism.* Berkeley: University of California Press.

Leslie, J. 1988: "No Inverse Gambler's Fallacy in Cosmology." *Mind* 97: 269-272.

———. 1989: *Universes,* London: Routledge.

Lewis, D. 1986: *On the Plurality of Worlds.* Oxford: Blackwell.

Linde, A. 1987: "Particle Physics and Inflationary Cosmology." *Physics Today* 40: 61-68.

Lloyd, G. 1994: *Part of Nature: Self Knowledge in Spinoza's Ethics.* London: Cornell University Press.

MacKay, D. 1988: *The Open Mind and Other Essays.* Edited by M. Tinker. Leicester: Intervarsity.

Mackie, J. 1982: *The Miracle of Theism,* Oxford: Oxford University Press.

Malebranche, N. 1980: *The Search after Truth/Elucidations of the Search after Truth.* Columbus: Ohio State University Press.

Mascall, E. 1956: *Christian Theology and Natural Science: Some Questions on Their Relations.* London: Longmans.

McGrath, P. J. 1988: "The Inverse Gambler's Fallacy and Cosmology — A Reply to Hacking." *Mind* 97: 265-268.

McMullin, E. 1978: "The Conception of Science in Galileo's Work." In *New Perspectives on Galileo,* edited by R. Butts and J. Pitt. Dordrecht: Reidel, pp. 209-57.

McMullin, E. 1981: "How Should Cosmology Relate to Theology?" In *The Sciences and Theology in the Twentieth Century,* edited by A. Peacocke. Stockfield: Oriel, pp. 17-57.

McMullin, E. 1993: "Indifference Principle and Anthropic Principle in Cosmology." *Studies in History and Philosophy of Science* 24: 359-89.

Merchant, C. 1980: *The Death of Nature — Women, Ecology, and the Scientific Revolution.* New York: Harper and Row.

Mermin, N. 1991: "Is the Moon There When Nobody Looks? Reality and the Quantum Theory." In *Philosophy of Science,* edited by R. Boyd, P. Gasper, and J. Trout. Cambridge, Mass.: MIT Press, pp. 501-16.

Mill, J. S. 1843: *A System of Logic,* London: Longman.

Moore, J. 1979: *The Post-Darwinian Controversies: A Study of the Protestant Struggle to Come to Terms with Darwin in Great Britain and America 1870-1900.* Cambridge: Cambridge University Press.

Morris, H., ed. 1974: *Scientific Creationism.* San Diego: Creation-Life Publishers.

Bibliography

Needham, J. 1954: *Science and Civilization in China*. Cambridge: Cambridge University Press.

Oldroyd, D. 1980: *Darwinian Impacts: An Introduction to the Darwinian Revolution*. Kensington, NSW: New South Wales University Press.

————. 1993: "Tiptoeing in Darwin's Footsteps." *The Australian*, March 20-21, 5.

Osiander. 1939: "Osiander's Preface to the 'De Revolutionibus' of Copernicus." In *Three Copernican Treatises*, edited by R. Rosen. New York: Dover Publications, pp. 24-25.

Paley, W. 1812: *A View of the Evidences of Christianity, in Three Parts*, 16th ed. London: W. Creech.

————. 1841: *The Principles of Moral and Political Philosophy*. London: Longman, Orme.

————. 1890a: "The Evidence of Design." In *Paley's Natural Theology*, edited by F. le Gros Clark. London: SPCK, pp. 9-28.

————. 1890b: *Paley's Natural Theology*. Edited by F. le Gros Clark. London: SPCK.

Peacocke, A. 1975: "On 'The Historical Roots of Our Ecological Crisis.'" In *Man and Nature*, edited by H. Montefiore. London: Collins, pp. 155-58.

Phillips, D. Z. 1965: *The Concept of Prayer*. London: Routledge and Kegan Paul.

————. 1976: *Religion Without Explanation*. Oxford: Blackwell.

————. 1991: "Religion in Wittgenstein's Mirror." In *Wittgenstein: Centenary Essays*, edited by D. Phillips. Cambridge: Cambridge University Press, pp. 135-50.

Plantinga, A., and N. Wolterstorff, eds. 1983: *Faith and Rationality: Reason and Belief in God*. Notre Dame: University of Notre Dame Press.

Plato. 1971: *Timaeus and Critias*. Translated by H. Lee. Harmondsworth: Penguin.

Polkinghorne, J. 1986: *One World: The Interaction of Science and Theology*. London: SPCK.

Rachels, J. 1991: *Created From Animal: The Moral Implications of Darwinism*. Oxford: Oxford University Press.

Roberts, M. 1997: "Darwin's Doubts About Design — The Darwin-Gray Correspondence of 1860." *Science and Christian Belief* 9: 113-127.

Robinson, J. 1963: *Honest to God*. London: SCM.

Ruhla, C. 1992: *The Physics of Chance*. Oxford: Oxford University Press.

Russell, B. 1946: *History of Western Philosophy*. London: George Allen and Unwin.

Salmon, W. 1984: *Scientific Explanation and the Causal Structure of the World*. Princeton: Princeton University Press.

Schlesinger, G. 1977: *Religion and Scientific Method*. Dordrecht: Reidel.

Smith, Q. 1986: "World Ensemble Explanations." *Pacific Philosophical Quarterly* 67: 73-86.

Spinoza, B. 1982: *The Ethics and Selected Letters*. Edited by S. Feldman. Indianapolis: Hackett.

Sproul, R. C. 1994: *Not A Chance — the Myth of Chance in Modern Science and Cosmology*. Grand Rapids: Baker.

Stich, S. 1990: *The Fragmentation of Reason*. Cambridge, Mass.: MIT Press.

Swinburne, R. 1991: *The Existence of God*, rev. ed. Oxford: Clarendon.

Tipler, F. 1996: *The Physics of Immortality*. London: Macmillan.

van Fraassen, B. 1980: *The Scientific Image*. Oxford: Clarendon.

————. 1989: *Laws and Symmetry*. Oxford: Clarendon.

van Inwagen, P. 1988: "The Place of Chance in a World Sustained by God." In *Divine and Human Action*, edited by T. Morris. Ithaca: Cornell University Press, pp. 211-235.

Venn, J. 1888: *The Logic of Chance*. London: Macmillan.

Waterworth, R. 1848: *The Canons and Decrees of the Council of Trent with History*. London: C. Dolman.

Wenham, G. 1987: *Genesis 1–15*. Word Biblical Commentary, ed. D. Hubbard and G. Barker. Waco, Texas: Word Books.

Whitaker, M. 1988: "On Hacking's Criticism of the Wheeler Anthropic Principle." *Mind* 97: 259-64.

White, A. D. 1960: *A History of the Warfare of Science with Theology*. New York: Dover Publications.

White, L. 1967: "The Historical Roots of our Ecological Crisis." *Science* 155: 1203-07.

Wilberforce, S. 1860: "Darwin's Origin of Species." *Quarterly Review* 108: 225-264.

Wittgenstein, L. 1958: *Philosophical Investigations*. 3d ed., New York: Macmillan.

————. 1961: *Tractatus Logico-Philosophicus*. London: Routledge.

Wolterstorff, N. 1995: *Divine Discourse*. Cambridge: Cambridge University Press.

Index

accommodation, 28

Al-Ghazali, A. H., 143-44

anthropic principle, 148-51

antirealism, 40; and religion, 49-56; and science, 41-45, 80-81, 148. *See also* realism

Aquinas, St. Thomas, 104-8, 112, 143, 154

arguments for the existence of God: anthropic design, 154-58, 169, 193, 195; design, 104-6, 108-13, 193; Kalām cosmological, 143-45, 148, 186; quantum cosmological, 186; success of science, 79-81

Aristotle, 10-11, 43, 57-59, 72, 104-5

Atrahasis epic, 21

Augustine, St., 16, 22-26, 29-30, 35-36, 39, 49, 56, 134, 141, 154, 194

Ayer, A. J., 53

Bacon, F., 5, 16, 27, 57, 62, 65-72, 76, 154

Barbour, I., 2

Barrow, J., 150

Beecher, H., 133

Bell, J., 179

Bellarmino, Cardinal, 4, 30, 32-34, 36-38, 43

Bell's theorem, 170, 178, 183, 186, 189

Bentham, G., 124

Berkeley, G., 154

Berkov, L., 176

Blur, E., 136

Bohr, N., 178

Brahe, Tycho, 45

Bree, G., 135

Brown, W., 183

Bryan, W., 132

Buffon, Comte de, 145

Calvin, J., 16, 26-29, 39, 50, 53, 56, 173

Carter, B., 159

chance worldview, 170-72

Cicero, 104

Clifford, W. K., 84

Copernicus, N., 13-14, 29, 38, 41, 43, 46

Cosmology: big bang, 146-48; Copernican, 13-14, 31, 41, 144; Greek, 10-12, 26

Craig, E., 61-62

creation science, 4, 104, 131, 137-38

Curtis, G., 136

Darrow, C., 132

Darwin, C., 1, 104, 108, 141, 191-93, 195; and God, 125-26; and Asa Gray, 127, 129-30; *Origin of Species*, 113-18

Davies, P., 143, 149-50, 157-58, 160

Dawson, J., 135-36

deep ecology, 75
Descartes, R., 57, 62-65, 69-71, 154
Duhem, P., 40, 42-44, 53

Einstein, A., 5, 179
Emerson, R., 154
Enuma Elish, 21
Erickson, M., 175
Euclid, 57, 59, 63
Eudoxus, 10-11
evolution: and creation, 104, 125-27; natural selection, 113-18; and special creation, 118-24, 129
explanation: mechanical, 106-8, 110; teleological, 104-6

Feuerbach, L., 40, 50-51, 53
Foscarini, 29-30, 33
Francis, St., 74
Frazer, J., 2, 52
Freud, S., 51-52

Galilei, G., 29-32, 35-39, 43, 46, 47, 50, 53, 56-57, 62, 64-65, 69, 79, 81, 101, 141, 144, 154, 191-92, 194
Gamow, G., 146
Gardner, M., 151
Genesis 1–3, 16-22, 28, 50, 59-60, 70-71, 75, 77, 104, 134, 137
god of the gaps, 156-57, 193-95
Gould, S. J., 158, 169
Gray, A., 104, 114, 127-31, 141

Hacking, I., 160-63
Hawking, S., 1, 3, 142-43, 146-47, 191, 194
Hegel, G., 154
hermeneutics, 17, 24, 29, 34, 50
Hodge, C., 133-35
Hooker, J., 118
Hoyle, F., 145-46, 149, 151, 154
Hume, D., 3, 51-52, 82-88, 90-98, 100, 194
Hutton, J., 145
Huxley, T., 1, 3, 125, 131

image of God, 59-62, 64-65, 71, 77, 80, 132
inference to the best explanation, 46-49, 80, 99-100, 102, 119-24, 155
Inverse Gambler's Fallacy, 160-63

James I, 76
James, W., 84
Jeffrey, R., 101, 103

Kant, I., 144-45
Kelvin, Lord, 124
Kepler, J., 14, 44-46
Kierkegaard, S., 84
Koestler, A., 172

Lamark, J.-B., 118
Lane, Craig W., 146
Laplace, P., 144
Leibniz, G., 144, 154, 171, 175-77
Leo XIII, 32
Leslie, J., 151, 157-58
Lewis, C. S., 17
Lewis, D., 160
Linde, A., 168
Locke, J., 154
logical positivism, 3, 53-54
Lloyd, G., 78
Locke, J., 84
Luther, M., 26
Lyell, C., 145

Mackie, J., 3, 83, 88-90, 95-96, 98
Maimonides, 43
Malbranche, N., 129, 176
Malcolm, N., 54
Manicheans, 22
many worlds, 159-60, 162
Marx, K., 51-52
McCosh, J., 136
McMullen, E., 25, 34-36, 164
Merchant, C., 75-78
Mill, J. S., 112
miracles, 81-83, 87-92, 94-101, 103

Moore, J., 131, 135-37
Morris, F., 135
Morris, H., 4, 138-41

Needham, J., 79
Newton, I., 5, 15-16, 69, 81, 108, 156

observer selection effect, 164-67
Orwell, G., 17
Osiander, A., 30, 40-42, 49-50, 53, 56

Paley, W., 5, 104, 109-13, 131, 156, 192-93
pantheism, 78, 154, 157-58
Pascal, B., 84
Paul, St., 53
perspicuity of nature, 62-64
Phillips, D. Z., 54-55
Plato, 22-24, 43
Polkinghorne, J., 143, 184-85
postmodernism, 18
providence, 173, 183-84, 187-89; concurrence, 176; Leibniz's theory, 176-77; occasionalism, 175-76
Psalms, 28-29
Ptolemy, 12, 43-44

Ramsey, F., 84
realism, 40; and religion, 56; and science, 46-49. *See also* antirealism
Rheticus, J., 41
Robinson, Bishop J., 52-53
Royal Society, 69
Ruhla, C., 170
Russell, B., 3

Schlesinger, G., 83, 99-103

Schopenhauer, A., 154
science and religion: conflict view, 2, 6, 34, 38, 53, 141, 194; harmony view, 4, 6, 34, 38-39, 52-53, 56, 141, 191; independence view, 4, 6, 39, 56, 191; interaction view, 5, 6, 39, 52, 57, 79, 191; neutrality, 25, 32, 35, 36, 39, 50; relevance, 25, 34-36, 39, 50, 194; religious science view, 3, 6
science, success of, 80-81
Scopes Trial, 132, 137
Sextus Empiricus, 104
simplicity, 101-3
Spinoza, B., 78
Sproul, R., 172-73

Tegwell, M., 160
testimony, 86-87, 93-94
theism, 79-81, 100, 103, 154
Tillich, P., 40, 52-53
Tipler, F., 143, 150
Torricelli, E., 107
Townsend, L., 136

van Fraassen, B., 40, 44-46, 53
van Inwagen, P., 187
Venn, J., 93

Warfield, B. B., 136-37, 141
Wheeler, J., 151
White, A. H., 52
White, L., 73-75
Wilberforce, W., 1, 131-32
Wittgenstein, L., 4-5, 41, 53-56

Zoroastrians, 22